# Sacred Play

# Sacred Play

## *Ritual Levity and Humor in South Asian Religions*

Edited by

Selva J. Raj

and

Corinne G. Dempsey

SUNY
PRESS

Cover photo taken by Corinne Dempsey in Trissur, Kerala, at the 1994 Onam festival.

Published by State University of New York Press, Albany



Printed in the United States of America



For information, contact State University of New York Press, Albany, NY
www.sunypress.edu

Production by Diane Ganeles
Marketing by Anne M. Valentine

**Library of Congress Cataloging-in-Publication Data**

Sacred play : ritual levity and humor in South Asian religions / edited by Selva J. Raj and Corinne G. Dempsey.
p. cm.
Includes bibliographical references and index.
ISBN 978-1-4384-2979-3 (hardcover : alk. paper)
ISBN 978-1-4384-2980-9 (pbk.: alk. paper)
1. South Asia—Religion. 2. Religion—Humor. 3. Ritual—South Asia. I. Raj, Selva J. II. Dempsey, Corinne G.

BL1055.S33 2010
203'.8—dc22 2009017904

10 9 8 7 6 5 4 3 2 1

*In memory of Selva J. Raj whose joyful spirit endures.*

# Contents

## PART 2
## Gods and Humans at Play: Religious Humor and Divine Intimacy



## PART 3
## Playing to Win: Edging Out the Competition

# List of Figures

# Acknowledgments

Selva Raj, my coeditor and friend, had hoped that we would grace the back cover of this volume with a black-and-white snapshot of the two of us, smiling, with martinis in our hands. Although I regret that this photo never materialized, it is my hope, for Selva's sake, to at least plant the image in the reader's mind.

As many of you who read these acknowledgments know, Selva did not live to see this book through to publication. His sudden death from a heart attack in March 2008 is something from which many of us will never fully recover. For those who never met Selva, he was the engine behind countless collaborative projects into which he infused a bountiful, joyful spirit. Selva greatly enriched our field of study through his research and writing on popular Catholicism in India, yet one of his most constant priorities was to humanize our scholarly community by imbuing it with a sense of camaraderie and fun. It is therefore fitting that I acknowledge him here for the pivotal role he played in organizing and editing this collection of chapters on—of all subjects—levity. I am grateful to the volume's contributors for their part in seeing this book through to completion, as one way among many that we honor the memory of our colleague Selva, his passion for the study of South Asian religions, and his enormous capacity for levity, laughter, and light.

At State University of New York Press, I would like to thank first and foremost Nancy Ellegate, who has graciously advocated for and ushered through—for the third time—a volume coedited by Selva and me. Thanks also to the ever-efficient Diane Ganeles, senior production editor, and to copy editor Michele Lansing, whose attention to detail is awe-inspiring.

# 1

# Introduction

## *Ritual Levity in South Asian Traditions*

Selva J. Raj and Corinne Dempsey

The comic is not a wart on the human soul but a part of the soul.

—Walsh, in *Holy Laughter*

Humans have long been classified as Homo Sapiens, Homo Faber (Man the Worker), and Homo Religiosus. Half a century ago, in his seminal work *Homo Ludens* (1950), Johan Huizinga coined a fourth functional designation: Man the Player. Huizinga's comment, that "ritual grew up in sacred play" (173), furthermore suggests the role and significance of play in rituals. Since the publication of this influential work, some scholars, such as Peter Berger, have called our attention to the religious aspects of playfulness as a human phenomenon, arguing that humor is "a necessary constituent of humanity" that cuts across ethnic, cultural, historical, geographical, temporal—as well as religious—divides (Berger 1997, x).

Despite such recognition and connection between humor and religiosity, the scholarly community has demonstrated only a marginal interest in the ludic dimensions of religious rituals, leading scholars such as Conrad Hyers to bemoan the paucity of literature on the subject. "[F]or all the wealth of material produced on the general subject of religion," he observes, "the amount of attention devoted to the place of humor in religion, and to the manifold relationships between the sacred and the comic, is almost infinitesimal by comparison" (Hyers 1969c, 4). Ingvild Gilhus attributes this neglect to the Western academy's focus on Christianity. "The separation between religion and the ludicrous," she observes, "has long been inherent in the mainstream of Christian tradition. This is perhaps the main reason why the relationship between religion and laughter is seldom realized and investigated" (Gilhus 1991, 257).

While the Western academy's focus on Christianity might have contributed in some measure to the current lack of interest in the study of religious levity, it is also due—at least in part—to the general tendency among scholars and nonspecialists alike to view ludic expressions and behaviors as no more than superficial and marginal aspects of human life, incongruent with the seriousness and solemnity normally associated with religion. Not surprisingly, therefore, scholars of religion traditionally have overlooked playfulness in ritual—let alone considered it a legitimate interpretive category—except to treat it as an occasional aside in ethnographic encounters and narratives. This perceived estrangement between religion and humor has led many to see them at best as strange bedfellows, if not enemies (Capps 2006b, 413). Commenting on this perceived estrangement, Doris Donnelly suggests that "something has gone wrong with our perception of the alliance between being religious and having a sense of humor" (Donnelly 1992, 386).

More recently, however, a new generation of scholars of religion trained in ethnography has shown an interest in this subject. A tangible sign of this growing interest is the number of panels and sessions focusing on this theme at the annual meetings of professional and scholarly associations. For example, the Midwest American Academy of Religion devoted its 2001 annual meeting to exploring the theme Religion and Humor. The following year, two contributors to this volume organized a panel focused on ritual levity and ritual play in South Asia for the national meeting of the American Academy of Religion (AAR) in Toronto. Envisioned as a prelude to this volume and cosponsored by three separate program units of the AAR, seven contributors to this book presented papers on levity and play in South Asian traditions at this well-attended and well-received session. Originating from the Toronto panel, this work is a modest interdisciplinary attempt to fill a void in current scholarship on an important aspect of religious practice.

That said, we hasten to add that this book is not simply about humor. Nor is it about religious jokes or about divine escapades and tricks. Its limited and specific focus is on the levity and playfulness that religious devotees manifest in structured as well as spontaneous ritual contexts. Our resolve is to offer some preliminary generalizations regarding ritual levity in South Asian traditions and to propose ritual levity and play as a viable hermeneutical tool and a legitimate analytical category for exploring religion in general and of South Asian religions in particular, worthy of further study and scrutiny.

## Ritual Levity: Its Nature and Function

Webster's *New World Dictionary* defines levity as "lightness or gaiety of disposition, conduct, or speech; especially improper or unbecoming gaiety or flippancy; lack of seriousness; frivolity" (1966, 842). A similar definition can be found in the *American College Dictionary*, which describes levity as "lightness of mind, character, or behavior; lack of proper seriousness or earnestness" (1964, 701). These conventional definitions suggest that, in common parlance, levity denotes lightheartedness and playfulness, lacking appropriate seriousness. However, ritual levity—as we understand it—denotes playful ritual actions that are at once lighthearted and serious. This may include and evoke an array of moods, attitudes, and expressions, such as mocking, clowning, play, parody, imitation, jest, laughter, fun, role reversal, and competition. There is a protean quality to ritual levity that makes it difficult to pin down. This very plurality of significations and the inherent elasticity of the concept present scholars of religion with both challenges and opportunities to isolate, decode, and articulate the themes and lessons implicit in ludic expressions.

What constitutes ritual levity and what function it serves in a particular instance will depend on, among others things, its context, its constituency, the intentionality of participants, and the desired and/or anticipated outcomes. As readers will discover, our contributors neither ignore nor dismiss the diversity of associations. In fact, in their efforts to isolate the meaning, significance, and nuances of ludic expressions in their respective case studies, they take refuge in and employ a wide array of concepts and terms. As editors, we have not imposed or proscribed particular definitions or understandings of ritual levity but have let authors articulate their own conceptions of levity drawn from the specific socioreligious contexts of their case studies. As scholars of religion continue to search for fuller and more comprehensive understandings, the wealth of ethnographic data furnished here offers rich fodder for cross-cultural study and comparison.

In proposing ritual levity as a category of analysis for religious practices, we draw on the insights of ritual theorists such as Victor Turner and Tom Driver. Turner developed his theory of ritual based on Arnold Van Gennep's (1960) notion of limen, expanding its significance beyond rites of passage to the processes of ritual themselves.[1] For Turner, when people perform rituals, they separate themselves, at least partially, from their traditional roles and statuses and enter into a privileged state of play. "Just as the subjunctive mood of a verb is used to express supposition, desire, hypothesis, or possibility, rather than stating actual facts," argues Turner, "so do liminality and the phenomena of liminality dissolve all factual and common-sense systems into their components and 'play' with them in ways never found in nature or in custom" (Turner 1986, 25; quoted in Driver 1998, 159). For Turner, liminality "is a phase particularly conducive to . . . ludic invention" (Turner 1982, 31–32).

Given that play is integral to ritual contexts, ritual participants are afforded an opportunity to engage in lighthearted "play" with symbols and symbol vehicles such as masks and costumes, meanings and words, and creatively to imagine, invent, and introduce new symbols, meanings, and words (Turner 1982, 85). Speaking of various forms of play in tribal and agrarian rituals, where "work and play are hardly distinguishable in many cases" (34), Turner notes that

> Huizinga's *ludic* abounds in many kinds of tribal rituals, even in funerary rituals. There is a play of *symbol*-vehicles, leading to the construction of bizarre masks and costumes from elements of mundane life now conjoined in fantastic ways. There is a play of *meanings*, involving the reversal of hierarchical orderings of social values and statuses. There is a play with *words* resulting in the generation of secret initiatory languages, as well as joyful or serious punning. Even the dramatic scenarios which give many rituals their processual armature may be presented as comedic rather than serious or tragic. Riddling and joking may take place, even in the liminal seclusion of initiatory lodges. . . . Liminality is particularly conducive to play, where it is not restricted to games and jokes, but extends to the introduction of new forms of symbolic action, such as sword-games or original masks. (Turner 1982, 85, emphases in original)[2]

Building on Turner's concept of liminality, Tom Driver also highlights the playful dimension of ritual.

> If there is any one thing that clearly distinguishes performance in the ritual mode from other kinds of events, it is that the performer assumes roles and relates to what is going on in an "as if" way not appropriate to the workaday world. As Victor Turner insisted, ritual realizes itself in the subjunctive mood. The so-called "sacred space" and "sacred time" of religious rituals are, above all, imaginative constructions, "rules of the game." . . . The playfulness of rituals, however, does not mean that they are nothing more than play-acting, much less that they cannot be efficacious. . . . In short, rituals are a kind of playful work. . . . We may speak of ritual, then, as work done playfully. Wherever the spirit of play enters in, work starts to become ritualized." (Driver 1998, 98)

According to Driver, such play and levity, contrary to popular assumptions, are not fleeting or flighty in nature. "However playful, foolish . . . and pretense-ridden liminality may be, there is a substance to it" (Driver 1998, 160).

If one subscribes—as we do—to Turner's theory of ritual and his interpretation of liminality further expounded by Driver, then ritual levity might well be described—to use Turner's phrase—as a "liminoid phenomenon," in that it occurs in borderline spaces and moments, "in a zone between the sacred and the profane" (Hyers 1969a, 23). As such, ritual levity is neither wholly sacred nor simply profane but "sacrafane," in that it exhibits both sacred and profane traits.[3] Thus it is the liminal character of ritual and the freedom inherent in liminality that provide the space and stimulus for creative imagination, empowering ritual performers to engage in what ordinarily might be considered "improper behavior." Ritual liminality allows participants to step out of the normal order (divine or human) to challenge, defy, invert, or subvert established conventions, ritual etiquette, and religious protocol, to poke fun at social and religious categories, distinctions, and cultural norms, and to "play" with gods and sacred realities with certain temporary impunity. Levity, therefore, is neither an anomaly nor an aberration but an essential, intrinsic part of ritual that serves multiple—both tangible and intangible—functions.[4]

If "play" is intrinsic to ritual, as several ritual theorists have persuasively argued, then what considerations—religious and otherwise—lead religious practitioners to engage in ritual levity and play? More specifically, what benefits do participants hope to reap by periodic and prescribed excursions into ritual playfulness? And what social role does ritual levity serve for the average religious practitioner? At the systemic level, what clues does levity reveal about the core values, aspirations, hopes, and traditions of the community sponsoring such play? Quite clearly, religious practitioners resort to levity and play not simply for temporary comic relief but also for the social, religious, and psychological dividends they yield. As a multivalent and polyvalent category, evoking a spectrum of meanings and significances for different constituencies in different settings, ritual levity's function for practitioners will depend on the individual and collective contexts. For example, in a particular instance, social aims might be of foremost importance, while in another instance, psychological and religious considerations might be of greater consequence. While sociologists, psychologists, and pastoral counselors have highlighted the social, psychological, and cathartic advantages of play, historians of religions who acknowledge these social and psychological dimensions will add to them potential religious and transcendental benefits.[5]

Chief among the socioreligious values of ritual levity is the context and platform—both structured and informal—it provides to find relief, albeit temporary, from inbuilt conventions. While ritual levity often softens distinctions and hierarchies among humans, it can narrow the divide between human and divine realms as well. Highlighting the socioreligious function of religious levity, Gilhus thus observes: "In a religious system, one of the functions of the ludicrous is to raise doubt about the hierarchic order of the cosmology, blur the relation between its elements, and bring about the collapse of the established order . . . the ludicrous intervenes in the interaction between cosmos and chaos, to the point that it allows chaos to get the upper hand. The ludicrous creates a chaos which is creative, but short-lived, and whose possibilities are never realized in a new world-order. The ludicrous chaos . . . can be experienced as laughable. . . . The ludicrous appears in myths and rituals, both verbally and non-verbally" (Gilhus 1991, 258). As readers make their way through the various chapters in this book, they will find that Gilhus's observations mostly ring true, yet as some chapters demonstrate, ritual levity in South Asian religious contexts indeed can provide lasting challenges to the earthly and cosmic order, affecting hierarchies within and outside the ritual context.

In spite of these exceptions, we find that the majority of case studies here demonstrate how ritual levity often plays with and indeed defies established religious beliefs and social conventions, yet it does not radically or permanently displace them. Such temporary playful defiance can in fact help reinforce and restore the value and significance of the status quo. It is this restorative quality implicit in ritual play that ensures not only its repeated occurrence in institutionally sanctioned arenas but also elicits institutional endorsement for such play. However, the temporary relief ritual levity produces is obviously not its sole value or function.

Also of interest are the ways in which levity and play respond to specifically transcendent concerns. In *Redeeming Laughter*, Peter Berger goes to some length to highlight this dimension that, although involving abstraction, invokes a function of levity that has more permanent religious and therapeutic implications. He maintains:

> The comic transcends the reality of ordinary, everyday existence; it posits, however temporarily, a different reality in which the assumptions and rules of ordinary life are suspended. This is, as it were, transcendence in a lower key; it does not in itself have any necessary religious implications. But . . . certain manifestations of the comic suggest that this other reality has redeeming qualities that are not temporary at all, but rather that points to that other world that has always been the object of the religious attitude. In ordinary parlance one speaks of "redeeming laughter." Any joke can provoke such laughter, and it can be redeeming in the sense of making life easier to bear, at least briefly. In the perspective of religious faith, though, there is in this transitory experience an intuition, a signal of true redemption, that is, of a world that has been made whole and in which the miseries of the human condition have been abolished. . . . The experience of the comic presents a world without pain. . . . It is, above all, an abstraction from the tragic dimension of human existence. (Berger 1997, 205, 210)

## Levity in South Asian Religions

Much has been said and written about the rich philosophical, theological, mystical, and mythological traditions of various South Asian religions. Supplementing this scholarly body of work are more recent ethnographically based writings, published primarily in the second half of the twentieth century, on lived and grassroots religious practices. These works have provided important balance to the textual and classical focus that has enriched South Asian scholarship for decades, if not centuries. Despite the wealth of available literature on South Asian religious traditions—both classical and contemporary ethnographical—the ludic dimensions of religious practices seen from the standpoint of human agents have remained largely overlooked. Almost all available literature on the subject focuses on play, tricks, and escapades instigated by divine entities, collectively termed *"lila,"* enacted for didactic purposes on behalf of humanity (Siegel 1987). Even when *lila* enlists human actors as, for example, in Ramlila, a popular devotional performance tradition in north India in which human devotees reenact, recreate, and retell the deeds and play of the Hindu god Rama, these are essentially plays in the sense of drama and artistic performances—not in the sense of playfulness or levity.

This book therefore marks an intentional departure from the usual focus on divinity-centered play, or what ritual theorist Jonathan Z. Smith refers to in the concluding chapter as the "cosmologized and ontologized notion of *lila* as an explanatory principle" within traditional South Asian scholarship. If *lila* is "top-down humor," then the ritual levity our contributors explore here might be described as "bottom-up humor" or "grassroots humor," in which human devotees "play with" established norms, institutions, and figures—both religious and secular. Apart from providing an outlet for transgressive experiments, these grassroots ludic expressions provide valuable clues to participants' earthly and existential concerns and relationships and to the ambiguities of devotion and religious expression. This grassroots levity, like the practice of making and fulfilling vows (Raj and Harman 2006, 1–13), is a common ritual thread running throughout all the major religious traditions of South Asia, providing a spacious window from which to view worlds of human contingency and belief.

Although this book focuses on human expressions of ritual levity, the gods and sacred realities are not merely passive or silent spectators, nor are they simply the butt of jokes. Deities frequently emerge as active participants in ritual levity, joining their human devotees in "playing with" the inadequacy of conventional norms and institutions. In this sense, ritual play in South Asia has both a vertical and a horizontal dimension. Indeed, religious practitioners rely on and resort to ritual levity and play—investing much individual and collective energy, emotion, and resources in them—because, as we established earlier, ritual provides one of the most potent outlets for "play," offering a tangible means for negotiating with these revered sacred figures, realities, institutions, and beliefs.

How might we classify the various ludic expressions prominent in South Asian ritual practices? Given the inherent diversity of South

Asian religious traditions and of their ritual performances, developing a typology of South Asian ritual levity is a daunting task. Nevertheless, based on our analysis of discernible common ludic threads and patterns woven throughout the diverse traditions represented here, we propose a working "functional" (pun intended) typology encompassing six basic types. Before doing so, however, we must offer the following three caveats. First, although each type of ritual levity highlights a distinctive trait or feature, it is not mutually exclusive. For example, transgressive levity that challenges an existing social or religious order often contains, as Turner has pointed out, restorative value that simultaneously works to cement order and convention. Our second caveat is that the proposed functional types apply to ritual participants and not to outsiders viewing the ritual for whom the same playful instance might have a very different—as in ludicrous or debasing—significance. Third, the effects of all categories can either be temporary or permanent, to different degrees.

The six basic types of ritual levity we propose are (1) *vertical levity*, which bridges the gulf between human and divine realms and establishes intimacy between the two, (2) *horizontal levity*, which softens social divides among humans and enhances human relationships and intimacy, (3) *transgressive levity*, which challenges established conventions, hierarchies, and institutions, often through role reversals, (4) *restorative levity*, which restores order, hierarchy, and conventional distinctions, (5) *redemptive levity*, which provides a glimpse into the meta or transcendent dimension of existence and bridges both vertical and horizontal distinctions and hierarchies, and (6) *competitive levity*, which is designed to edge out competition and display contests (religious, professional, and ritual) between rival participants within a religious group or between competing, if not conflicting, traditions. This type of levity also helps mark and reinforce boundaries.

## The Book

Drawing primarily on original ethnographic research, contributors to this book offer a panoply of playful ritual expressions, displaying the spectrum of functional types. The chapters furthermore represent all of the major religious traditions practiced in South Asia—Hindu, Muslim, Christian, and Buddhist—and provide a generous view into the various occasions and venues that engage levity within ritual.

The most widely represented occasion for ritual levity in this book is the annual festival, a ritual context most likely to involve actors and audience members from multiple religious groups. North Indian festivals include A. Whitney Sanford's description of a raucous Holi celebration in Braj and Rachel McDermott's exploration of humor and spectacle at Kolkata's Durga Puja. In Tamil Nadu William Harman investigates multilayered, multicommunal joking at a traveling festival in Madurai and Selva Raj finds teasing and laughter as well as serious play at a Catholic festival in rural Arulanandapuram. Dealing with somewhat less public terrain are the two chapters exploring levity and joking at ritual gatherings performed exclusively by women: Tracy Pintchman investigates playful humor at an annual ritual performance honoring Krishna and Tulasi in Benaras, and Amy Bard analyzes women's laughter at the Shiah Muslim Muharram festival in Pakistan and India. Unearthing play at a women's life-cycle rite, Liz Wilson explores Newari "mock" marriages in Nepal. Finally, three chapters focus more generally on laughter and playfulness in relation to ritual settings: Mathew Schmalz describes the religious play of a Catholic charismatic healer in Delhi, Jonathan Walters reflects on ritual levity in the context of Buddhist Sri Lankan healing practices, and Corinne Dempsey and Sudharshan Durayappah consider rambunctious playfulness at a diaspora Hindu temple in Upstate New York.

To optimize analytical potential, chapters in this volume allow the topic of investigation to speak for itself, in all of its diversity and complexity. In other words, contributors do not frame the issue of levity—or language describing levity—in any particular way except from within the context of ritual performance. Terms commonly used throughout this book, such as levity, play, and laughter, thus derive shades of meaning that shift depending on the context and perspective. In some cases, notions of levity, play, and laughter can accrue very different, if not opposite, values, depending on circumstances or viewpoints.

For example, many of the chapters demonstrate the positive aspects of what we have termed horizontal and vertical levity—practices that invite and welcome intimacy among human participants and between humans and divinity. Theologically speaking, levity, connoting lightness and lightheartedness, can elicit rather straightforward, positive associations as seen in Walters's and Schmalz's respective descriptions of Sri Lankan Buddhist and Catholic charismatic healers. They note how, in similar ways, religious joy or playfulness represent religious aims of transformation and redemption; lightness and levity emerge when released from the weight of worldly entrapments or sin. This is not to say that lightness, within a religious context, is trouble free, as the risk of trivializing religion through levity consistently seems to loom.

McDermott discovers how the Kolkata Durga Puja's incongruous—and, therefore, to some, humorous—display of the Goddess in everything from computers to the Titanic ship raises theological concerns for a vocal minority who consider such spectacle to border on the irreverent. Tracy Pintchman notes how her male research assistant deemed women's ritual levity to be frivolous, interpreting women's laughter as reflecting a lack of commitment to serious ritual work. Pintchman argues that raucous joking in the ritual context is far more complex and far from trivializing for the women themselves. In the end, none of the chapters argues that laughter, for true devotees, diminishes ritual's serious intent. Moreover, levity never manages to belittle divinity. Demonstrated by Sanford's portrayal of Balarama's raucous proclivities, Harman's discussion of Shiva's pranks, or Walter's description of gods who outlandishly possess healers, divinity may be lighthearted but never trivial. Divine levity enacted through ritual and ritual narrative is most often deliberate, with good cause, and sometimes performed at humanity's well-deserved expense. Although gods and goddesses may seem funny, the joke, in the end, is not on them.

A term with multiple, and sometimes boldly contrasting, implications in this collection is "play." Depending on the context, ritual play can refer to a range of activities, from spontaneous revelry to highly scripted performances; it includes "make-believe" play-acting and fiercely competitive play that produces winners and losers. Play can also connote movement or artistic license available within ritual that confounds convention. Representing spontaneous play that defies normative social and religious prescription—described earlier as transgressive levity—is Sanford's vivid description of Holi participants engaging in activities not dreamed of outside of festival time, Dempsey and Durayappah's recounting of instances when liquid ritual materials become grist for nonscripted messy fun, and Raj's description of a ritual on church grounds in which spontaneous teasing breaks out among women at the expense of men. In regular defiance of verbal scripting, charismatic glossolalia, as described by Schmalz, emerges as playful, childlike babble with serious religious implications. Highly orchestrated performance, on the other hand, also can be central to a range of ritual play. Ritual play in this mode is somewhat similar to theatre play, yet it distinguishes itself most fundamentally due to divinity's explicit inclusion as a member and, in some instances, as an active participant. Throughout this book, gods and goddesses are invoked or themselves perform ritual play through possession rites, divine imagery, ritual speech, choreographed movement, and festival fanfare. As Pintchman's and McDermott's chapters demonstrate, divinity can be made present and engaged, respectively, through simple handcrafted mud figurines or in extraordinary public display.

Ritual events that bring us closest to theater play-acting include a practice that takes place at a Tamil Catholic church, described by Raj, in which lay authorities auction babies to the highest bidder who, everyone knows, always ends up being the parents. The event is more than theater, however, due to the participation of St. Anne, who has blessed the previously childless couple with the child. The ritual encounter is thus ultimately not play-acting but ensures the fulfillment of a promise in return for the saint's favor. Likewise, the Nepalese Newar *ihi* ceremony that enacts a wedding between young girls and a divine spouse is, as described by Wilson, much more than theater acting due to its lasting consequences. Although the "play" of the ceremony for ritual participants involves subtle nuances of levity—witnessed by warmhearted joking to this effect—a sense of serious performance emerges, as Wilson sees it, through the ritual vocabulary of normative wedding rites. On the other end of the play spectrum, distinct from spontaneous unscripted play and theatrical play-acting, is that which we characterized earlier as competitive levity. Herein emerges the decidedly serious side of ritual play, performed with considerable stakes for winners and losers. As demonstrated by the exquisite Durga pandals described by McDermott, playful charismatic healers recounted by Schmalz, and Shiah women's laughter chronicled by Bard, the point of play for some individuals or groups is to distinguish themselves as different from—and better than—other players.

As witnessed by the array of examples in this book, laughter within ritual can build or break human connections and community, depending on the arena and tenor in which ritual levity gets played out. Laughter can enhance or create cooperation among and between groups, or it can deepen division and difference. Particularly in the ritual context that, by nature, resonates with meaning and emotion, laughter can be reassuring in transformative ways, disrupting powerful hierarchies and inviting otherwise impossible inclusivity. While offering a formidable means for connection and the mending of severed ties, laughter in its derisive and divisive modes can sever and break ties as well. This volume as a whole reminds us that while accounts of levity and play often evoke notions of light and lightheartedness, their dark and demeaning side, particularly in socially and theologically loaded ritual settings, must not be ignored. The following chapters take into account the many points along the spectrum, exploring the ritual play of light and dark humor as well as the nuanced shades of grey.

We have divided the chapters in this book into three parts having to do with three main characteristics of levity. Chapters in part 1 explore ritual levity that challenges or reverses—temporarily or permanently—social and religious norms. Part 2 views humor and playfulness ritually expressed by deities themselves, reflected in the practices and perspectives of their devotees, and resulting in greater and lesser degrees of human-divine intimacy and communal cohesion. Part 3 describes ritual levity as providing a platform for playful competition and, in some cases, dissension between competing religious, sectarian, or secular groups. Needless to say, although the three views of levity organizing this book reflect resonant and repeating themes, they do not exhaust available types of ritual levity. Moreover, instances of laughter described in the chapters themselves are always more complex than indicated by the part's title. The "play" or movement within ritual levity is not something one can or would want to neatly pin down; yet for the sake of a modest sense of direction, we must start somewhere.

The book's first part, "Laughing Inside Out: Playful Breaks with Convention," is led by Raj's chapter that features two Tamil Catholic rituals that he labels "Men Who Cook" and "the Baby Auction." Here he highlights how these highly scripted performances—and the non-scripted humor intrinsic to them—help demonstrate the absurdity of gender hierarchies and alleviate the usual distance between the resident saint and her human devotees. Viewed as a totality, these festival rituals offer a moment of comic relief to a community that experiences year-round hardship and isolation; they bind past and present members and allow the saint access to involve herself in human affairs. Sanford's "Don't Take It Badly, It's Holi: Ritual Levity in Balarama's Holi" likewise demonstrates how the Braj celebration—performed with particular gusto compared to other regional Holi events—offers an annual opportunity for participants to whisk away gender and caste hierarchies through raucous playfulness. Sanford argues that this suspension of social comportment helps renew and maintain everyday familial and social bonds as well as affirm important ties between the agricultural cycle and community health. Giving added contour to the event's transgressive nature is the way participants "play" Holi in the spirit of the resident deity, Balarama, whose anti-authoritarian irreverence they celebrate during this festival.

Wilson's exploration of the *ihi* wedding ceremony in "Playing the Married Lady: Primary Marriage among the Newars of Nepal" focuses on how this ritual event, often amid good-natured teasing, allows young girls to defy normative wedding tradition by maintaining and strengthening ties to their natal family. These ties are further enforced after the girls undergo their "secondary" marriage to a human male later in life. The *ihi* ceremony, forever ensuring that the girl will remain an auspicious married woman, even after her human husband passes away, effectively plays with or "mocks" traditional expectations for married and widowed women. Dempsey and Durayappah's chapter, "The 'Artful Trick': Challenging Convention through Play in Upstate New York," focuses on the prominent theme of laughter and fun that permeates ritual interactions at a Hindu diaspora temple. They argue that the temple's challenge to caste and gender convention, also a pervasive theme, is further enhanced and supported by ritual levity that binds members to one another as well as to divinity. They juxtapose insider playfulness with the nervous laughter of critical outsiders who might view the temple's unconventional ritual performances as ludicrous and perhaps even dangerous. Temple practitioners who revel in access to divine power—due to their unique ritual approach—invariably seem to get the last laugh.

Part 2, "Gods and Humans at Play: Religious Humor and Divine Intimacy," investigates instances in which deities themselves are portrayed as playful or humorous, often inspiring reciprocal playfulness among their devotees in the form of ritual levity. We begin this part with "Friendship, Levity, and Love in a Hindu Women's Ritual Tradition," in which Pintchman describes the Benaras Kartik *puja* performed by women whose laughter, lighthearted antics, and occasional bawdy humor reflect the playful behavior they admire in their god Krishna. Pintchman notes how Krishna's humorous escapades, representing sacred freedom and play existing outside of ordinary time, provide him with a means for forging intimacy with his devoted *gopi* cowherdesses who live and play in his midst. Devotion to Krishna furthermore draws this community of women to one another in loving friendship. Women who together perform Kartik *puja* become, like Krishna's *gopis*, bonded as playful, loving devotees and friends, sharing jokes that are not simply a fringe benefit of ritual performance but are indispensable to it. Harman's chapter, "Laughing until It Hurts . . . Someone Else: The Pain of a Ritual Joke," discusses ritual levity enacted during Vishnu's Journey Festival to Madurai, in which devotees reenact his travels to his sister Minakshi's wedding to Lord Shiva. Alas, he arrives too late and, according to tradition, the snubbed Vishnu takes refuge for a night with a Muslim courtesan. Harman notes how this ritual detail evokes appreciative laughter from Hindus, while Muslims often attempt to ignore it. Festival tradition thus portrays Muslims in a negative light and Vishnu in an only slightly better one. Yet Harman notes how

Shiva, the dominant deity in the region, nonetheless chooses to display self-deprecating behavior—pulling gags or pranks to get devotees to pay attention—in narrative traditions. When viewing these narrative and ritualized festival accounts in light of the social and religious hierarchies they reflect, one can see that laughter is the domain of the dominant, often at the expense of others. Walters, in "Gods' Play and the Buddha's Way: Varieties of Ritual Levity in Contemporary Sinhala Practice," describes the two strands of religiosity engaged by Sinhala Buddhists, involving what he calls a pre-Buddhist Theistic layer and a more conventional Buddhist layer. Based on interviews with Sinhala Buddhist healers, Walters argues that while levity plays a crucial role in the Theistic layer, it is nearly absent in the Buddhist layer. In the Theistic realm, gods are understood to tease and joke when enacting the "play" of possession; they furthermore expect and receive tangible human offerings for their own sense of entertainment and fun. The Buddhist layer, reflecting the fact that the Buddha, unlike the gods, rises above human needs, emphasizes moral discipline and asceticism that, according to strict monastic codes, strictly eschew the trappings and varieties of ritual levity.

Chapters featured in part 3, "Playing to Win: Edging Out the Competition," lead us to consider instances when ritual levity helps establish religious, social, or political supremacy over opponents. In some cases the competition plays by slightly different rules but ultimately takes part in the same game. In other instances ritual play and laughter distinguish and differentiate between those who play from those who do not, the latter of whom often provide the butt of the joke. McDermott's "Playing with Durga in Bengal," recounting the six-day Durga Puja in Kolkata, relates the gaiety and carnivalesque atmosphere that prevails throughout this Bengali megafestival. Elaborately displayed throughout the region are Durga's images, crafted in *pandal* "homes" and designed to articulate carefully considered themes such as current political events, famous people, and recent movie sets. Amid the nostalgia and a certain level of devotion characterizing the event, the predominant mood surrounding the city's omnipresent and sometimes outrageous display of the goddess is the spectacle of artistic, social, and political competition. McDermott argues that while outsiders might be tempted to read theological meaning into the dizzying array of Durga *pandals*, it is, for those most deeply invested, all about notoriety and winning. Bard, in "Turning Karbala Inside Out: Humor and Ritual Critique in South Asian Muharram Rites," investigates laughter surrounding all-women's *majlis*, or mourning assemblies, during the Sh'i Muslim rite of Muharram. In such instances, women poke fun at female lay preachers as a form of critique. Critical laughter ranges from inappropriate giggles during the event itself, aimed at incongruous regional or outdated styles, to jokes outside of the ritual context at the expense of someone whose arrogant or "masculine" delivery strikes listeners as comically odd. The celebration that concludes Muharram, ending this somber period on a note of levity, has an even sharper edge. Disdained by many Shiahs for a variety of reasons, the event raucously reenacts the death of Sunni caliph Umar and, as such, provides potential fodder for sectarian unrest. Viewing Muharram levity as a whole, Bard observes that laughter at difference and incongruity can devolve into intolerance. Schmalz's "A Catholic Charismatic Healer at Play in North India" concludes this part by describing the life, theology, and practices of Jude, a North Indian Catholic charismatic healer, originally from Kerala. Focusing on Jude's ideologies and actions, Schmalz characterizes the charismatic movement as one that revels in play—from the freedom of glossolalia as a source for divine messages to the joy of healing that incarnates what it means to be redeemed. Schmalz suggests that the key to the charismatic movement is to play through life, in spite of its troubles, into hope and beyond hope. Jude's success as a healer is reliant not only on the fact that he plays the charismatic life and ideology well, but that he is recognized by his clientele as one who plays better than the competition.

## Notes

1. Van Gennep (1960) identified limen as the crucial second phase in the tripartite structure he outlined for all rites of passage.

2. Turner believes that while play continues to be a constitutive element of ritual in what he calls Oriental religions, such as Hinduism, Taoism, Tantrism, and Buddhism, industrialization has displaced or eliminated this element of play in the religions of the book, giving birth to new forms and forums for play such as theater. He writes: "It would seem that with industrialization, urbanization, spreading literacy, labor migration, specialization, professionalization, [and] bureaucracy, the division of the leisure sphere from the work sphere is the firm's clock; the former integrity of the orchestrated ritual *gestalt* that once constituted ritual has burst open, and many specialized performative genres have been born from the death of that mighty *opus deorum hominumque*. These genres of industrial leisure would include theater, ballet, opera, film, the novel . . . rock music, carnivals, processions, folk drama, major sports events, and dozens more" (Turner 1982, 86).

3. Selva Raj (playfully) coined this term to illustrate the coexistence and fusion of sacred and profane characteristics of ritual levity.

4. Particularly in small-scale and traditional societies, periodic excursions and engagement in ritual play can be deemed essential for religious vitality, communal well-being, and social cohesion. Ritual thus becomes a symbolic vehicle to help level, however temporarily, vertical and horizontal barriers and boundaries. As Walsh observes, it is "a great leveler of barriers between man and man, and between man and God" (Walsh 1969, 235), a theme richly illustrated by several chapters in this volume. This theme is further corroborated by Lorna Rhodes (1983) in her analysis of the Sri Lankan exorcist ritual. In this particular ritual, participants poke fun at the Buddhist practice of "giving" (dana), which ordinarily entails deferential treatment of monks who receive regular gifts from the laity. However, during the exorcist ritual, the monks are referred to with disrespect, if not contempt. Rhodes discerns in this deliberate deed "the themes of reluctance to give, the absurdity of the body, and the mocking of hierarchy" (Rhodes 1983, 980).

5. On the psychological benefits of comedy, levity, and humor, see Capps (2002, 2006a) and Berger (1997). In a recent essay (2006a, 393–411), Capps maintains that levity helps negotiate and moderate stress. In the final pages of this essay, he writes: "Humor may help a person cope with negative life experiences. . . . [Humor] seems to mitigate anxieties relating to one's loss of control or inability to determine what happens" (409). In an earlier work, *Men and Their Religion: Honor, Hope, and Humor* (2002), Capps proposes that people have two primary ways of being religious—through a religion of honor and a religion of hope. And because these two modes of religion do not fully satisfy humanity, he argues that we have developed a third religion, "the religion of humor" which, in his view, is the greatest of the three.

## Works Cited

*American College Dictionary*. 1964. 20th ed. New York: Random House.

Berger, Peter L. 1997. *Redeeming Laughter: The Comic Dimension of Human Experience*. New York: Walter de Gruyter.

Capps, Donald. 2002. *Men and Their Religion: Honor, Hope, and Humor*. Harrisburg, PA: Trinity Press International.

Capps, Donald. 2006a. "The Psychological Benefits of Humor." *Pastoral Psychology* 54:5: 5: 393–411.

Capps, Donald. 2006b. "Religion and Humor: Estranged Bedfellows." *Pastoral Psychology* 54:5: 413–38.

Donnelly, Doris. 1992. "Divine Folly: Being Religious and the Exercise of Humor." *Theology Today* 48: 385–98.

Driver, Tom F. 1998. *Liberating Rites: Understanding the Transformative Power of Ritual*. Boulder, CO: Westview Press.

Gilhus, Ingvild S. 1991. "Religion, Laughter and the Ludicrous." *Religion* 21: 257–77.

Huizinga, Johan. 1950. *Homo Ludens: A Study of the Play-Element in Culture*. Boston, MA: Beacon Press.

Hyers, Conrad M., ed. 1969a. "The Comic Profanation of the Sacred." In *Holy Laughter: Essays on Religion in the Comic Perspective*, 9–27. New York: Seabury Press.

Hyers, Conrad M., ed. 1969b. *Holy Laughter: Essays on Religion in the Comic Perspective*. New York: Seabury Press.

Hyers, Conrad M., ed. 1969c. "Introduction." In *Holy Laughter: Essays on Religion in the Comic Perspective*, 1–7. New York: Seabury Press.

Raj, Selva, and William Harman, eds. 2006. "Introduction: The Deal with Deities—Ways Vows Work in South Asia." In *Dealing with Deities: The Ritual Vow in South Asia*, 1–13. Albany: State University of New York Press.

Rhodes, Lorna A. 1983. "Laughter and Suffering: Sinhalese Interpretations of the Use of Ritual Humor." *Social Science and Medicine* 17:14: 979–84.

Siegel, Lee. 1987. *Laughing Matters: Comic Tradition in India*. Chicago, IL: University of Chicago Press.

Turner, Victor. 1982. *From Ritual to Theater: The Human Seriousness of Play*. New York: Performing Arts Journal Publications.

Turner, Victor. 1986. *The Anthropology of Performance*. New York: Performing Arts Journal Publications.

Van Gennep, Arnold. 1960. *The Rites of Passage*. Translated by Monika B. Vizedom and Gabrielle L. Cafee. Chicago, IL: University of Chicago Press.

Walsh, Chad. 1969. "On Being with It: An Afterword." In *Holy Laughter: Essays on Religion in the Comic Perspective*, ed. Conrad M. Hyers, 241–51. New York: Seabury Press.

Webster's *New World Dictionary of the American Language*. 1966. College edition. New York: World Publishing Company.

Part 1

# Laughing Inside Out

*Playful Breaks with Convention*

## 2

# Serious Levity at the Shrine of St. Anne in South India

SELVA J. RAJ

## Introduction

If there is any one thing that clearly distinguishes performance in the ritual mode from other kinds of events it is that the performer assumes roles and relates to what is going on in an "as if" way not appropriate to the workaday world. As Turner (1969) insisted, ritual realizes itself in the subjunctive mood. The so-called "sacred space" and "sacred time" of religious rituals are, above all, imaginative constructions, "rules of the game." The playfulness of rituals, however, does not mean that rituals are nothing more than play-acting, much less that they cannot be efficacious. "When a Christian priest lifts a chalice, or a New Guinea man greases a sacred stone, each really *does* what she or he is doing. Such a performer does not only pretend, as might an actor on a proscenium stage. In rituals, for the most part, there is no question of illusion. Gestures are actually performed, and these gestures have social, personal, and religious consequences. In short, rituals are a kind of playful work" (Driver 1998, 98).

Fifty years ago, in his seminal work *Homo Ludens*, Johan Huizinga (1950) called our attention to the close relationship between ritual and play. Subsequent cross-cultural studies and ethnographic data suggest that not only are rituals and play intimately related, producing a substantial similarity between these two forms, but that frequently this union gains dialectical expression. To scholars engaged in cross-cultural and comparative studies, this dialectic presents a new hermeneutical category, the category of ritual levity or ritual play, where seriousness and playfulness, or, in Huizinga's words, "sacred earnest and 'make-believe' or 'fun,'" coexist as the twin faces of public rituals (Huizinga 1950, 24). This dialectic of seriousness and levity—more simply serious ritual levity—gains special prominence during annual or grand religious festivals. In this chapter, I examine two public rituals typically performed during the annual festival at a Catholic shrine in the south Indian state of Tamil Nadu. Though each reveals a distinctive form of ritual levity, taken together they well illustrate the dialectic of serious ritual levity. In the concluding section, I offer some reflections on the social and religious significance for the devotees and the social and religious institutions that endorse and legitimize such public displays.

## The Shrine of St. Anne at Arulanandapuram

Fifteen miles south of the city of Madurai in the south Indian state of Tamil Nadu lies the tiny village of Arulanandapuram in the civil district of Shivaganga. After a half-hour bus trip from Madurai, on a sunny summer afternoon in July 2003, I arrived at Sampranendal, a small village on the main highway connecting Madurai and Manamadurai. Having been to this village before on prior research trips, I was quite familiar with the local landscape. Getting off the bus, my research assistant and I walked through rice and sugarcane fields to reach the banks of the Vaigai River, the major water resource for the region's farmers. While there was a steady flow of water in the central areas of the river, the outlying areas were notably dry. Those familiar with the river and the region know full well that except for the monsoon season, when the water level rises significantly, for much of the year segments of the Vaigai River dwindle into a trickle, though waist deep in the deeper parts of the river. A fifteen-minute walk through the river brought us to the outskirts of the village of Arulanandapuram, surrounded by tall palmyra and coconut trees. Most prominent in the village landscape is a large but aging Gothic Catholic church towering above clusters of tiny mud huts and brick houses. Located within the church compound are the parochial elementary school and the shrine priest's residence.

The village name "Arulanandapuram," meaning "the village of Arulanandam," reflects the Catholic religious identity of the villagers. "Arulanandam," literally "bliss of divine grace," is the Tamil name for St. John de Britto. Britto was a seventeenth-century Portuguese Jesuit missionary saint who was beheaded at the orders of the Hindu king of Ramnad in February 1693 in Oriyur near the ancient port town of Thondy, sixty-five miles northeast of Arulanandapuram. Hailed as the Marava saint—that is, the saint of the Marava caste groups, such as the Pallars, Kallars, and Udayars, widespread in the vicinity of Oriyur—St. John de Britto is a popular Catholic saint in the region, renowned for his ability to bestow fertility and healing. So revered is this European saint that not only has the local Catholic diocese adopted him as its patron, but it is customary for devotees to name their children, settlements, and villages after him. Interestingly enough, though the village is named after the Marava saint, none of the Marava caste groups is represented in the village's homogenous population. Its 150 households belong to the Vellala caste.

In terms of caste hierarchy in Tamil Nadu, the Vellalas are ranked higher than the socially humbler Nadar, Udayar, Kallar, and Pallar caste groups. Though originally an agricultural caste, a sizable segment of the Vellalas—due to the support of European Jesuit missionaries—has had greater access to formal education and white-collar jobs. Detached from social commerce with other caste or religious groups necessitated by both geographical and social realities, the villagers of Arulanandapuram live a fairly insulated existence. Given that intracaste and intrareligious marriage is the prescribed cultural protocol and accepted social practice, its inhabitants only marry Vellala Catholics from the village, its diasporic population, or neighboring Vellala Catholic villages. Consequently, with the exception of the annual festival, intercaste and interreligious fellowship is not only unknown but constitutes a major taboo.

Cut off from the mainland by the Vaigai River, Arulanandapuram is an isolated interior village that, like many villages in rural India, has been left out of recent developments and lacks access to such basic modern amenities and services as running water, electricity, indoor plumbing, and transportation. Of the 150 households, only a dozen or so can boast of electricity. Between my first visit to the village as a young boy in the mid-1960s and my recent visit in 2003, there has not been any notable change in the village's geophysical landscape or infrastructure. In some ways, it has remained frozen in time. Apart from the lack of basic amenities, the village does not have the resources to introduce public means for social and cultural interaction, such as movie theaters, clubs, playgrounds, and shopping centers. To procure basic necessities such as groceries, its residents have to cross the sometimes waist-deep Vaigai River and travel approximately five miles on foot or by bus to neighboring small towns such as Thiruppachethi in the north and Rajagambeeram in the south.

In the absence of basic social outlets, the parish church serves as the sole locus of social interactions and cultural activities. The parochial elementary school administered by the local Catholic diocese is the lone symbol of progress. After completing elementary education, economically well-off families send their children to boarding schools in neighboring cities, where many of these children eventually choose to settle down. Not surprisingly, therefore, during the past five decades, a large number of natives have migrated to urban areas and major cities such as Madurai and Trichy in search of white-collar jobs and better living conditions. This exodus has not only caused a steady and severe brain drain but has adversely affected the village's labor pool and economy. Of those who remain in the village, a negligible number of men work in textile mills and factories in the neighboring town of Manamadurai, while the vast majority of men and women work in sugarcane, rice, and beetle-leaf fields.

Whereas the village is named after the powerful Marava saint John de Britto, the shrine itself is dedicated to St. Anne, a popular Catholic saint and mother of the Virgin Mary, who attracts large numbers of devotees from all castes and creeds from the economically depressed civil districts of Ramnad and Shivaganga, particularly during the annual festival. Well known in the southeastern part of Tamil Nadu for her powers of fertility and healing, St. Anne is the revered recipient of various votive performances and vow rituals locally known as *nercchai*. By its association with two sacred figures (Britto and Anne), this rural shrine is believed to contain the combined sacral powers of the two Catholic saints most revered in the region. The annual festival, when devotees draw the statues of saints Anne and Britto enthroned in colorfully decorated chariots through the village streets, is a public declaration of their dual patronage.

At the social level, its patron, St. Anne, supports the rigid indigenous social order insofar as she enables its Vellala residents to differentiate themselves from the humbler Marava Catholics through their prominent place in festival procedings. Though sponsored by the dominant Vellala Catholic group, the festival also attracts some Marava Catholics and Hindus from the vicinity. This practice of constructing churches and church festivals along caste lines is not peculiar to this village but fairly widespread in rural Tamil Nadu. Unlike other more famed regional shrines in Tamil Nadu, the Vellala-associated shrine of St. Anne enjoys the limited patronage of the local village, its diasporic community, and its more immediate neighbors. In contrast, the shrine of Britto at Oriyur or the pan-Indian basilica of Our Lady of Good Health at Velankanni on the Coromandel Coast in the Bay of Bengal attracts tens of thousands of devotees from diverse ethnic, linguistic, caste, regional, and religious groups.

The annual festival observed on the titular feast of St. Anne in the last week of July is undoubtedly the high point of the village's cultural and religious life. Celebrated over five days, the festival season transforms this otherwise sleepy farming village into a site of intense social interaction, cultural activities, and religious fervor. The entire village wears a festive look. Merchants set up temporary shops and stalls for brisk business among visiting pilgrims and local residents. Banana trees and mango leaves—common festive symbols in Tamil Nadu—adorn the main street leading to the shrine. Bright electric illuminations, powered by rented generators, give a fresh look to the aging Gothic church. Throughout the day, loudspeakers blare devotional and film songs. A feature film shown free of cost on the penultimate day of the festival is a major attraction among the villagers and their neighbors. On the last day of the festival, a band of Hindu musicians and drummers hired for the occasion is in attendance, providing live music for the special festivities of the day, including the chariot procession. Scores of visiting pilgrims set up temporary residence in the parochial school. Locals who have migrated to urban centers make it a point to return to the village during the festival season, receiving hospitality from relatives and childhood friends. Despite the obvious hardships and inconveniences of rustic living, many emigrants look forward to this annual trip to the village with palpable anticipation, as it affords for many an opportunity to express their spiritual loyalty to the patron saint and renew social bonds and cultural ties with kinfolk. The more devout among them treat such hardships and inconveniences as temporary forms of asceticism and as expressions of personal devotion to the saint. For the vast majority, these annual sojourns serve as the only surviving link to their native, cultural roots.

## The Men Who Cook: A Ritual of Serious Levity

Observed on the last day of the festival on July 23, the Men Who Cook ritual marks the culmination of the five-day festive celebration. It is eagerly anticipated by the village community, particularly the village women and visiting pilgrims.[1] Preparations for this day-long ritual begin in the early hours of the morning. At the break of dawn, the menfolk of the village march in groups to the banks of the Vaigai River, carrying empty silver, aluminum, earthen, and plastic water pots. After their purificatory bath in the river, they fill the pitchers with water. Even as they go about this obligatory task, they do so in a playful spirit, throwing water at each other and poking fun at other men struggling to balance the water pots on their waists. But as they line up for the ensuing solemn procession, there is a notable seriousness in their demeanor and deportment. With water pots on their waists, heads, or shoulders, and drenched in wet *veshti* (a long, white cloth worn by men in Tamil Nadu) wrapped around their waists, the men solemnly proceed in single file through the main streets of the village toward the shrine as loudspeakers blare devotional songs. Women and children stand along the processional route and watch the spectacle with delightful glee and laughter. Upon reaching the portico of the shrine, the pots are placed in the shape of a giant cross. Placed above the metallic cross are large aluminum drums and trays containing rice, vegetables, spices, and other culinary ingredients. Dressed in formal liturgical attire, the shrine priest now stands in front of the cross and welcomes the men bearing water pots. When the last pot is placed on the ground, he blesses the pots with holy water and incense, recites a few prayers, and concludes this para-liturgical rite with a formal blessing on the assembly of men as women and children congregate in the background.

As soon as the blessing ceremony is over, the men set out on the most important task of the day—cooking the festive communal meal to be served later in the evening for the entire village and for the visiting pilgrims. Some men set up three huge temporary stoves on the shrine premises, while others go about chopping onions, vegetables, and other ingredients required for the sumptuous vegetarian meal.[2] As elsewhere in rural south India, at Arulanandapuram, fetching water and cooking are considered female tasks. However, on this day, men assume these conventional female roles and duties. I was told that in the past women never went near the stoves, nor did they assist in the preparation of the meal. Nowadays, however, some women and children assist the men by cutting vegetables or peeling onions. When the meal is ready, the village catechist makes a public announcement over the loudspeaker inviting visiting female vow-takers, village women, children, and visiting pilgrims of both genders. Village tradition requires that men serve the meal first to children followed by female votaries, women, and visiting pilgrims of diverse castes. This pattern is a reversal of the traditional norm and practice of women serving the men first and eating the leftovers as well as societal rules regarding intercaste commensality. According to one estimate, the village men feed an average of about 1,000 people. Village tradition requires that only after all of the children, women, and visitors are fed can the men partake of the leftovers of the communal meal.

The prevalent mood among male actors and female spectators, both during the preparation and the serving of the meal, is one of seriousness and joviality. From fetching water to serving the meal, the men go about their tasks with notable seriousness. Accompanying this manifest seriousness is a latent spirit of levity. Throughout the day, the Men Who Cook are the butt of female parody, ridicule, and jokes. Relieved of their usual kitchen duties for a day, women spend the entire day in leisure in the company of other women, either in their homes or on shrine premises. Women who volunteer to assist in the cooking do not miss a single opportunity to poke fun at men's culinary skills or lack thereof. Others who opt to observe the goings-on from a distance narrate humorous anecdotes about their husbands' cooking skills and domestic prowess. Except for an occasional joke, men generally abstain from poking fun at the women and diligently go about their ritually prescribed duty. The entire sequence is interspersed with an admixture of prescribed and obligatory seriousness and playfulness. The men are obligated to perform their duty seriously, and the women are expected to poke fun at the men. Thus each group performs its respective playful duty with appropriate, obligatory seriousness. Even as they play their respective scripted roles, all of the prominent actors in this drama—men, women, children, and the clergy—are fully cognizant that the entire ritual is make-believe, temporary, and playful. The rest of the year, men will not cook for women, and women will not eat before men. Nor can or do women poke fun at the men in public. Similarly, the rest of the year, Vellala Catholics will neither eat nor share commensality with people of other castes or religions.

An additional level of role reversal emerges during the serving of the communal meal. Childless women praying for the gift of children form an important cultic constituency of St. Anne. Considered ritually inauspicious due to their inability to bear children, these socially marginalized women subject themselves to public social humiliation during the communal meal in an effort to redress a physical malady and its social implications. In the days and weeks preceding the festival, these female votaries commit themselves to a strict ascetic regimen observing a series of taboos and prescriptions including, though not limited to, regular fasting, abstinence from sexual activity, dietary restrictions, and self-selected devotional exercises.

The last day of the festival marks a day of obligatory ritual fasting for these women votaries, beginning with a pre-dawn purificatory bath at the shrine well. After the purificatory bath, the petitioners proceed in wet clothes to the shrine and drink a glass of margosa juice prepared by a village woman noted for her pious devotion. Following this preliminary ritual, each petitioner—accompanied occasionally by a female relative—goes separately on a begging round. Local tradition requires each votary to beg uncooked rice and vegetables from five different households, declaring to her donors the specific favor hoped for. The items thus collected are then taken directly to the shrine staff. Votaries spend the remainder of the day continuing to fast until the shrine staff issues a call on the public speaker inviting them for the first serving of the communal meal. Prepared by men in a socially inverse ritual, this festive meal is said to be particularly auspicious and efficacious for childless women. After the meal is served to children and before the children begin eating, each petitioner—occasionally accompanied by her spouse—kneels in front of the children, recites a prayer, and begs food from ten children. With the food thus collected, the petitioner sits beside the children and eats it. It is believed that consuming the food donated by the children will yield offspring. Devotees say that St. Anne rewards those women who humble themselves in this fashion with the boon solicited. Local residents and visiting pilgrims never tire recounting stories about women who were blessed with children after undertaking this socially humbling yet salutary rite.

## Playing with the Saint: The Baby Auction Ritual

The ludic aspects of public rituals at Arulanandapuram gain dramatic expression in yet another ritual, which also occurs on the last day of the festival: the ceremonial baby auction.[3] Although symbolic auctions are a common devotional exercise in rural Catholic shrines throughout Tamil Nadu, the live Baby Auction sponsored by visiting pilgrims and local residents is unique to the shrine of St. Anne at Arulanandapuram. Couples seeking children indicate in a promissory note (*muri*) that if and when their prayer is granted they would surrender the child to the saint. Signed by two witnesses and notarized by the village catechist, the *muri* is kept in the shrine until its fulfillment. If and when the prayer is answered, couples pay off their debt by surrendering the child to the saint in a carefully orchestrated ceremonial auction. One such auction that I witnessed in July 1990 well illustrates the dialectic of seriousness and playfulness, a trademark feature of Arulanandapuram's public ritual performance and tradition.

Joseph Thomas, a police officer in the city of Madurai, and his wife Mary, an elementary school teacher, got married in 1982 but were childless for seven years. After persistent admonition and prompting from family and friends, they went on a pilgrimage to several shrines—Catholic and Hindu alike—including the popular shrine of Our Lady of Good Health at Velankanni, and they offered numerous *nercchai* rites praying for a child, but to no avail. In early July 1988, they met a native of Arulanandapuram who testified to the special sacral powers of the shrine and its patron St. Anne, persuading the young couple to offer *nercchai* rites during the annual festival. Desperate to have a child, Joseph and Mary went on pilgrimage to Arulanandapuram in July 1988 and submitted a *muri* pledging to return the child to St. Anne if she would grant their prayer. Later that year, Mary conceived, and in 1989 she gave birth to a baby girl.

The following year, the couple returned to the shrine with the ten-month-old baby during the annual festival to pay off their debt. At the couple's express request, the village catechist rang the church bell announcing the couple's intention to fulfill their promise and inviting the entire village to witness the ritual. After placing various votive offerings at the altar of St. Anne in thanksgiving for favors received, the couple entered the vestibule and handed over the infant to the village catechist. Conspicuous by his absence was the shrine priest, who stayed back in his residence just 100 yards away. With the whole village now in attendance, the catechist received the baby, called for bids on the infant, and proceeded to auction off the baby. All members of the family—men and women, young and old, local villagers and visiting pilgrims—enthusiastically participated in the auction by making bids. Joseph and Mary stood on the side and watched, with some mild trepidation, as the ceremonial auction gained momentum. When the bidding reached Rs 100, the child's father made a bid for Rs 101 (a paltry sum, even by local economic standards), at which time the auctioneer quickly concluded the auction and handed the baby to the highest bidder: the child's natural father!

During my interview with the couple soon after the auction, I learned that prior to the ceremony they had made a private deal with the auctioneer so that when the father bid Rs 101, the auctioneer would quickly conclude the auction. Thus the auction proceeded as scripted, with everyone taking an active part. All participants in this ritual drama knew their respective roles and played their part diligently and seriously—some by their presence and others by making bids—knowing full well that there were no real losers in this game, and that everyone would come out winners. The auctioneer knew full well that he was presiding over a pretend auction that nevertheless had serious implications for the family and the shrine. Members of the assembly were serious about making bids on the child, fully aware that they would never make the final bidding. Yet they played a crucial role insofar as they helped the parents fulfill their promise to pay off the debt. The parents initiated the auction, confident in the knowledge that they would not in fact lose the baby, even if the ritual did cause some internal anxiety. Devotees claim that the saint—given her supranormal powers—also knew the eventual outcome, as did the parish priests and church officials. With the exception of the screaming baby—the central character in this ritual drama who was blissfully ignorant of the multiple and multilayered negotiations—everyone knew that it was a pretend action, conducted with dead seriousness, yet laced with a subtle dose of playfulness.

By participating in this ritual drama, votaries fulfill their part of the deal, and they signal to the saint, church officials, and the village community that the transaction is complete. While they acknowledge the ritual maneuvering and manipulation implicit in this transaction, devotees do not believe that they are shortchanging the saint. Nor do they believe that the saint is wholly duped. Certain spiritual and social benefits accrue to the saint as well, in the form of renewed faith in her powers and a stronger commitment to her cult. The audience at this auction is what Huizinga calls "the chorus to the play" that knows it must not be "spoil-sports" (Huizinga 1950, 23). What matters to the saint, devotees insist, is not the child per se but votaries' resolve and commitment to live up to their part of the bargain in some form. This ceremonial auction benefits all concerned: parents have the satisfaction of living up to their end of the contractual agreement; the shrine gains additional revenue and prestige; the villagers gain renewed confirmation in the efficacy of their rituals and the sacred powers of their local shrine; and the saint's sacral powers are authenticated, enhancing her spiritual prestige and gaining her some new devotees. I learned that, on average, a half dozen such ceremonial auctions take place on the last day of the festival every year.

Let me close this ethnographic account with a brief comparative overview of the two examples of ritual levity, discussed earlier. While both occur in the shared spatial and temporal context of the shrine and its annual religious festival, one can discern significant differences. First, while the Men Who Cook ritual occurs in a predominantly social setting involving a full cast of human characters consciously mixing up and parodying socially constructed categories of gender and gender roles, the second ritual occurs in an overtly religious context involving both human and sacred characters. The temporary communion of two distinct categories of beings (human and sacred), notable in the second example, provides clues to the reciprocity that is a hallmark of divine-human relationships in Tamil Nadu. Second, the patron saint who was merely a distant and silent spectator in the Men Who Cook ritual, providing tacit approval and legitimacy to social constructions, is chosen by her human devotees as an active participant in the ceremonial Baby Auction. Her inclusion infuses a sacred character to an otherwise material, economic transaction, transforming it into a sacred covenant.

On the theoretical level, the two examples help differentiate two types of ritual levity. Although both involve play-acting, one is more overt and the other more subtle and invisible. Thus whereas levity is quite palpable in the Men Who Cook ritual, elements of levity are more subdued and invisible in the Baby Auction example. Nevertheless, if pretense is an essential characteristic of play, as Driver (1998) and Huizinga (1950) have convincingly argued, then the Baby Auction is playful, since its entire cast is conscious of the pretension that dominates its conceptual framework and ritual performance. These differences notwithstanding, both reveal the dialectic of serious playfulness. Finally, not only are these expressions of levity and play distinct in form and content, but they also serve two distinct yet related goals and functions. Whereas the former helps maintain and reinforce the efficacy of social order, the latter serves to reinforce important indigenous religious assumptions about ritual efficacy and about sacred figures and their powers. The Men Who Cook ritual reveals intravillage social dynamics, while the Baby Auction reflects the dynamics between the human and divine realms.

## Concluding Reflections

Role reversal and status reorganization constitute a common thematic thread in the two examples just documented. Anthropologists such as Turner (1969) and Marriott (1986) and other scholars such as Hunt (1977) and Kretzer (1988) have explored the social, cultural, psychological, and even political significance of role reversals and status elevation rituals that often occur during religious festivals.[4] Religious festivals, these scholars argue, provide a culturally prescribed moment to indulge in antistructural and chaotic behavior in order to experiment with other redemptive possibilities unavailable within a conventional structure. It is a suspended, liminal moment when human and divine realms merge. That moment is sacred and charged with the freedom to experiment with new possibilities. Consequently, traditional roles and norms are temporarily reversed so that everyone can return at the conclusion of the festival to their traditionally assigned roles and positions with a renewed sense of structure and order.

These features are clearly apparent in the Men Who Cook ritual. Men who normally do not cook assume the lowly role of cooks for a day. Women who ordinarily eat after men not only eat before them but are served by the men they normally serve. Thus the lowly are elevated, and the powerful are made low, though just for a day. This role reversal pattern—though in a slightly different form impelled by a human need—is also manifest in the communal meal where socially marginalized childless women seek to redress personal crisis and regain social status by humbling themselves before children who are also marginalized. Lowly children, in turn, gain ritual elevation over their social superiors, albeit temporarily. Religiously, this reversal rite also exhibits the classic traits of sympathetic magic, insofar as devotees hope to attain the privilege to feed and nurture children by being fed and nurtured by them.

Although less apparent, the themes of role reversal and status adjustment are also prominent in the Baby Auction. Occurring at a liminal moment, this rite involves a cast of liminal characters and entities, those whose identities and roles are temporarily unhinged or shifted. For the duration of the ritual, the child's natural parents return to their precontractual state of childlessness, awaiting the outcome with mild trepidation, while the witnessing crowd acts as the child's potential parents. Conspicuously absent and ritually invisible, the shrine priest, who ordinarily is the proper ritual specialist, is relegated to the role of a passive, distant spectator, while a simple orderly of the priest, the village catechist, assumes the coveted role of ritual proxy for his ritual and spiritual superiors: the priest and the saint.

Conversely, the transcendent saintly intercessor is also temporarily brought from the divine/sacred realm into a personal encounter with the harsh realities and earthly needs of her human devotees. Humanized by her devotees, she presides over the fulfillment of a sacred contract modeled after an economic human transaction. Like the child's parents, St. Anne also enters into a liminal state, becoming humanized and accepting a temporary reduction in status. Ultimately, however, both the saint and the parents—the principal actors in this ritual drama—regain their status in the process. The saint gains fame and notoriety for her ritual power, while the latter attains social esteem. Having had the privilege of participating in a sacred drama, the audience too emerges from the ritual with an elevated sense of self and sacred connection.

Apart from the themes of status reversal and enhancement, other scholars discern the roles that laughter and levity play in role-reversal rituals. In *Humor and Laughter*, Apte (1985) discusses sex-role reversal rituals associated with ritual humor or ritual play and cites several cross-cultural examples from Nigeria, Mexico, and Native America. In all of these instances, the role-reversal rite provides a ritual outlet for its members to step out of ordinary life and laugh at the absurdities of the social constructions and structure they have embraced or inherited. To turn to the two rituals described in this chapter, the Men Who Cook ritual affords the villagers an opportunity to temporarily transcend and laugh at the inbuilt shortcomings and inherent absurdities of the social structures in which they ultimately find meaning and order. They laugh at the rigidity of the order when they step out of it. However, even as they parody and ridicule them, social constructions—more precisely, gender role determinations—are neither aggressively rejected nor permanently altered but only temporarily reversed and exchanged in a playful manner in a seriously constructed make-believe ritual framework.

Similarly, in the Baby Auction ritual, the unhinging of realms temporarily brings about a new order between humanity and divinity. This shifting of realms places devotees in a different space and time and makes efficacious their contract; the vow turns effective in the space where roles and realms are temporarily rearranged. And playfulness is crucial to this shift. Rooted in popular devotional practice, the mechanics of the Baby Auction vow performance are in some ways a transgression of religious prescription, asserting the efficacy of nonorthodox rituals and, by implication, the inefficacy of normative religion. To this extent, the auction becomes a parody of official, normative religion, a feature that explains, in part, the shrine priest's absence from the auction.

While inversion characterizes the Men Who Cook ritual, subversion is the dominant motif and strategy in the Baby Auction ritual, though both ultimately acknowledge the respective values of social order and official religion. Though their strategies and targets might differ, in both cases ritual humor, levity, or play is neither spontaneous nor haphazard. On the contrary, playfulness is carefully prescribed, orchestrated, structured, regulated, and executed. Whether executed in a strictly religious context, as in the case of the Baby Auction sponsored by Joseph and Mary, or a socioreligious context, as in the case of the

Men Who Cook ritual, these rites emerge with predictable regularity at the prescribed calendrical moment of the annual festival.

Upon closer scrutiny of the social realities and cultural dynamics of Arulanandapuram, we discover that something besides status and role realignment is at work in these playful rituals. Its residents live amidst two distinct yet interlocking realms of absurdities: the realm of social absurdity and the realm of existential absurdity. The former refers to social dyamics mentioned earlier: the absurdity of rigid societal constructions, especially those that regulate gender relations. The latter refers to villagers' existential absurdities and frustrations of isolated existence bereft of life's basic amenities and comforts. As Huizinga (1950) has argued, levity, humor, and play are "the accompaniment, the complement, in fact an integral part of life in general. It adorns life, amplifies it and is to that extent a necessity both for the individual—as a life function—and for society by reason of the meaning it contains, its significance, its expressive value, its spiritual and social associations, in short, as a culture function" (9). For the residents of Arulanandapuram, periodic ludic excursions in the ritual context help enhance and complement an otherwise insulated rustic existence, rife with social restrictiveness and cultural confinement, investing meaning and significance in their commonly held social values and cherished collective faith in St. Anne and her sacral powers.[5]

Ritual levity and playfulness discussed herein are therefore not merely social and cultural expressions but are charged with profound religious meaning and significance. This is evident in the preferred religious context and framework for communal playfulness and in the religious behavior and sentiments these events evoke in the participants. These levity rites accrue a certain weightiness precisely because they take place in the sacred space of the shrine—rather than in a secular or neutral site—and at the religiously auspicious time of the annual festival in the context of a paraliturgical service with the tacit approval of the clergy. In the case of the residents and pilgrims of Arulanandapuram, these public festive rituals place them in the good graces of the powerful patron saint who is capable of answering their manifold mundane needs, particularly fertility. These rituals also help them overcome structural difficulties, even if only for a brief moment, having to do with the frustrations of an insulated social life, the rigidities of caste structure, the inbuilt tensions associated with rural farming existence, and the gender inequalities embedded in a strict patriarchal system. Within the ritual context, these social discourses are imbued furthermore with a sense of the sacred.

Even as ritual participants seek to transcend, however temporarily, the ordinariness and absurdity of mundane life, their playfulness is inscribed with a notable seriousness in which they, as Driver describes it, "are almost always conscious of the absurdity, the contradiction lying within ritual pretension" (1998, 99). In other words, while ritual participants are serious about executing these rituals, they are playfully and painfully aware of the inability of the ritual to lift them above the ordinariness of their mundane rural existence. Play, humor, and laughter thus become an acknowledgment of this imperfect existential condition. In this regard, Driver's comment, that "in ritual, sacrality and sacrilege are twins" (1998, 99) seems appropriate. It is this unholy alliance between sacrality and sacrilege, between seriousness and playfulness, that sustains and provides vitality to the serious levity amply embedded in the ritual tradition at Arulanandapuram.

## Notes

I am grateful to Albion College for a Hewlett-Mellon grant in 2003 that provided funds for summer field research at Arulanandapuram. I also am grateful to my colleagues Corinne Dempsey and William Harman for their valuable comments and suggestions regarding earlier drafts that aided in the revision of this chapter.

1. A regular social fixture in the ethnically and racially diverse city of Albion, Michigan, the Men Who Cook ritual is a popular social event, attracting large numbers of local residents of diverse races. The role-reversal aspects of this social ritual are quite obvious. When first introduced twenty years ago, its founders envisaged this annual social tradition primarily as a community-building strategy and as an occasion and a venue for fostering intracity communion and interracial fellowship in an ethnically diverse city. The founders also viewed this tradition as a unique way to raise funds for the beautification of the city. Since it was not a common cultural practice then for men to cook, city residents welcomed this tradition as a novel experiment intended to level conventional gender role constructions. Though humor elements are not overtly expressed or talked about, these are neither absent nor entirely lost among the participants.

2. Some elderly residents of the village told me that in the past nonvegetarian meals were the norm. The flesh of goats and chickens offered by pilgrims in fulfillment of *nerccai* vow rituals was cooked and served as a main dish during the communal meal, but today only vegetarian dishes are prepared for the communal meal.

3. A differently focused discussion of this ritual appears in *Dealing with Deities: The Ritual Vow in South Asia* (2006), where I explore the dynamic of ritual exchange between Hindus and Catholics in south India.

4. Kretzer maintains that role-reversal rites are "mechanisms through [which] the oppressed can release pent-up frustrations and hostilities, and, by so doing, preserve the status quo." Through such rituals, "the powerless switch places with the powerful on the designated day" (Kretzer 1988, 131).

5. In *The Sacred and the Profane*, Eliade (1959) suggests that rituals help humans overcome the ordinariness and absurdity of life by placing them in the company of gods and in primordial time.

## Works Cited

Apte, Mahadev. 1985. *Humor and Laughter: An Anthropological Approach*. Ithaca, NY: Cornell University Press.

Driver, Tom. 1998. *Liberating Rites: Understanding the Transformative Power of Ritual*. Boulder, CO: Westview Press.

Eliade, Mircea. 1959. *The Sacred and the Profane: The Nature of Religion*. San Diego, CA: A Harvest/HBJ Book.

Eliade, Mircea. 1974. *Patterns in Comparative Religion*. New York: A Meridian Book.

Firth, Raymond. 1973. *Symbols: Public and Private*. Ithaca, NY: Cornell University Press.

Huizinga, Johan. 1950. *Homo Ludens: A Study of the Play-Element in Culture*. Boston, MA: Beacon Press.

Hunt, Eva. 1977. "Ceremonies of Confrontation and Submission: The Symbolic Dimension of Indian-Mexican Political Interaction." In *Secular Ritual*, ed. Sally F. Moore and Barbara G. Myerhoff, 127–47. Aseen: Van Gorcum.

Kretzer, David, I. 1988. *Ritual, Politics, and Power*. New Haven, CT: Yale University Press.

Marriott, McKim. 1986. *Village India: Studies in Little Community*. Chicago, IL: University of Chicago Press.

Raj, Selva, J. 2006. "Shared Vows, Shared Space, Shared Deities." In *Dealing with Deities: The Ritual Vow in South Asia*, ed. Selva J. Raj and William Harman, 43–64. Albany: State University of New York Press.

Singer, Milton. 1980. *When a Great Tradition Modernizes*. Chicago, IL: University of Chicago Press.

Turner, Victor. 1969. *Ritual Process: Structure and Antistructure*. Ithaca, NY: Cornell University Press.

3

# Don't Take It Badly, It's Holi

## *Ritual Levity, Society, and Agriculture*

A. Whitney Sanford

India's springtime festival Holi enlivens the months of February and March in north India. During the six weeks of the Holi season, the telltale splotches of red, yellow, and pink on hair and clothing mark the enthusiastic celebration of this festival. While Holi is celebrated throughout India, residents of Braj—a cultural and geographic region approximately 150 miles southeast of Delhi—are arguably the keenest participants. The dominant religious expression in the Braj region is devotion to the Hindu deity Krishna, his consort Radha, and his brother Balarama, and the Holi celebrations in Braj are intimately tied to this devotional tradition. Visitors observing the Holi festivities might be struck by the raucousness of the festival, as water fights and the throwing of colored powders, some of the most obvious manifestations of Holi, are par for the course.

Holi is a festival of frivolity and celebration, not one of solemnity and dignity, so in this contribution to the discussion of ritual levity, it is not hard to argue that Holi is fun and funny. After all, water fights are fun, and throwing things is fun. However, I contend that the ritual festivities associated with Holi—elements we might call ritual levity—provide important social functions as well. I will further argue that the "fun" of Holi is not incidental but critical for these social goals. In particular, the Holi festivities provide a means to renew and maintain social bonds, and in doing so they celebrate the continuity of the agricultural cycle and demonstrate the important connections between social and agricultural health.

This chapter will specifically discuss the Holi festivities as they are celebrated in Baldeo, a village in Braj that is known as Balarama's place. Just east of an oxbow on the Yamuna River, it lies eighteen kilometers downstream of Mathura, a holy city located approximately fifty kilometers north of Agra, which is reputed to be the birthplace of Krishna, itself over 100 kilometers downstream of Delhi. Baldeo lies in a primarily agricultural district, and the roads to the village are lined with fields of mustard, wheat, and barley. Baldeo is the center of Balarama pilgrimage and houses his image worshipped as Dauji or Baldev. Temple guides and hereditary priests from the Panda community perform service rituals (*seva*) for Balarama that are patterned on worship rituals of the Vallabh Sampraday, one of the two major devotional communities of the sixteenth century. Local temple priests emphasize that Balarama is the king of Braj, yet Braj is divided in half, with the Yamuna River as the dividing line. Krishna reigns supreme in his half, which includes Mathura, Govardhan, and Vrindavan, while the other side of the Yamuna River, including Gokul and Baldeo, belongs to Balarama.

Baldeo has a specific set of devotional practices that center on Balarama, not the more famous Krishna. Balarama is Krishna's elder brother and is himself a deity often associated with agricultural concerns, responsible for the region's fertility. Most images of Balarama depict him as carrying a plow and a mace, tools that denote his agricultural and protective responsibilities. Holi in Baldeo reinforces Balarama's status as the king and protector of Braj, emphasizing his capacity for both social and agricultural renewal. In this chapter, I will discuss some Holi practices in Baldeo that one might identify as ritual levity, and I will explain their contextualization within Baldeo lore and practice. These events during Baldeo's Holi appear riotous like much of Holi in India, but they have a specific meaning in Baldeo. Residents note that Holi activities in Baldeo both contribute to the renewal of social bonds as well as reinforce a sense of Balarama's rectitude, even when at first glance these raucous events might be seen as encouraging the exact opposite. To begin this discussion, I will first broadly address the Holi festival itself and then explore how Holi is a particularly special festival for devotees of Balarama.

Holi marks the arrival of spring and the harvesting of the winter's crops, and by February most of north India is eager to celebrate the passing of winter. Many ritual elements of Holi, such as the hobbyhorse, the bonfire, and the temporary abandonment of behavioral codes, bear structural similarities to other historical and contemporary springtime agricultural festivals, such as, for example, the burning of the straw man in Celtic traditions (Crooke 1896, 315–18). Most forms of revelry in Braj have no textual referents, but the agricultural and fertility elements of the Holi festivities are clear in both text and practice (Haberman 1994, 174–75; Marriott 1966, 204–205). Balarama's dragging the Yamuna River with his plow has obvious sexual connotations, as I will describe later, and contemporary Holi festivities demonstrate a sexual license that would be inappropriate at any other time. The importance of seeds, plows, and bonfires in Holi ritual demonstrates that the celebration of spring and its fertility is an essential aspect of the festival. The ritual exchange of seeds and the ubiquitous throwing of color furthermore reveal connections between agriculture and social relationships.

Like most Indian festivals, the celebration of Holi is determined according to the lunar calendar (each month has a dark half when the moon is waning and a bright half when the moon is waxing). As such, the dates of Holi shift by a few days each year. This calendrical system ensures that most festivals are intimately linked to natural and agricultural cycles. Most devotees play Holi over a week-long period so they can travel throughout Braj to enjoy Holi on different days in villages significant to Krishna and Balarama. On the full-moon day of the lunar month Phalguna (February–March), avid devotees arrive in Balarama's village in Baldeo to play Holi with Balarama.

The entire Holi season lasts approximately six weeks, starting on Vasant Panchami, the fifth day of the bright half of January–February (Magh). Vasant Panchami is considered the start of spring; from this day on, the temperature begins to rise and signals the end of the cold winter months. The Balarama temple in Baithain (named for the fact that Balarama and his friends once rested there) inaugurates Holi on Vasant Panchami with a processional singing of Holi and spring (Vasant) songs as well as the throwing of color. Some devotees travel to Baithain to begin Holi on Vasant Panchami, but most devotees outside of Baldeo begin to play only in the last week of Phalguna (February–March), actually the fifth week of the Holi season. The six-week Holi season ends with a final blast of color on Rang Panchami, the fifth day of the dark half of Chaitra (March–April).

While Holi is played throughout India, it is most enthusiastically observed in north India, tied in practice and myth to Krishna devotion. Holi in Braj has a dual significance. Braj Holi incorporates motifs and practices that exist widely in north India, such as the throwing of color, the lighting of the bonfire, and carnivalesque role reversals, yet it accrues an additional layer of significance because Krishna and Balarama themselves played Holi in Braj. While most devotees recognize the agricultural aspects of Holi and some rituals, such as the bonfire, have clear agricultural roots that predate the sixteenth century, contemporary Holi rituals are primarily understood through the lens of Krishna devotion. Balarama devotees playing Holi in Baldeo provide the exception to the exclusive emphasis on Krishna.

To celebrate Holi is to "play Holi." The throwing of color commemorates Krishna's play not only with his brother but with his beloved consort Radha and her friends, the cowherd girls of Braj. On the days leading up to Holi and on the day of Holi itself, devotees exchange color with fellow devotees. Devotees note that exchanging color is a means to renew social bonds (Sanford 2005, 18). This color takes the form of powder or colored water, and methods of exchange range from tenderly applying color to another's cheek to dousing crowds with buckets of colored water. Typically Holi and the days leading up to the festival are times when social norms are temporaily abandoned, so, for example, women and the poor are given license to verbally abuse men and the rich, respectively (Haberman 1994, 174–75; Marriott 1966, 204–205). By the actual day of the Holi festival, the streets become a battleground of color, and anyone not prepared to get doused should just stay home.

Baldeo, Balarama's village, is one of the more important stops on the Holi pilgrimage tour, where residents identify with a deity who is subordinated—or less obvious—beyond the village of limits. Most residents refer to Balarama affectionately as Dauji, Daubaba, or Baladev. Dau means elder brother in Brajabhasha, the local dialect of Hindi, and "ji" and "baba" are appended honorifics. Devotees' reference to Balarama's status as elder brother to Krishna is not without significance: it denotes Balarama's pride of place as elder brother to his more popular younger brother and, additionally, the status as elder confers upon Balarama the role of guardian. Devotees in Baldeo emphasize Balarama's capacity as protector, an emphasis that makes Balarama devotion in Baldeo unique. This association as elder and protector is thus important and all-pervasive: locals refer in shorthand to the temple, deity, and the village using the honorific term for big brother, "Dauji."

Every year on the second day after the full moon of Chaitra, boisterous crowds fill every millimeter of the Dauji Temple in Baldeo. Pilgrims arrive by bus, train, and tractor to play Holi with Balarama. Locals hail Balarama by his popular names of Dauji and Baladeva, and shouts of "Jai Baldeva" (Hail Baladeva) and "Jai Dauji" fill the air. Some of these devotees have been playing Holi for just the previous week, while others have been playing Holi for the entire six weeks of the Holi season. One of the most obvious signs of Holi in Baldeo is the ubiquitous yellow splashes of color that stain virtually everything. Balarama plays with yellow dye made from safflower, which devotees claim is good for the skin, and everyone who has been spending time in Baldeo now sports a conspicuous (and seemingly permanent) yellow tint.

The anticipation of the crowds escalates as the midday start of the festival approaches. The hereditary priests and guides of the temple (Pandas) stand before the image of Balarama and sing to him, inviting him to play. It is important to note that devotees "play" Holi and that much of Holi appears to be a game. To use the word "play" invokes the notion of *lila*, which describes the divine presence on earth and human interaction with the divine as a form of play. That is, *lila* is the spontaneous play of the divine, and all existence results from the spontaneous outpouring of divinity. Devotees describe Krishna's and Balarama's adventures in Braj as play and note that none of their activities is done of necessity. This notion of play as the underlying cause and structure of being is particularly appropriate in Braj devotion. Much of Braj devotion is irreverent, and Krishna's and Balarama's games manifest a spontaneous rebellion against authority, poking fun at conventional norms and decorum. The actual Holi activities translate the abstraction of divine play into real and spontaneous human play and, in Baldeo, negotiate tensions between impropriety and decorum.

As soon as the crowd sees, or takes *darshan* of, Balarama's temple image, devotees begin to play Holi, or Huranga, as it is called in Baldeo, by throwing colored water and powder. The crowds on the ledge above the temple courtyard (including myself) throw out handfuls of colored powder until the scene below is barely visible through the cloud of color. When the sprinklers that line the roof are turned on, this powder turns into paste and floods the courtyard's marble floor. This pasty mix of water and powder covers the dancers; Panda men dance with their sisters-in-law (specifically their elder brother's wife), holding colored scarves between them. Amidst the dancers, two groups of men each carry a pole adorned with mango buds (*baur*), balloons, and ashoka leaves (*jhands*), offering a connection to spring fertility rituals. Mango buds not only remind participants of spring and Holi, but they also have medicinal value as antisnake venom.[1] The game ends when the adorned poles are toppled (after about one hour), and materials are stripped from the poles and distributed.

While the mood of the festival is certainly exuberant and raucous and, to an outsider, might appear chaotic or even violent, devotees understand that these events play important social functions. Holi is a time to reaffirm social bonds and to celebrate spring and its harvest—two concerns that are, furthermore, intimately related, since agricultural success and prosperity underlie social connections and harmony. The levity embedded in the stories and practices associated with Balarama in Baldeo also, as we shall see, reaffirms his status as a protector, as both the king of Braj and as the premier agriculturalist.

While many devotees honor Balarama in his capacity as the elder brother of Krishna and are familiar with his strength and prowess in the battles of the epic *Mahabharata*, few devotees outside of Baldeo and fewer outside of Braj know why Holi is such a special festival for Balarama. This significance is best understood in the context of Balarama's own Holi story that relates two important events: first, Holi is the time when Balarama (unlike his younger brother) returns to Braj after a long absence, and, second, Balarama, upon his return, alters the Yamuna River's course with his plow. These two events demonstrate Balarama's protective relationship with Braj, both in social and agricultural terms and, as a result, shape the ways his devotees understand the rituals of Holi.

## The Story of Holi

To situate his return, let us begin with the eve of Balarama's departure, his last night in Braj before he and Krishna left for Mathura to defeat the demon Kamsha. This night is particularly memorable to devotees because, on this night, the night of the romantic October full moon (Sharad Purnima), Krishna danced with the cowherd girls who adored him. In this dance called the *Maharasalila*, Krishna multiplied himself 16,000 times so that each and every girl thought that she alone was dancing with Krishna. These girls abandoned their chores and homes, such was their love for Krishna. It is striking and significant that Balarama, as the elder brother, was not invited to dance. While Krishna and the girls danced in the moonlight, Balarama hid behind a rock and watched (*Bhagavata-Purana* [hereafter BP], 10.33). The next day, Krishna and Balarama left for Mathura to slay the demon Kamsha and promised to return in a week's time. Krishna never returned to Braj, and the trope of this lengthened separation from Krishna is the basis for many devotees' emotional stance toward Krishna (BP, 65). However, Balarama, the elder brother, did return to Braj during Holi, and this return makes all the difference. For devotees in Baldeo,

Balarama's homecoming reflects his commitment to the people of Braj. For them, he is king of Braj.

The *Bhagavata Purana* tells the story of Balarama's return to Braj at Holi, but the *Balabhadra Mahatmya* (a chapter of the *Gargasamhita,* hereafter GS) provides an even more detailed account of Balarama's return (BP,10. 65: 1–32; GS, 2:1–20). According to the *Balabhadra Mahatmya,* Balarama's return satisfied a promise he made in a previous life when he took the form of the serpent lord Ananta, or Shesha. Lord Ananta reigned over the underworld kingdom that is the traditional abode of serpents (*nagas*). The serpent lord announced that he would take birth as Balarama to assist Krishna in liberating the earth; his wife Nagalakshmi would take birth as Balarama's wife Revati. The serpent princesses who served in his underworld court were eager to join him in Braj (as were all those attending in the court). Shesha promised the princesses that they had earned future births in the homes of the cowherd girls and women of Braj (*gopis*) due to their devout asceticism. Shesha proclaimed to them, "I will dance the *Maharasalila* with you on the banks of the Kalindi (another name for the Yamuna) and fulfill your desires." (Recall that Balarama had been excluded from the dance with the women on the eve of his and Krishna's departure from Braj years before.) The serpent princesses received the boon of rebirth as the *gopis*, the cowherd girls of Braj, who later danced and frolicked with Balarama after his return during Holi.

The *Bhagavata Purana* simply states that Balarama missed his friends and family and decided to return to Gokul, his childhood home, and the textual accounts are in accordance with this point. His family and friends were overjoyed to see him and greeted him with warm embraces and tears of joy. As etiquette required, the villagers asked about the health of their relatives in Dwarka and wondered if Krishna ever remembered them. Balarama remained in Braj for the two spring months—Chaitra and Vaishakha—and frolicked with the women every night. Balarama was so infatuated with the charms of the cowherd girls that his two-month visit seemed as if it were one long night. On one particularly romantic spring night, Balarama had his own Maharasalila dance with the cowherd girls of Braj, and the repercussions of this event are critical to understanding Balarama's responsibility for Braj's agrarian fertility.

The lyrical narrative illustrates a scene designed for romance: fragrant breezes redolent of night lotuses wafted over the banks of the Yamuna, and the rays of the spring full moon bathed the revelers. Varuna, sovereign of all waters, dispatched his wife Varuni, the Goddess of wine, to Braj. Ambrosia flowed from the hollow of a kadamba tree, and its fragrance permeated the forest. The exquisite beauty of this sight captivated the deities who gazed, rapt from their sky-vehicles, and joyfully sang of Balarama's wondrous exploits. Enticed by the scent of the ambrosia, Balarama and the women found the honey-beverage and drank. After drinking his fill, Balarama regaled the women with song and staggered through the forest, unable to focus his eyes. Yet, despite—or perhaps due to—this condition, this handsome youth appeared resplendent, wearing a wreath of five flowers and only a single earring.

It is at this point that the second critical feature for devotees unfolds: Balarama's diversion of the Yamuna River. The act of diverting the Yamuna is clearly important, as it reinforces Balarama's role as the patron of agriculture and fertility; it is an event furthermore articulated in every ritual in Baldeo.

After their evening of dancing and drinking, Balarama and his friends wanted to play in the water. In Braj lore, this is a standard chain of events, as water play (*jala-krida*) usually follows the Maharasalila dance. However, this time, the Yamuna (or the Kalindi) River—a Goddess herself—had not watched or even come near Balarama's games. Balarama demanded that she approach him so he and the cowherd girls could play in her waters. She hesitated. Enraged, in his intoxication he interpreted her hesitation as contempt for him as king of Braj. (It is important to note that Balarama made a reasonable assumption: typically when a devotee calls upon a deity, he or she appears.) Balarama thrust the pointed edge of his plow into the earth and dragged Yamuna to his feet. He rebuked her, "Oh you sinner! You scorned me. I summoned you, and you delayed. Now you will flow in one hundred directions!" The terrified Yamuna lay prostrate at his feet and implored him to show mercy. She praised his majesty, wisdom, and immense strength and, invoking his merciful nature, she begged him to free her. Satisfied, he released her. That he forever changed the Yamuna River's course testifies to Balarama's infinite strength, one of Balarama's definitive characteristics.

Balarama then entered the river and bathed, cavorting with the cowherd girls. When Balarama emerged from the water, the Goddess Kanti gave him the blue clothes that, according to Vaishnava tradition, he traditionally wears. She further adorned him with precious jewels and a dazzling golden necklace. Kanti, meaning lovely, is a name for the Goddess Lakshmi, who is associated with the home and wealth and is the consort of Vishnu.[2] Kanti, interestingly, is also associated with Durga, a warrior Goddess who, like Balarama, fiercely protects the world.

## Contextualizing Balarama's Story

These stories provide the background against which Holi is played and interpreted in Baldeo. Ganashyam Pandey, founder of the Baldev Research Institute in Baldeo, emphasized to me (as did other devotees in Baldeo) the agricultural implications and interpretations of Balarama's relocation of the Yamuna. Devotees worship Balarama as a guardian of sustenance and fertility; diverting the Yamuna River provided water for a desert-like agricultural region. As noted earlier, the village Baldeo lies on an oxbow of the Yamuna River, and this oxbow created by Balarama resembles an irrigation canal.

Interestingly, the rendition of this story appearing in the *Harivamsha*, an older set of stories about Krishna and Balarama, states that Braj had become barren since Balarama and Krishna's departure, and that Balarama returned to restore this fertility (Vemsani 2006, 116). Balarama's act ameliorates the frustrating reality that natural forces such as rain are capricious. It is important to recall that Pandey's understanding is consistent with traditional concepts of the relationship between a male deity and the feminine waters, that this deity performs a protective function through releasing the life-giving waters to the earth. This relationship between a male deity and the waters emerges in both Shaiva and Vaishnava paradigms of protection, and it does raise questions about connections between agricultural productivity, aggression, and gender relations. The Yamuna River—as are all rivers—is the Goddess; Balarama's restoration of the region's fertility required that he drag the river—the Goddess—unwillingly to his feet.

The Vaishnava paradigm of protection shapes how devotees interpret Balarama's diversion of the Yamuna River; the importance of this act cannot be overstated for Balarama devotion. Balarama's root mantra (mul-mantra), "Om, the Kalindi, split by Samkashana, svaha!," which literally restates that Balarama split the Yamuna River, is recited in every ritual for Balarama in Baldeo and specifically uses a name for Balarama, Samkarshan, which refers to creating a furrow. The verse encodes the story of Balarama's diversion of the Yamuna to provide water for Braj, and its continued recitation means that Balarama's agricultural connections and his relationship to the Goddess are consistently central to Baldeo ritual practice. This episode is critical to understanding Balarama devotion and certainly bears multiple interpretations. Devotees in Baldeo view this episode as a testament to Balarama's status as a guardian, both of society and of agriculture, yet at the same time Balarama's actions also reveal gender and power inequities that exist in agriculture and society.

For Baldeo temple priests, Balarama's actions identify him as an exemplar of maryada, a term that translates best as ethical propriety or decorum and is applied to a righteous and upstanding person. These qualities are intrinsic to a protector or guardian such as Balarama, and devotees praise Balarama for these qualities. They furthermore cite his rectitude and care for the social order as depicted in the *Bhagavata Purana* and the *Mahabharata*. As an agriculturalist and a protector, Balarama's actions fit within a set of social and familial obligations of protection and sustenance.

It is also worth noting that while devotees praise Balarama for his *maryada* characteristics, in the theologies of both Gaudiya Vaishnavism and the Vallabha Sampradaya, the two major devotional communities of the sixteenth century, *maryada* is subordinated to *pushti,* a term that literally means grace or nourishment but connotes the ecstatic devotion that transcends social norms. Thus Balarama is being praised with a term that many would consider a lesser form of devotion. For devotees in Baldeo, though, Balarama's *maryada* persona is a high form of praise; Balarama maintains order and decorum, as should a king or guardian.

Balarama's relationship with the Yamuna River is complicated, because it has multiple dimensions. The Yamuna River as Goddess is clearly situated within Vaishnavism; the Yamuna is often identified as the Goddess Lakshmi, Vishnu's consort and the queen of his celestial heaven; as such, she is sometimes understood to be Krishna's wife—and Balarama's sister-in-law. However, Balarama has an even closer relationship with Mahasarasvati, the form of the Goddess who is both a river and the embodiment of wisdom. In the Dvapara era, she granted Balarama the great strength and wisdom that rendered him the proper groom for Jyotishmati, or Revati. Mahasarasvati's great power (*shakti)* and wisdom furthermore helped Balarama fight evil. Balarama's worship of the Goddess is proper (*maryada*), because it both fulfills his familial duty and gives him the necessary strength to maintain the moral and social order.

Balarama's association with the Yamuna emerges on a number of levels as well. His desire to worship the Yamuna after dancing with the cowherd women, a pattern that appears several times in the

*Bhagavata Purana*, is mirrored by Krishna's worship of the Yamuna after dancing with the gopis. Balarama and the Yamuna are similar in that they both embody the concept of propriety and so uphold social norms, thus Balarama assumed that Yamuna would respond to his invocation. Also, theYamuna is Balarama's family Goddess; by worshipping her, he observes his familial duty. Yet Balarama appears to dominate the Yamuna. He forcibly relocates this river and demonstrates his power over her. That Balarama is obliged to worship the Yamuna complicates their relationship, making it one that does not fit into a clear hierarchical pattern.

The relationship is further complicated if viewed in light of ritual practices and the attendant dynamic between devotee and the divine that is structured by reciprocity and obligation. Jamison and Witzel note that Vedic sacrifice can be likened to a contract, or at least a form of mutual obligation. That is, the human performance of the ritual obligates the deity to provide results, so ritual becomes a mode of mutual exchange (Jamison and Witzel 2002, 68). In this way, Balarama and the Yamuna are also bound by mutual obligation: Balarama is obliged to worship the Yamuna, and the Yamuna is obliged to provide water.

Balarama's close relationship with the Yamuna thus helps him fulfill his agricultural duties. Balarama's diversion of the Yamuna River's waters furthermore recapitulates human agricultural practices; the human actions of tilling and plowing the earth in turn replicate Balarama's actions that ensure the earth's fecundity. He is a deity of place, and his actions that result in sustenance fulfill this role. If Balarama's relocation of the Yamuna appears to be a sexualized act, then it is because agriculture itself is a sexual and potentially violent activity that results in sustenance. That is, most forms of agriculture require the rending of the earth's surface to implant seed, and this act reflects the ambivalence of human relationships to the earth as experienced in agriculture. In Baldeo, the motif of agricultural fertility is clearly situated within notions of kingship, and the king's authority and the earth's productivity are mutually reinforcing (Kinsley 1987, 67, 70). Actions that appear aggressive toward the earth are read as protective (and necessary) toward both the earth itself and her flora and fauna. Balarama's relocation of the river makes water accessible for agriculture; Balarama is, after all, the king of Braj and is responsible for protecting the life and sustenance of the region.

These texts and stories offer the narrative context for Holi ritual practice. The following section will discuss in more detail the ritual events of Holi itself, and we will see how these events (which manifest the themes of aggression, sexuality, and intoxication) translate into events through which Balarama, the elder brother and king, can best serve and protect his devotees.

## Balarama's Holi in Baldeo

Residents of Baldeo stressed repeatedly that Baldeo's Holi is different from the rest of Braj, and they remarked that Holi in Baldeo is played with love. (Of course, residents of other Braj villages might take exception to this distinction.) These statements were in response to the reality that, throughout much of north India, Holi has become synonymous with egregious behavior. Many residents (particularly women) simply stay inside for the duration.

During the Holi period in 1999, I was a guest of the Yogendra Pandey family. The Pandeys are an important family in Baldeo for at least two reasons: first, they run a clinic and fulfill much of the community's medical needs; second, the Pandeys organized the Baldev Research Institute, an organization dedicated to Balarama. Dr. Pandey and his family are Ayurvedic doctors and run a clinic in Baldeo; they are also Ahivasi Brahmans and thus hereditary Pandas as well, acting as ritual servants when it is their family's turn to do so. Ravi Pandey, the youngest of the Pandey brothers, explained that Holi is a game of love, or *prema*. Friends renew bonds, and it is a time to make amends and let bygones be bygones. After all, Holi is the time when Balarama came home to Braj and reunited his friends and family for the first time since he left for Mathura long ago.

The throwing of color is but one aspect of Holi that, both in text and practice, displays strong aggressive and sexual undercurrents. Pranks and outlandish behavior are common, for this is a time when the strictures of normal society are loosened—to a point, anyway. Women tease men, younger people gang up on elders, and lower castes wreak havoc on the upper castes. However, this reversal should not be overstated. Certainly everybody has more license than usual; yet despite claims to the contrary, those wielding power, such as men or the higher castes, have considerably more license to violate social boundaries. The phrase on everyone's lips in Baldeo at this time was, "Don't take it badly, it's Holi." It was considered poor sportsmanship to complain about rough behavior. Certainly these activities are ripe for interpretation; my focus is on how Baldeo residents enacted and viewed Holi activities.

When I observed a typical Holi in Baldeo, the priests and residents played Holi for the entire six-week season, though the most significant days are those surrounding the full moon of Phalguna, the night when Balarama danced with the cowherd women of Braj. The color, the singing, and the festivities of the previous weeks were all merely a prologue. The real Holi revelry in Baldeo began on the late afternoon of the full moon. On this afternoon, the residents of Baldeo proceeded in groups through town, winding through the village to a site where villagers were preparing for an enormous bonfire. The Pandas, the largest group, led the procession, followed by the Sanadhya Brahmans, and finally the merchants (Baniyas) and others who had far smaller processions. The Sanadhyas are Brahmans but have no official function in the temple. I walked with the Pandas as they proceeded through town, singing and throwing powder. They carried the temple's large red anthology of devotional poetry that leaves the temple only once each year for this procession.

This procession of Baldeo residents suggested an atmosphere of revelry befitting a springtime festival linked to fertility. One older man with a tri-color beard danced suggestively with a pole. Some carried plows, one of Balarama's trademark items, while others carried an adorned pole (*jhand*) that reappeared in Balarama's official Holi celebration in the temple several days later. Approximately thirty minutes after the Pandas' procession, the Sanadhya Brahmans paraded through town, also carrying a similarly adorned pole. Their numbers were smaller, and some danced. The procession of the Sanadhya Brahmans revealed the first evidence of Holi's carnival aspect. Men wore fake beards and funny hats, several rode backwards on an ass, and one, encouraged by the crowd, danced in a stuffed bra. This revelry and flouting of social decorum has parallels in springtime fertility festivals in other cultures that mock class roles and, in some instances, include partipants who ride backwards on asses (Bose 1953, 98–99; Marriott 1966). Although the reversal of gender roles is central to Holi play, women did not participate in this parade.

The procession led to the Holika bonfire that would be lit later that night when devotees throughout Braj set alight bonfires to commemorate Prahlad's devotion to the deity Vishnu. The *Puranas* tell the story of Prahlad, a young devotee of Vishnu. Prahlad's father, the king Hiranyakashipu, however, was a dedicated enemy of Vishnu and was infuriated by his son's steadfast devotion. Hiranyakashipu made many attempts to sway his son from his devotion, but the boy was immovable. Eventually, Hiranyakashipu called upon his sister Holika to enter a bonfire carrying Prahlad, assuming that she was impervious to fire. Holika entered the fire holding the boy on her lap, but to the king's surprise, Prahlad was untouched by the flames, while Holika perished. The Holi bonfire reenacts this story and celebrates Prahlad's steadfast devotion to Vishnu. Before the fire was lit, a statue of Prahlad was placed in the woodpile. After the fire had been burning for some time, and just when it appeared almost too late, a young boy leapt up and rescued Prahlad from the fire. The crowds cheered the boy for his daring rescue.

During the day mostly everyone, and especially women, went to the bonfire and performed ritual service, primarily offering sticks and branches, cow dung (*govar*), rice, wheat, roasted barley, and *ghee* (clarified butter). All of these materials have both symbolic and practical relevance to agricultural fertility and sustenance. The sticks and branches were draped with strings of *govar*, a traditional fertilizer and emblem of hope of future fertility; this *govar* was shaped into small round balls and strung together as necklaces. Devotees received these necklaces as a sanctified offering (*prasad)* and wore them around their necks or on their hats. This ritual offering (*puja)* included rice, but homegrown roasted barley was the most important contribution, indicating Holi's origins as an agricultural festival. While the bonfires were public events, most families replicated these offerings in their own homes as well. The big Holi bonfire was lit at around midnight, and at about 4:30 a.m., house fires were lit with materials from the primary fire. The barley was roasted and handed out to family and friends to strengthen and display bonds of friendship and intimacy.

Later that morning friends and families visited one another to exchange color and celebrate the day. I spent most of this morning with the elder Pandey brothers in their clinic. As a service for Balarama and the village, they offered anti-snakebite venom to the town's residents on the morning of Holi. The main ingredient for this concoction is the mango blossom, a sign of spring, and a teaspoon of the anti-snakebite venom is meant to last an entire year. Virtually all of Baldeo's residents visited the clinic, played a mild Holi, and paid their respects to the Pandey family. The family's services and the responses of the town's residents demonstrated how Balarama's ties to protection, agriculture, and health get carried into the social sphere.

By 11 a.m., Holi festivities for the morning had concluded, and everyone returned home to bathe and don new clothes for the afternoon's *Maharasalila* dance in the temple. This dance was the first of several ritual activities that highlighted the *devar-bhabhi* relationship between the younger brother and his elder brother's wife. In Krishna's familial structure, Krishna and Revati, Balarama's wife, are the *devar* and *bhabhi*. Traditionally, a joking and an implicitly sexualized relationship exists between these two, offering a friendly outlet for women marrying into an extended family. Her relationship with her husband, her husband's elder brother(s), and her in-laws is formal. That is, the bride (particularly if she is a new bride) must show humility (*lajj*) before her in-laws and husband's elder brother(s). Showing *lajj* means that the bride must speak softly with downcast eyes; she often covers her face when conversing with elder members of her new family. Her relationship with her husband's younger brother is more relaxed, and she can speak freely and laugh in this context. Technically, Balarama, or the elder brother, does not play, although devotees insist that all of Balarama's family play Holi.

Most of the Panda families sported silk pieces of cloth, mostly yellow and pink scarves, once worn by the image of Balarama in the temple. Many of the temple priests dressed as cowherd women, some wearing green for Rukmini, Krishna's wife, and yellow for Radha and Revati. At 2 p.m., the temple opened for a special viewing before the *Maharasalila* in which pairs (or triads) of *devar* and *bhabhi* danced, each holding one end of a scarf so that they did not actually touch. Traditionally, only the Panda families could participate in this dance and the next day's Huranga, although these rules are less strictly observed today. Women of the more prominent priestly families did not participate in any of the public *devar-bhabhi* activities.

The following morning, the second day of the dark half of Chaitra, Baldeo prepared for its big event: Huranga. Ghanashyam Pandey, current head of the Baldev Research Institute, stressed that the Huranga, which indicates the throwing of color, is unique to Baldeo. He stated that other villages, such as Barsana or Nandagaon, throw color, but, unlike in Baldeo, they also play with sticks, lathi-Holi. Lathi-Holi is a ritualized role reversal in which women dramatically overpower men. Each year, women from Barsana, Radha's village, travel to Nandagaon, Krishna's village, to protest Krishna's heartless—as they see it—treatment of the cowherd women when he danced with them under the full moon, then left town the next day. The women from Barsana who represent the cowherd women carry heavy sticks and beat the Nandagaon men. The men hold shields to protect themselves from the women's blows. This ritual, it would seem, provides a vent for women's frustration with men and exemplifies one of the major reversals of Holi.

There is no lathi-Holi in Baldeo, only the throwing of color. Ghanashyam Pandey's remarks parallel Ravi Pandey's comment that devotees of Balarama play Holi with love. Krishna, he said, plays Holi with sticks (lathi-Holi), while Balarama plays only with color, and that is Huranga. However, Holi and Huranga are joined: the pair are husband and wife. Holi is the wife (*patni*), while Huranga is the husband or lord (*pati*).

In anticipation of the Huranga, devotees filled the temple's courtyard and rooftop to capacity. Small boys dressed as Krishna and Balarama sat on a raised platform facing the image of Balarama; the VIPs sat under a canopy on the roof overlooking the courtyard. Others (including myself) sat on the ledge just below the temple roof with large bags full of colored powders. Sprinklers were attached to this ledge, and although they were not yet turned on, the courtyard floor was flooded with several inches of water. The priests in the courtyard below, dressed in silks and as cowherd women, began to dance, and revelers threw buckets of color and water balloons at the watching crowd. The mood in the courtyard was enhanced by the vast quantities of the intoxicating drink of *bhang*-laced thandai (a cooling drink made with milk, sugar, and almonds) offered to Balarama in the morning.

I sat on the ledge just in front of the VIPs. After about twenty minutes of play, the VIPs realized the effect of my presence: they were being doused with all the color aimed at me—clearly a target—and did not seem altogether pleased with the extra color. After the dancing had begun, an engineer sitting next to me leaned over and told me that it would start soon. It looked to me as if something has already begun; I wondered what more would start?

The priests stood in front of Balarama's image singing *samaj*, a form of group singing that frequently occurs immediately prior to *darshan*. The lyrics invited Balarama to come play Holi. The two poles that the Pandas and the Brahmans carried in the procession to the bonfire areas appeared in the courtyard, signaling the start of the Huranga. The play would continue until both poles fell over. Once toppled, they would be broken into small pieces that would be offered to devotees. The poles were placed before Balarama, and there was a brief *darshan*. In the courtyard, the *devar-bhabhi* pairs danced, and soon the women began to rip off the men's shirts. They twisted the shirts, dipped them into the water on the floor, and beat the men with their own wet clothing. No boy or man on the courtyard floor was exempt from this beating.

Then it started: everyone (but me) knew it was time. Those sitting on the ledges threw powder on those dancing below, and those not dancing threw buckets of color. A dense cloud of red, yellow, and silver powder made it difficult to see across the temple courtyard. Below, several men paraded the poles around the courtyard, while others danced, beat someone, or tried to avoid being beaten. Some men were raised overhead and carried about. On and off the cloud of color thinned and rendered visible the frenzied activity below. The water on the courtyard floor was almost four inches deep, and wet, colored powder stuck to everything. After forty-five minutes, the poles fell, and the offerings were distributed. Everyone then returned home to share a traditional meal of fried bread *(puris)* and rice pudding *(khir)*, two of Balarama's favorite foods.

The final throwing of color occurred on Rang Pancami, the fifth day of the bright half of Chaitra. Afterwards the *devar-bhabhi* relationship was highlighted once again through an exchange of gifts: younger brothers gave their elder brothers' wives a sari, and women offered their brothers-in-law a sweet rice dish.

## Conclusion

The rituals and practices of Baldeo's Holi that I witnessed and describe here reveal the tensions of sexuality, production, and aggression that threaten and sustain social stability. While previous scholars have demonstrated how the rebellious aspects of Holi provide vents for social tensions, I direct my study to the ways in which residents of Baldeo envision Holi and, as such, the important role that Balarama and agriculture play in balancing these tensions.

Residents of Baldeo rightly emphasize that Holi is a time of social renewal. They commemorate the time when Balarama returned home to renew his bonds and to fulfill his promise to the serpent princesses. Krishna never returned to Braj, and devotees emphasize this difference. Holi rituals that emphasize social bonds also demonstrate an important link to agriculture and fertility, and given that serpents are typically associated with water and fertility (and Balarama and the cowherd women are incarnations of the serpents), this connection is further strengthened. The fact that Balarama's plow enabled him to divert water upon the earth further offers for him the role of an agriculturalist who protects his devotees.

Holi ritual practices mediate agricultural and social tensions through comedic performances that in the end emphasize restoration and resolution. As philosopher Susanne Langer notes, springtime fertility festivals are comedic because they celebrate both social and agricultural life and vitality (Langer 1953, 331). Yet Balarama's Holi narratives and associated practices have to do with resolution and wholeness amid tension and ambiguity; the satire and frivolity that enliven these narratives and practices may appear to further subvert hierarchies and stability, while in fact they work to strengthen them. Balarama's actions and Holi's carnivalesque activities may mock social norms, but in the end these norms and their associated social bonds are fortified.

Many of the riotous activities at Holi are understood as defiance against social decorum, yet Balarama's qualities of aggression and intoxication underscore his status as protector and elder brother. As noted earlier, kings are responsible for agricultural fertility. The story of Balarama and the Yamuna fits the paradigm of a deity releasing life-giving water, yet it is a product of an aggressive act. While aggression and, more so, intoxication can weaken social bonds, devotees understand that Balarama uses these qualities for their benefit. Balarama's aggression helps him protect his devotees, and his intoxication helps him ready himself for battle. Since Balarama uses aggression and intoxication only in the service of righteousness and to protect his devotees, devotees deem these qualities appropriate.[3]

Holi manifests tensions mixing sexuality and aggression in its general teasing and prank playing, particularly in the *devar-bhabhi* activities, which are central to Holi. The actions of the *devar-bhabhi* pair exemplify this ambivalent mix of sexuality and aggression that is seen in Balarama himself: the pairs dance together in the temple during the Huranga, after which the women thrash their brothers-in-law. This thrashing looks like nothing less than a war. These activities and associations manifest the flexibility of the *devar-bhabhi* relationship itself. This relationship provides a space for an informal bond, yet this informality also provides perhaps women's only opportunity to vent anger and frustration not allowed within the more formal interactions with other family members. Situated within the husband's family unit, this flexible space nonetheless has its boundaries.

Holi narratives and practices also can be seen to adjudicate tensions having to do with the reality of agriculture—and basic survival—in which something must die if we are to eat. Since the Panda community is strictly vegetarian, I am not speaking here of the obvious give-and-take of hunting. In the play of Holi, survival anxieties emerge in the guise of gender relations and fecundity. Balarama's aggression toward the earth and the Yamuna River might be seen to address and allay fears that the forces of nature will not provide. Since devotees explain Balarama's aggression as socially necessary and look to Balarama for, among other things, healing, protection, and agricultural benefits, his violence becomes justified. Balarama's violence toward a gendered river divinity and source of fecundity, ensuring fertility and prosperity of the land, simultaneously ensures the health, prosperity, and stability of society and societal relationships.

In the context of Holi, ritual levity provides a means to negotiate a variety of social tensions. Baldeo's Holi demonstrates the tensions and ambivalences between the properties of protection and aggression and between fertility and sexuality, and these anxieties have the potential to destabilize society. Baldeo's springtime festivities celebrate earthly fertility, and at the same time they alleviate social tensions, thereby recognizing the integral connection between agrarian abundance and social order. The exuberance and spontaneity of these ritual practices offer the flexibility and freedom to work out ambivalences in realms such as sexuality and aggression that are not typically part of public discourse. These rituals are thus not only funny (although it might be difficult to imagine Holi as not funny), but levity is intrinsic to their performance and to the successful meeting of their social goals. Without fun and levity, Holi would be an entirely different festival; it is defined in many ways by lightness and fun, if not raucous hilarity. At the same time, the fun and lightness of Holi enable practitioners to deal with real concerns of social and agricultural survival, concerns that are anything but light.

Each of these Holi activities in Braj also reflects a spontaneous grassroots expression of play, allowing devotees the opportunity to freely cavort with the divine and with each other. While the central ritual itself, the *Huranga*, is scheduled to occur at a particular time, and the play of devotees in these ritual spaces reconciles a variety of serious social and personal matters, the events within are not strictly scripted. Like a game, the ritual offers a context and structure for play and humor but does not control the event itself or the outcome.

The spontaneous activities within the ritual play may ultimately be shaped by the needs of the participants, yet in the end if it is to remain play, games must be fun—otherwise, there is no point in playing.

## Notes

1. Today the goddess Shri-Laksmi is primarily associated with monetary wealth. However, later Vedic texts associate this deity with the earth's fertility and agriculture. Her symbolic association with the lotus (itself a symbol of fertility) reveals this connection with the life-giving potency in terms of agriculture (Kinsley 1987, 20–21).

2. This understanding echoes the Rajput (one of India's warrior dynasties) linkage of lust, wine, and strength. Meat and wine are important for male Rajputs, because they build lust and strength, important traits for professional warriors and kings (Harlan 1992, 127).

## Works Cited

Bose, Nirmal Kumar. 1953. *Cultural Anthropology and Other Essays*. Calcutta: Indian Association Publishers.

Crooke, William. 1896. *The Popular Religion and Folklore of Northern India*. Vol. II. Delhi: Munshiram Manoharlal.

Entwistle, Alan W. 1987. *Braj, Centre of Krishna Pilgrimage*. Groningen: Egbert Forsten.

Haberman, David. 1994. *Journey through The Twelve Forests*. New York: Oxford University Press.

Harlan, Lindsay. 1992. *Religion and Rajput Women: The Ethic of Protection in Contemporary Narratives*. Delhi: Munshiram Manoharlal.

Jamison, Stephanie, and Michael Witzel. 2002. "Vedic Hinduism." http://www.people.fas.harvard.edu/~witzel/vedica.pdf, 65–113.

Kinsley, David. 1987. *Hindu Goddess: Visions of the Divine Feminine in the Hindu Religious Tradition*. Delhi: Motilal Benarsidass.

Langer, Susanne K. 1953. *Feeling and Form*. New York: Scribner's Sons.

Marriott, McKim. 1966. "The Feast of Love." In *Krishna: Myths, Rites, and Attitudes*, ed. Milton Singer, 200–12. Chicago, IL: University of Chicago Press.

Sanford, A. Whitney. 2005. "Holi through Dauji's Eyes: Alternate Views of Krishna and Balarama in Dauji." In *Alternative Krishnas: Vernacular and Regional Views on a Hindu Deity*, ed. Guy Beck, 91–112. Albany: State University of New York Press.

Shastri, Pandey Ramtej, ed. 1996. *Gargasamhita*. Delhi: Chaukhamba Sanskrit Pratishthan.

*Srimad-Bhagavata-Mahapurana: Sri Subodhini*. Jodhpur: Sri Subodhini Prakashak Mandal.

Van Buitenin, J. A. B., ed. and trans. 1973. *The Mahabharata*. Chicago, IL: University of Chicago Press.

Vaudeveille, Charlotte. 1991. "Multiple Approaches to a Living Hindu Myth: The Lord of Govardhan Hill." In *Hinduism Reconsidered*, ed. Gunther Sontheimer and Herman Kulke, 105–26. New Delhi: Manohar.

Vemsani, Lavanya. 2006. *Hindu and Jain Mythology of Balarama: Continuity and Change in an Early Indian Cult*. Lewiston, NY: Edwin Mellen Press.

4

# Playing the Married Lady

## *Primary Marriage among the Newars of Nepal*

Liz Wilson

Bharati Mukherjee's 2002 novel *Desirable Daughters* begins with a dramatic marriage between a five-year-old human bride and a nonhuman groom (Mukherjee 2002). The narrator describes the wedding of her great-great-aunt Tara Lata to a tree in a ceremony performed in Bangladesh in 1879. That Tara Lata marries a tree is necessitated by the untimely death of her fiancé, who dies of a snakebite en route to their wedding. The bridegroom's family blames the premature death of the boy on the bride, impugning her character. Tara Lata's father, an attorney by day who reads Hindu legal treatises at night, avoids carrying out a marriage contract with a dead groom and condemning his daughter to the restrictive life of a prepubertal Brahmin widow by marrying Tara Lata that very day to a proxy bridegroom: a tree deity identified as the god of the Beautiful Forest. Although it would seem that Tara Lata's father denies her the possibility of future marital felicity by marrying her to a tree deity at the tender age of five, what she gains as a treebride is a level of autonomy of which most of her elite Hindu peers could never dream.

Mukherjee indicates in an interview with a journalist that she based the tree-marriage episode on practices observed by members of her family's Bengali Brahmin Kulin subcaste. "Women could only go to heaven by worshiping god through their husbands," the author explains (Amirrezvani 2004). "If something happened to the groom, they were married off to a proxy—a tree, a stone or a crocodile." Treatises on Hindu religious law codified in Sanskrit *dharmashastra* collections mention precedents for such practices as those of Mukherjee's family. Mitramishra's *Samskaraprakasha,* for example, describes a number of ceremonies for averting widowhood that require the bride to marry such ritual substitutes for the groom as an *ashvattha* tree (Ficus Religiosa) or a water pot (*kumbha*).[1] The oldest precedents for Mukherjee's tree wedding are found in the *Rig Veda.* The Vedic marriage hymn (*vivaha-sukta; Rig Veda* V.X.85) presumes that what the marriage ceremony celebrates is not in fact the bride's first marriage but her fourth.[2] A girl marries the god Soma first, then the Gandharva, and then Agni. The three divine husbands function sequentially as celestial protectors or guardians of the bride. Each enjoys her favors before passing her along to the next deity. Each endows her with a divine gift, for example, she receives cleanliness in her girlhood from Soma.

While I am aware of no evidence that Kulin Brahmin Hindu communities of Bengal celebrate such proxy marriages with any regularity today, matrimony by substitution does occur in contemporary South Asia. The Hindu-influenced Newars of the Kathmandu valley of Nepal marry their daughters to ritual stand-ins when initiating their prepubertal girls. In a collective ritual that is central to the life cycle of Newari women, Newar girls between the ages of five and nine are symbolically wed to an immortal deity in a ritual sequence known as *ihi.* Being married in this manner to an eternal mate does not prevent the child from entering into later marriage to a human mate (a key difference between this Newar practice and the tree-marriage narrative that Muhkerjee presents in *Desirable Daughters*). But the Newar girl who marries an immortal in the *ihi* ceremony relegates her subsequent marriage with a human bridegroom to a lesser status. Since a Newar woman's human spouse constitutes a secondary or stand-in husband, his death need not have the devastating consequences for her that the death of a husband can have for Hindu women. Newars assert that the primary marriage ritual protects women from the stigma of widowhood, that women who have undergone the ritual do not suffer a loss of status upon the death of their mortal husbands.

While the *ihi* ritual is not overtly playful in the sense of general mirth or hilarity, it is a rite that seizes upon the play or scope for movement afforded by the use of a ritual surrogate standing in for the human bridegroom. The *ihi* ceremony draws upon the ritual lexicon of the orthodox Hindu rite of marriage, or *vivaha.*[3] The *ihi* rite follows much of the ritual procedure of the *vivaha* but functions primarily as a collective coming-of-age ritual that endows girls with adult privileges and allows them to play adult social roles without abandoning their status as members of their natal households. What the orthodox marriage ceremony accomplishes is a sending off or separation between the bride and her natal family. Indeed, the very word for the orthodox ceremony (Sanskrit: *vivaha*) means "separation." The primary marriage ceremony uses the ritual forms of the orthodox rite to achieve the opposite result: a strengthening of the bonds between the girl and her family.

## "You Say Good-bye, I Say Hello": Pretending to Sever Ties

Before turning to the particulars of the *ihi* ceremony, a few words on the orthodox *vivaha* rite on which it draws are in order. The literal meaning of *vivaha* is "separation." Much of the ritual work performed in the orthodox Hindu ceremony of *vivaha* entails the severing of a girl's kinship ties with her natal family. Symbolically disaggregated from her father's family, she is remade into a member of her husband's family. In the crucial ritual step of the *kanyadan,* or gift of the maiden, the father or male guardian of the bride makes a gift of the maiden, or *kanya,* with no expectation of return. The groom accepts this gift by taking her hand in his to the accompaniment of Vedic mantras. The wife is understood to become the "half-body" of the husband, ontologically merged with her husband and his line.[4] Should her husband predecease her, she is subject to many of the avoidances associated with death. Moreover, there is no assurance that her natal family will care for her.

Hindu legal treatises identify marriage as the female rite of passage to adulthood.[5] Where Brahminical Hindu legal traditions give boys the ritual means to become men before they marry, girls must leave home as brides in order to become women. The *ihi* ceremony makes a girl into a woman without the obligation to leave home and take up virilocal residence with her husband's family. *Ihi,* then, is a marriage that is not a marriage: it enables the girl to perform as an adult when the dominant ideology holds her to be a child, and it makes her a woman without having to leave home. The ceremony subverts normative expectations (at least those of the north Indian Hindus who migrated to Nepal and whose rites and norms became fashionable to emulate) that a girl cannot become a woman and exercise adult responsibilities in her own natal home.

The Newar primary marriage rite draws on the ritual vocabulary of the *vivaha* while reinforcing the bonds that tie a girl to her home. The *ihi* ritual enfranchises women in their father's lineages and ensures that women will be able to call upon the privileges that such lineage membership entitles them. Young girls can thus play the social roles of married ladies without relinquishing the emotional comforts and privileges associated with being daughters.

In this way, the *ihi* ritual might be said to play with normative expectations of female behavior derived from Brahmanical literature. Where Brahmanical authorities suggest that the *dharma,* or religious duty of women, is epitomized in the devoted wife (*pativrata*) whose role in life is service and devotion to her husband, the girl who plays the married lady has no such obligation to orient her life around her husband and his family. Her nuptial joining with an immortal husband may be seen as an ironic statement. She has been "given away" in marriage, but the local nature of her spouse ensures that ties to her birth family are strengthened rather than severed. She "merges" with her husband and his line, but due to his divine nature and the connections ritually forged between him and her father's line of descent, her primary source of identity comes from her own natal rather than affinal ties. She is now a devoted wife who "serves" a husband, but her husband is not of this world (or at least he has fewer mundane needs than the typical spouse).

## The Newars

The Newars are descendants of the indigenous inhabitants of the Kathmandu valley. There are over 250,000 Newars living in the valley today, and an equal number of Newars live in other parts of Nepal. Although the ancient Newars were in all likelihood predominantly Buddhist, the Newars have long been conversant with Brahmanical Hindu practices due to the establishment in Nepal of a number of immigrant Hindu dynasties of north Indian origin. The Newars today include both Hindu and Buddhist practitioners and are subdivided into many castes. The highest Newar castes tend to identify as either Hindu or Buddhist; as one moves down the caste hierarchy, the distinction becomes less and less relevant.[6] Ritual leadership is provided by both Hindu Brahmins and a priestly Buddhist caste, the Vajracaryas, who have been dubbed Buddhist Brahmins, as they constitute a hereditary married priesthood (Greenwold 1974, 101–23; see also Gellner 1995).

## The *Ihi* Ritual

Newars regard the primary marriage ceremony as the most important of all domestic rituals (Allen 1990, 182). No other Newar life-cycle ritual is as minutely choreographed as this elaborate rite. It is unique among domestic ceremonies, in that it is a collective ritual involving girls of different castes, castes among whom normally one would not find intermarriage or commensalism. Primary marriage is celebrated by all clean castes (*ju pim*) that fall in the complex Newar caste system between the Rajopadhyaya Brahmins at the summit of the system and the Untouchable groups at the bottom (Vergati 1982, 272). The numbers of girls who participate in a given *ihi* ritual in the Kathmandu valley can range from fifty to as many as 300 or 400.

One reason for the collective nature of the ritual is the considerable expense involved. The ritual expenses are underwritten by a person of some affluence who wishes to earn merit. The sponsor may also be someone undergoing his or her own life-passage ritual. Primary marriage is often held in conjunction with some other ceremony, such as the old-age ritual performed when a person reaches seventy-seven years, seven months, and seven days. For Buddhists, the ritual is generally held in conjunction with the consecration of a new religious monument, such as a *stupa* or Buddhist reliquary monument.

Informants give various reasons for performing the *ihi* ritual. Parents suggest that it will protect their daughters from malicious spirits, that it will preserve their daughters' virginity until a human mate is selected and the girl is married to that mate, and that the ritual will ensure that their daughters marry men as beautiful as the deity who serves as the ritual bridegroom in the primary marriage ceremony. But the most common reason given is that the ritual prevents widowhood.[7]

Newars tell a legend about the origins of the *ihi* ceremony that emphasize this protective function (Levy 1990, 666). According to this legend, it was Shiva's wife, Parvati, who interceded on behalf of human women to prevent widowhood through the institution of mock marriage. Parvati is the daughter of Himavan, god of the Himalayas. Her father gave her the Kathmandu valley as her dowry when she married the god Shiva. One day, as Parvati was walking through the valley, she heard an old woman crying. Parvati asked the woman why she was crying. The old woman explained that her husband had died and that ever since his death her life had been terrible. Parvati took pity on the old woman and asked Shiva to do something to prevent the women of the valley from becoming widows. Shiva replied that he and Narayana (Vishnu Narayana, the form in which the Hindu sustainer god Vishnu is most commonly worshipped in Nepal) would arrange it so that women did not suffer this fate. Thus the Newars were given the *ihi* ceremony, with Narayana as the groom and Shiva as the witness.

Primary marriage is an elaborate ceremony lasting two to three days. While a narration of every step of this complex sequence of events is beyond the scope of this chapter, I will summarize some of the key moments in the ritual, emphasizing those that draw most heavily on the ritual lexicon of Hindu marriage ceremonies.

On the first day, the girls rise early in the morning and perform purificatory rituals at home. They dress in new clothes and ornament themselves with some jewelry. After a ritual meal, the girls assemble in a courtyard. They take seats around the edge of the courtyard, accompanied by their mothers or paternal aunts. The highlight of the day is a rite unique to the *ihi* ceremony called *sat brindika*. The woman in charge of the ceremonial procedure carefully measures each girl from head to toe with a yellow thread. The thread is shaped into the form of a necklace that is later placed in an unbaked clay bowl, where it remains until the next day. When the girl later in life marries a human bridegroom, she gives him the yellow "necklace" as proof that she has undergone the primary marriage ceremony and as a means of assimilating him to her divine bridegroom. After the necklaces are placed in the bowls, the girls are led in worship directed toward a gilded image of Suvarna Kumara, the golden bachelor son of Shiva.

On the second day, the girls assemble again in the courtyard. Where the clothes they wore on the previous day were simply presentable, everyday outfits augmented with a little jewelry, on this day the girls wear much more elaborate outfits in bridal colors. In addition, they wear gold and silver jewelry. The bridal appearance is enhanced by the application of kohl around the girls' eyes as well as the marking of the forehead with a red *tika* or forehead mark. Following a sequence of purification rites involving the feet and head, the woman who measured the girls the day before now goes down the line and rubs vermillion paste into the part of the girls' hair. This action is clearly indicative of marriage, since in the adult marriage ceremony, the groom's rubbing of vermillion in the part of his bride's hair constitutes a key moment in the marriage rite. The girls are then given the yellow necklaces that were measured out the day before and also a strip of material of the sort used to make *sari*s for married women. A female relative then pins a piece of paper that bears a sacred image onto the girl's hair. The paper given to Buddhist girls depicts a sacred water pot; for Hindu girls, the paper bears an image of the god Vishnu Narayana.

Now purified and adorned, the girls begin the main ritual sequence of the day, the *kanyadan,* in which the girl is given away. The events that follow establish a relationship between each girl and the deity she marries. In front of each girl is a clay bowl, into which is deposited a fruit from the wood-apple tree (Newari, *bya* fruit; Nepali, *bel* fruit; Sanskrit, *bilva* fruit).[8] The priest then puts a red thread about six to eight inches long into each bowl and rubs some purifying yellow powder in the upturned hands of the girls. At this point, the fathers of the girls become active participants in the ritual for the first time. Each father takes the *bya* fruit and puts it in his daughter's hand. Another male relative adds a rupee note and also pours flower petals and rice over the hands of the girl. The girl's hands are folded over the *bya* fruit, and the red thread is tied around her wrists (recall that in the sharmashastra description of the water-pot wedding, the water pot is connected to the bride by a network of threads).

The gifting of the girls to an immortal deity can occasion some good-natured teasing during this key moment in the ceremony. A grandfather participating in the *kanyadan* portion of a primary marriage ceremony performed in Kathmandu in 1979 adopted a jocular tone of voice with his ten-year-old granddaughter, telling her, "You're going to be 'sent off' now" (Allen 1990, 189). Would this be best described as ritual levity? Does grandfatherly teasing make light of the situation by highlighting the discrepancy between the state of separation from home suggested by the ritual forms and the cementing of ties to home that the ritual actually achieves? The grandfather's comment is amusing (though probably a great deal more amusing to knowing bystanders than to the young girl herself!), precisely because it is not true—the girl is not being sent off. She in all likelihood will not leave home for some time.[9]

Hindu celebrations of the primary marriage ceremony include at this point the requisite walk around the sacred fire. The fathers take their daughters in their arms and carry them in a clockwise direction three times around the sacrificial fire. In Buddhist primary marriage ceremonies, the girls are led by their fathers three times around the courtyard. Whether they have proceeded around the fire or around the courtyard, the girls then resume their seats, and the red threads are removed. The *bya* fruits are rolled in the hands of the girls' fathers and then placed into the clay bowls in front of each girl.

The question of whom the girls marry in the ritual can be answered in a variety of ways. Many of the girls involved in Buddhist performances of the ceremony held in Kathmandu in 1974 told Michael Allen that the fruit itself was the bridegroom (Allen 1990, 190). More sophisticated informants see the *bya* fruit as a natural representation—an *avyakta,* in Sanskrit—of a deity or sacred principle. Buddhist priests told Anne Vergati that the girl marries a personification of *bodhicitta*—the thought of awakening or determination to reach enlightenment (Vergati 1982, 271–87). Most of Vergati's Hindu informants declared that the divine husband in the ritual is Vishnu Narayana, with the fruit representing Shiva as a witness to the marriage (Vergati 1982, 278). The dominant Buddhist theory, reflected by the majority of Allen's informants, is that the girl marries Shiva's son Kumara, the eternal bachelor god.

Although there may be little consensus as to the identity of the deity the girl marries, both Hindu and Buddhist participants view primary marriage as a rite of passage that entails the assumption of adult duties and privileges. Girls who have undergone primary marriage accompany their fathers at the annual celebration of the lineage festival, where they offer the *bya* fruit to the lineage deity.[10] Like the Newar boy's initiation rite, primary marriage confers upon the girl membership in her father's lineage and caste. Hindus refer to it as the girl's *upanayana,* since it confers caste membership in the manner of the investiture of the sacred thread for twice-born castes. The change in the girl's status after primary marriage is reflected not only in her observance of caste commensal rules but also in the case of the girl's death, in the right to be carried to the cremation ground on a ceremonial platform.

## Secondary Marriage: The Truncated Marital Rite

The ceremony of marriage to a human mate that typically occurs around age sixteen or seventeen for most Newar girls includes neither the *kanyadan* nor the circumambulation around the sacred fire, and therefore it lacks the sacramental qualities of the *ihi* ritual (Bajaracharya 1959, 418–29; Nepali 1965). It consists mainly in the groom's gifting of clothing to the bride. Marriages by elopement are also common among Newars. A Newar girl who has undergone primary marriage retains close ties to her parents' kinfolk, especially her paternal kin and her mother's brothers. Even after marriage to a human spouse, daughters are invited home for a variety of family ritual occasions, where they are fed certain ritually prescribed foods and perform a number of ritual functions. Because most Newar marriages are contracted between families within easy visiting distance from one another, married daughters spend a considerable amount of time fulfilling ritual obligations at their natal homes.

Primary marriage, utilizing as it does the ritual idiom of the *vivaha,* parallels the orthodox wedding ceremony in form but inverts many of the social meanings of the ceremony. It is a rite of separation that in fact binds the girl to her natal family, a "sending off" that in practice unites the girl more closely than ever to her natal home and lineage.

It makes sense that Newars attribute the origin of this ritual to the goddess Parvati, that it was Parvati who heard the cries of the widow and persuaded her husband Shiva to institute the ritual of primary marriage. Parvati excels at finding work-arounds while appearing to conform to patriarchal norms. She, for example, succeeded in marrying a man her parents deemed an inappropriate spouse. Indeed, she bullied Shiva into falling in love with her (although he was an ascetic intent on maintaining his celibacy) by beating him at his own game by performing astounding feats of athletic asceticism. Parvati, tricksterlike, turns obstacles into opportunities, into springboards for achieving her own ends. The Newar girl's *ihi* ceremony likewise subverts norms limiting female autonomy without directly contravening those norms.

The *ihi* ceremony might be described as a form of play-acting in which a child performs a public role that is dissonant with her actual social role. The young bride acts out an adult ritual in a ceremony that endows a ritual stand-in with the properties of a bridegroom. But like the turn-of-the-century ceremony that Mukherjee invokes in *Desirable Daughters*, the *ihi* as a proxy wedding is more than a simulation, more than mere play-acting. This Newar conjugal rite has very real consequences for the girl, and so it is more than make-believe. Thus I would take issue with the body of ethnographic literature that translates the term *ihi* as "mock marriage" in the sense of simulation or mimicry without consequence.[11] We can perhaps call such marriages "mock marriages" in the sense that these ceremonies may be said to mock or subvert normative north Indian Hindu prescriptions for females. But these marriages-by-proxy have very real consequences for the brides involved. Following the suggestion of Dumont, *ihi* is best translated as "primary marriage."[12] This translation underscores the idea that the *ihi* ceremony is the "real" sacrament; it is the definitive, socially legitimating marriage. Later marriages to human males lack the level of ritual finality, legitimacy, and irrevocability that the *ihi* rite entails.

## The Tree Bride: Playing With Normative Expectations of Hindu Women

We return to Tara Lata, the Tree Bride, by way of conclusion. Tara Lata never takes a human spouse. She rejects the pursuit of religious excellence through service to one's husband and serves her country instead. She never leaves her home until the day she is arrested and made a martyr to the cause of Indian independence. In becoming a Tree Bride, Tara Lata thus subverts the usual pattern of virilocal residence after marriage. She lives the rest of her life in her father's house. In fact, she appropriates her father's study, after his death, and conducts much of her political work there. Indeed, Tara Lata takes over many features of the patriarch's role and assumes many of the privileges of the head of the household. While the girls who undergo *ihi* in the Kathmandu valley today need not eschew human spouses in order to assume the privileges of patriarchal social configurations, they can be said to enjoy similar levels of enfranchisement in the lineages of their fathers, as well as something of the dignity, independence, and autonomy with which Mukherjee endows her heroine.

## Notes

1. See Kane 1974, II: 546. Mitramishra's *Samskaraprakasha* and other dharma treatises go into some detail on the ritual procedure for the water-pot wedding (*kumbha-vivaha*) and the *ashvattha*-tree wedding (*ashvattha-vivaha*). Both weddings are to take place the day prior to the girl's marriage with a human mate. In the case of the water-pot marriage, a golden image of the god Vishnu is dipped in the water pot (*kumbha*) and the water pot is connected to the bride with a network of threads. The water pot is eventually broken, and the water is sprinked over the bride, to the accompaniment of mantras from *Rig Veda* VII.49. The *ashvattha*-tree wedding follows the same procedure, except that the *ashvattha* tree is substituted for the water pot.

2. For a detailed discussion of the Vedic marriage hymn, its various interpretations, and the implications for the proper marriage age for women, see Leslie 1989, 252–55; see also Menski 1984.

3. Hindu *dharmashastra* literature identifies eight forms of marriage. When speaking of the Hindu *vivaha* ritual, it is conventionally understood that the form intended is the Brahma *vivaha*. The Brahma *vivaha* is the highest of the eight forms. It is characterized by the presumption that the bride is freely given away by the father rather than (as in other of the eight forms of marriage) taken by force or given in exchange for goods. See Pandey 1949 [1969], 153–233; see also Sharma 1993.

4. On the mechanisms of transformation that achieve this ontological change with reference to the Bengali context, see Nicholas 1995, 140 ff.

5. For example, in the course of explaining the initiatory ceremony of investiture with a sacred thread (*upanayana*), the rite of passage that ushers upper-caste Hindu males into adulthood, the Hindu legal codifier

Manu explains (2.67) that, for females, the ritual of marriage serves the same initiatory function. "The ritual of marriage is traditionally known as the Vedic transformative ritual for women: serving her husband is (the equivalent of) living with a guru, and household chores are the rites of the fire." See Doniger and Smith 1991, 24. On rites of passage for Hindu females in Nepal, see Bennett 1978, 31–45.

6. For a discussion of caste and religious identity among Newars, see Gellner 1992, 41–72.

7. See Allen 1990, 190 ff. Even Gellner, who disputes Allen's claim that Newar women avoid the stigma of widowhood in actuality, nevertheless admits that this is what Newars generally assert about the *ihi* rite. The question for Gellner is whether in fact Newar women *do* suffer a loss of status when their human mates predecease them. In Gellner's experience of high-caste Newar groups, such as the Vajracaryas, Shakyas, and Sreshthas, widows do indeed suffer certain limitations in their ritual participation and must follow prohibitions associated with the state of inauspiciousness. See Gellner 1991, 116. As Gellner notes, other colleagues working among Newar groups in the Kathmandu valley have not observed status loss and stigmatization among widowed Newari women. See, for example, Toffin 1977 and Toffin 1978. For a discussion of the extent to which Toffin's informants are representative of core Newar values, see Gellner 1991, 117–19.

8. The *Aegle marmelos* Correa species produces an astringent, citruslike fruit. The fruit is used medicinally in South Asia, and its leaves are used in Shiva worship. See Monier-Williams 1974, s.v. *bilva*.

9. The secondary marriage to a human spouse typically follows some years later. A study done in 1985 suggests that the average age for marriage to a human spouse is about sixteen and a half for Newar girls, where the average age of marriage for non-Newar Hindu girls is thirteen and a half. See Tuladhar 1985, 55–62. Pandey distinguishes between first marriage (*prathamavivaha*) and the blessed fruit marriage (*shriphalavivaha*), conducted with the use of a *bya* fruit proxy for the groom. See Pandey 1972, 134.

10. That this enfranchisement in the lineage is accomplished through the medium of the *bya* fruit seems significant. Like the gifts with which the Vedic gods endow the young girl in the Vedic marriage hymn, the *bya* fruit ensures the girl's future security.

11. See, for example, Gellner 1992; Gellner 1991, 105–25; Levy 1990. Allen (1990), although quite clear about the ritually definitive and irrevocable role that the *ihi* ritual plays in contrast to the less ritually elaborate, less sacramental secondary marriage, also uses the phrase "mock marriage" in conformity with the dominant ethnographic convention. I thank Joyce Burkhalter Flueckiger for pointing out problems with the term "mock marriage" in oral communication, November 2002.

12. Dumont 1964, 77–98. See also Dumont's earlier reflections on marriage in Southeast India and Sri Lanka, in Dumont 1961, 75–95. See also Nepali 1965, 198; Pradhan 1986, 167.

## Works Cited

Allen, Michael. 1990. "Girls' Prepuberty Rites amongst the Newars of Kathmandu Valley." In *Women in India and Nepal*, ed. Michael Allen and S. N. Muiherjee, 179–210. New Delhi, India: Sterling Publishers Private Limited; New York: Apt Books.

Amirrezvani, Anita. 2004. "Bharati Mukherjee's Cultural Journey: Novelist and Characters Try to Balance Indian Values with Life in the U.S." *San Jose Mercury News*, August 26.

Bajaracharya, Purna Harsha. 1959. "Newar Marriage Customs and Festivals." *South West Journal of Anthropology* 15: 418–29.

Bennett, Lynn. 1978. "Sitting in a Cave: An Analysis of Ritual Seclusion at Menarche among Bramans and Chhetris in Nepal." *Contributions to Nepalese Studies* 6:1: 31–45.

Bennett, Lynn. 1983. *Dangerous Wives and Sacred Sisters: Social and Symbolic Roles of High-Caste Women in Nepal*. New York: Columbia University Press.

Doniger, Wendy, and Brian K. Smith, trans. 1991. *The Laws of Manu*. New York: Penguin Books.

Dumont, Louis. 1961. "Marriage in India, The Present State of the Question: 1—Marriage Alliance in South East India and Ceylon." *Contributions to Indian Sociology* 5: 75–95.

Dumont, Louis. 1964. "Marriage in India, The Present State of the Question: Postscript to Part 1—Marriage and Status, Nayar and Newar." *Contributions to Indian Sociology* 7: 77–98.

Gellner, David N. 1991. "Hinduism, Tribalism, and the Position of Women: The Problem of Newar Identity." *Man* 27:1: 105–25.

Gellner, David N. 1992. *Monk, Householder, and Tantric Priest: Newar Buddhism and Its Hierarchy of Ritual*. Cambridge and New York: Cambridge University Press.

Gellner, David N. 1995. "Sakyas and Vajracaryas: From Holy Order to Quasi-Ethnic Group." In *Contested Hierarchies: A Collaborative Ethnography of Caste among the Newars of the Kathmandu Valley, Nepal*, ed. David N. Gellner and Declan Quigley, 209–39. Oxford: Clarendon Press; New York: Oxford University Press.

Greenwold, S. M. 1974. "Buddhist Brahmins." *Archiv fur European Sociology* 15: 101–23.

Kane, P. V., ed. 1968–1974. *History of Dharmashastra*. 5 vols. Poona: Bhandarkar Oriental Research Institute.

Leslie, Julia. 1989. *The Perfect Wife: The Orthodox Hindu Woman according to the Stridharmapaddati of Tryambakayajvan*. Delhi and New York: Oxford University Press.

Levy, Robert. 1990. *Mesocosm: Hinduism and the Organization of a Traditional Newar City in Nepal*. Berkeley: University of California Press.

Menski, Walter. 1984. "Role and Ritual in the Hindu Marriage." Doctoral thesis, University of London.

Monier-Williams, Sir Monier. 1974. *A Sanskrit-English Dictionary: Etymologically and Philologically Arranged with Special Reference to Cognate Indo-European Languages*. Oxford: Clarendon Press.

Mukherjee, Bharati. 2002. *Desirable Daughters*. New York: Theia.

Nepali, G. S. 1965. *The Newars: An Ethno-Sociological Study of a Himalayan Community*. Bombay: United Asia Publications.

Nicholas, Ralph. 1995. "Caste, Marriage and Divorce in Bengali Culture." In *From the Margins of Hindu Marriage: Essays on Gender, Religion, and Culture*, ed. Lindsay Harlan and Paul Courtright, 137–59. New York: Oxford University Press.

Pandey, Rajbali. 1949. *Hindu Samskaras: Socio-Religious Study of the Hindu Sacraments*. Banaras: Vikrama Publications; 2nd ed. Delhi: Motilal Banarsidass, 1969.

Pandey, Roop Narayan. 1972. "Nepalese Society during the Malla and Early Shah Period." In C. R. Swaminathan et al., *Cultural Heritage of Nepal*, ed. Ravindra Sahai Varma. Allahabad, India: Kitab Mahal.

Pradhan, Rajendra P. 1986. "Domestic and Cosmic Rituals among the Hindu Newars of Kathmandu, Nepal." Doctoral thesis, University of Delhi.

Sharma, Bhaiyaram. 1993. *The Vivaha: The Hindu Marriage Samskaras*. Translated by R. C. Prasad. Delhi: Motilal Banarsidass.

Toffin, Gérard. 1977. *Pyangaon: Une Communauté Néwar de la vallée de Kathmandou, la Vie Matérielle*. Paris: Centre National de la Recherche Scientifique.

Toffin, Gérard. 1978. "O'Organisation Sociale et Religieuse d'une Communauté Newar." *L'Homme* 18: 109–34.

Toffin, Gérard. 1984. *Socie'te' et Religion chez les Newar du Népal*. Paris: Centre National de la Recherche Scientifique.

Tuladhar, Jayanti Man. 1985. "Factors Affecting the Age at Marriage in Nepal." *Contributions to Nepalese Studies* 12:2: 55–62.

Vergati, Anne. 1982. "Social Consequences of Marrying Visnhu Narayana: Primary Marriage among the Newars of the Kathmandu Valley." *Contributions to Indian Sociology* 16:2: 271–87.

Von Furer-Haimdorf, Christoph. 1956. "Elements of Newar Social Structure." *Journal of the Royal Anthropological Institute* 86: 15–38.

# 5

# The "Artful Trick"

## *Challenging Convention through Play in Upstate New York*

Corinne Dempsey and
Sudharshan Durayappah

Aiya, the guru and head priest at the Shri Rajarajeshwari Pitham in Rush, Upstate New York, is—and always has been—playful. If one is fortunate to be in Aiya's company while he is reminiscing about his childhood, then one would likely hear tales featuring his youthful antics such as snatching communion wafers from his kindergarten classroom, chasing girls with bags of cockroaches, or concocting elaborate pranks to play on his school chums. Reveling in his naughty past, Aiya often laughingly ends his stories with statements such as, "I was a little scamp." Those who knew Aiya when he was growing up in Sri Lanka—and have since lost touch—are often shocked to find that he has become a well-respected religious leader, responsible for establishing and maintaining a thriving temple dedicated to the goddess Shri Rajarajeshwari. Remembering him as a ringleader and mischief maker, out to have a good time with his raucous friends, they are understandably puzzled over the way his life's course has veered off in an entirely different direction.

It is our contention that Aiya's turn toward religion, founded on a dramatic conversion experience when he was a twenty-year-old atheist, allows for his role as ringleader and gleeful mischief maker to continue unabated. Aiya would be the first to agree with this assessment. While impish naughtiness is something he enjoys highlighting in stories of his childhood and teenage years, it is also foundational to his current self-perception as a temple priest, guru, and teacher. Foundational to his temple, housed in a one-story barn in rural Upstate New York since 1998, is in fact the work of goading convention. Unlike Aiya's youthful antics, likely propelled by his sense of adventure and pure mischieviousness, religious mischief at the Rush temple is founded upon convictions he considers quite serious, if not urgent. Most pressing is the obligation he feels, with blessings from his own guru, to offer his students—regardless of caste, gender, or ethnicity—special access to what he and they consider an unnecessarily restrictive, rigidly defined tradition.

Foundational to the Rush temple's convention-breaking mischief is its floor plan. Although it is a south Indian-style temple that in many aspects follows Vedic Brahmanical prescription, the interior does not enclose its deities within small shrines, accessible only to temple priests who mediate between these deities and lay devotees who must stand at a distance from their object of devotion. Rather, the Rush temple brazenly and incongruously sets its gods and goddesses out in the open, available for public access. During daily rituals, participants are encouraged, if not expected, to approach, touch, and receive the blessings of the temple deities.

Saturday *abhishekam* rituals further orchestrate communal participation. Organizers instruct the congregation to form a line down the left side of the temple to allow them to approach, one by one, the three main black granite images *(murtis)* of Shri Rajarajeshwari, Ganesh, and the aniconic Shiva lingam. Temple volunteers, waiting at the front of the line, hand over small vessels of watered-down milk to allow participants to perform the typically priestly function of pouring the contents of their vessels over each deity, lovingly rubbing in the liquid for good measure.

For first-time visitors, encounters with the temple's unusual floor plan and communal style can be surprising, if not startling. If they anticipate meeting a conventional guru who is reserved, perhaps bearded, and wearing ochre robes, expounding upon philosophical platitudes for his listeners, they will find Aiya clean-shaven, still youthful in his mid-sixties, and—if not in the midst of performing a ritual—in street clothes. Although he relishes philosophical and theological exchanges, Aiya may just as likely be holding forth in his irrepressible comical style, dodging the person sitting next to him whom he has just teased. If these visitors arrive at the temple during a ritual performance, they may furthermore be startled to find that the person acting as head priest—whether for daily worship (*puja*) inside the temple or for fire rituals (*homam*) in an adjoining hall—may

Figure 5.1. Temple participants line up to perform *abhishekam* during Shivaratri 2006; Aiya leads Sanskrit chanting in the background. *(photo by author)*

be non-Brahmn and/or non-male and/or non-South Asian. Finally, the tradition of meditation, mantra, and ritual practices that Aiya "mischievously" transmits to almost anyone genuinely interested in learning—regardless of gender, caste, or ethnicity—is of the Shrividya tradition, conventionally a highly secretive, male-oriented, and exclusively Brahmanical Tantric path.[1]

It is our contention that nothing, in the end, is intrinsically funny. Context and audience invariably determine whether a humorous moment will fly or fall flat. As a number of chapters in this book attest, what people perceive as funny in one situation may be sickening in another; what moves one person to tears might make another laugh. Set within the context of a temple that is considered both controversial and powerful, whose lighthearted and highly purposeful mischief reverberates with Aiya's trademark impishness and humor, this chapter explores two mutually exclusive dimensions of laughter and levity, viewed from opposite vantage points, potentially evoked by and enacted within Rush temple ritual.

The first section reflects upon instances in which elaborate rituals, earning for Rush a positive reputation for divine blessings and miraculous power, can stir up certain, if not serious, misgivings among the more traditionally oriented members of the Hindu community, particularly those who understand priesthood as an exclusively male Brahmanical right or who feel that the Shrividya tradition is best guarded more closely than at the Rush temple. Framing this issue in terms of ritual levity, this section views how the temple's reputation for institutional mischief, for breaking with traditional caste and gender restrictions, might evoke in avowed outsiders nervous if not derisive laughter at the practitioner's expense. From this perspective, Rush temple devotees might be understood as mischievous "clowns" who, upon further investigation, are not as laughable and without purpose as they at first seem.

The second section moves on to describe unmitigated, gleeful ritual levity enjoyed by dedicated temple insiders. Here we attempt to make sense of the fact that Rush temple rituals, although performed with deep sincerity and seriousness by a cadre of highly disciplined devotees (who understand themselves as anything but clownlike or laughable), can and do occasionally erupt into raucous playfulness. It is precisely in the midst of devotees' sincere devotion and serious discipline that ritual levity seems to flourish.

Assisting us in excavating the layers of levity at the Rush temple will be a cameo appearance by a Kattiyankaran, a professional clown figure from Tamil ritual theater. As we shall see, the role of the Kattiyankaran is to serve as a bridge that mischievously links and confounds the audience with actors as well as the mundane with sacred realms. As such, he offers a useful vantage point from which to examine and juxtapose insider and outsider perspectives of the Rush temple's ritual mischief and levity. The Kattiyankaran, master of bridging worlds, ultimately draws upon his skillful wit and humor to perform the artful trick of linking irreverence with piety, laughter with divine intimacy—contrasting modes that, at the Rush temple, are not only inextricably linked but dependent upon one other for their existence.

Whether viewed from the inside or the outside, lavishly performed rituals are foundational for exploring the complex, disparate forms of levity at the Rush temple. This is so, in large part, because much is at stake in ritual performance. Since ritual at the Rush temple serves as a vital means for harnessing the power of its goddess, Rajarajeshwari, the defiance of long-standing gender, caste, and ethnic conventions within the ritual context cannot be a neutral matter. On the one hand, such defiance runs the risk of the undesirable if not dangerous mishandling of sacred power, yet, on the other hand, it dramatically breaks open opportunities for otherwise unavailable divine-human interactions. Those uncomfortable with the Rush temple's ritual practices can try to diminish their undesirable impact by rendering practitioners laughable, so to speak. Those who embrace newfound possibilities often do so with humor and glee. Levity and laughter potentially exist around and within Rush temple rituals, but their manifestation in two very different forms is, in a sense, a response to two very different, and sometimes very serious, "jokes."

## A View from the Outside: Nervous Laughter

To offer a striking example of a ritual event regularly performed at Rush and likely to invoke nervous laughter—among other reactions—from traditionalist Hindus, imagine a Euro-American woman resplendently dressed in a colorful sari, performing a four-hour-long *shri chakra puja*, the intricate ritual core of the highly secretive, essentially male Brahmanical Shrividya tradition. She chants in perfect Sanskrit, something she has honed after countless hours and over a decade of practice, and she does so into a microphone for all present—initiates and non-initiates—to hear. She is seated in front of a *shri chakra meru*, a sacred, conical-shaped form intricately made from brass that represents the divine cosmos, yet whose features correspond to aspects of the human body as well.

By performing *puja* to the *meru*, the woman invokes the cosmos as divinity within the temple and within herself as the embodiment of divinity. The *meru* and the lead chanter-priestess sit at the feet of Sri Rajarajeshwari's granite form, the temple manifestation of the same, all-encompassing divinity. Seasoned fellow devotees sit nearby as well, many of whom supplement the ritual with synchronized chanting and sacred hand gestures (*mudras*). Other devotees struggle along, using the Shrividya book published by Aiya that boldly transliterates instructions for performing the otherwise exclusive and secret *shri chakra puja* ritual into vernacular, accessible, script—from Sanskrit into Tamil and English. Some present may be first-time temple visitors who come for the "show," struck by the sights and sounds that incompatibly coalesce for the evening.

As suggested earlier, possible shock or uneasiness provoked by such a ritual performance might well be mitigated through humor. Dismissive laughter arising from such misgivings would most likely not be directed at the intricate ritual itself but at those responsible for unhinging the status quo through the transgression of gender and caste conventions. As such, bold temple insiders could be portrayed, albeit loosely, as dignified yet mischievous jesters or clowns who, according to clown tradition, take part in outlandish activities that make certain audience members laugh nervously. This clown analogy becomes even more pertinent when we consider Don Handelman's (1990) work on ritual and humor that locates "clown types" within border zones between orthodoxy and anti-orthodoxy. As a result, they emerge not simply as comical but as dangerous and powerful.

Drawing from the work of Edmund Leach (1976) and Mary Douglas (1968), who describe boundaries just outside of cultural norms as both threatening and potent, Handelman (1990) argues that irreverent and provocative clowns do not in fact break boundaries; their power stems from their being *of* the boundaries, embodiments of status quo uncertainty. Likewise, Rush temple members, although they break with caste and gender conventions, do not leave convention completely behind. As demonstrated in the previous example, the elaborate and highly polished rituals they perform are the result of much discipline and close attention to ritual detail. While ritual actions ideally adhere closely to convention, ritual actors do not. Like clowns described by Handelman, it is precisely Rush devotees' position on the border between convention and nonconvention that makes them threatening and therefore makes some people uneasy.

To further flesh out and extend this reflection on the potency of clown figures, we introduce the Kattiyankaran, a figure from Terukuttu ritual theatre in Tamil Nadu. The Kattiyankaran is someone who, like Rush practitioners of Shrividya, mediates the boundaries between convention and nonconvention as well as between divinity and humanity. Tamil Terukuttu plays in village Tamil Nadu typically feature selections from Sanskrit epics such as the *Mahabharata* and the *Ramayana* or scenes from Tamil classics such as the *Chilappadikaram* and the *Periya Puranam*.[2] Terukuttu performances require a team of actors, typically low-caste men, drawn from the local village itself, who are adept at both singing and dancing. The single most demanding role of all is assumed by the Kattiyankaran, a semi-professional who is not necessarily from the local village. He is traditionally known and revered for his quick wit, sense of humor, and keen ability to improvise according to the needs of the audience and actors.[3]

The Kattiyankaran's role is, most basically, that of mediator between the worlds of gods and humans and between devotion and irreverence, an often precarious balance made possible by his skillful wit and humor. The Kattiyankaran stands on stage with the other Terukuttu actors, yet he is the only one who can address the audience directly. By humorously interjecting explanations of the plot as well as clever asides that weave present-day events and politics into the play, the Kattiyankaran links the lives of gods and kings with those of the mostly low-caste audience members. The Kattiyankaran further levels cosmic and social divides by poking fun at or making lewd comments about the divinities portrayed on stage and by cajoling Brahmins into the limelight where they are often verbally derided and physically abused (Link 1993, 32–33; Frasca 1984, 335–36).

The Kattiyankaran's dress and makeup further underscore his position as trickster mediator. Unlike the other Terukuttu actors who wear traditional clothing, his is often outlandishly and deliberately modern. His facial makeup is also unlike other actors, in that he looks neither male nor female, nor does he appear distinctly realistic or unrealistic. Playfully hinting at the Kattiyankaran's borderline stance between the higher and lower planes is his painted mustache, often curved up on one side and down on the other (Link 1993, 33).

As Handelman (1990) would argue, the Kattiyankaran's "clown" status amid boundaries—between time frames (cosmic and human), spatial settings (stage and audience, heaven and earth), and convention (between devotion and irreverence)—gives him the license and power, fortified by his humor, to threaten and challenge the status quo.[4] The Kattiyankaran's role as a skillful and an efficacious mediator is not lost on the actor, since he is self-described as a *chuttiram*, literally meaning thread or cord, as well as an artful trick, a puzzle, or a secret mystery (Link 1993, 34). The question remains, as is often the case in the realm of folk resistance, as to whether or not the Kattiyankaran simply acts as a release valve for devalued members of society—and thus a safety valve for the status quo—or whether he encourages actual change through his bold words and actions. In his study of folk clowns in south India, David Schulman less than optimistically notes that these clowns expose yet often reaffirm the inequities of society (1985, 213).[5]

To bring the discussion back to the Rush temple, the border regions inhabited by temple devotees enable them, somewhat like the Kattiyankaran, to strike a nerve. Chanting well-honed Sanskrit and performing complex Vedic rituals with grace and accuracy, the fact that they labor within the system makes them—in spite and perhaps because of their embodied critique of caste and gender restrictions—difficult to discount. Like tricksters who are difficult to ignore, Rush devotees are aware that they provide a kind of "show," the actors themselves playing along by assuming the clownlike role of goading convention. Aiya realizes that part of what draws people to the temple is its unconventional approach to ritual. Hopeful that their performances will inadvertently broaden the horizons of curiosity seekers among them, he deliberately pushes competent women into the limelight, assigning them ritual leadership roles during large festivals. These women are usually willing if not dedicated partners in mischief, for mischief's sake as well as for the greater good of breaking barriers.

The question as to whether embodied critique during Rush temple rituals promotes actual change within the larger system, or whether such performances are simply provocative, evoking little more than nervous laughter among detractors, brings us to the edge of our clown analogy. Unlike the Kattiyankaran, devotees at the Rush temple do not perform their ritual defiance on the edge of a stage bordering "real" time and space but in a temple that has earned legitimacy and respect within a wide segment of the North American Hindu community. The largest contingent of temple participants, typically 100 to 300 during nonfestival weeks, is Sri Lankan Tamils of all ages and backgrounds who live in Toronto and make the three-hour journey to Rush rather than attend one of over two dozen Sri Lankan Tamil temples in the Toronto area.

Furthermore, it seems that some of Rush's ideologies and practices are currently making an impact, not just on a growing number of participants but on portions of the greater south Indian Hindu community as well. Most noticeable is the fact that certain unconventional yet well-received practices at the Rush temple have prompted competing Sri Lankan Hindu temples in Toronto to add similar features to their rituals. For instance, several temples have begun to assign women an increased role by allowing female palanquin bearers to carry processional deities. This practice, performed as a matter of course at Rush, was earlier unheard of at these traditional south Indian temples. Two Toronto temples have also begun offering communal *abhishekam* deity-washing rituals. Although the ritual is performed outside of the temple to a proxy deity, such communal participation represents a dramatic shift in style. While it is impossible to say whether Toronto temple officials have altered their practices due to a genuine shift in ideology or to keep up with the local competition, it does not appear that Rush temple "mischief" functions merely as a release valve for insiders and thus as a reaffirmation of the status quo.

The Kattiyankaran clown analogy completely runs out of steam when we view Rush temple rituals through the eyes of devotee insiders. Aware that they occupy the margins within the South Asian temple culture, Rush participants validate and center their unconventional ritual performances through the backing of an esteemed guru lineage. Aiya's guru, affectionately known as Guruji, is a Smarta Brahmin and nuclear physicist from Andhra Pradesh who initiated Aiya, a non-Brahmin, into his Shrividya lineage under the condition that he teach the tradition to anyone interested in learning, regardless of her or his background. True to form, Aiya has taken on Guruji's request with gusto, gleefully breaking with convention and opening up otherwise exclusive practices and traditions for his students. If Rush devotees think of themselves as clowns, it is simply because laughter is such an intrinsic part of temple life. The joke, if there is one, is not at their expense. Rather than invalidating their practices, joking and laughter act to strengthen and enrich them.

## A View from the Inside: Serious Ritual Levity

Laughter and playfulness are such an intrinsic part of Rush temple life that Aiya is fond of telling people, in all seriousness, that joking is "absolutely central" to his guru lineage. He enjoys regaling listeners with examples of Guruji's irreverent sense of humor, although people who know both Aiya and Guruji often insist that Aiya is the master teaser. In reference to Aiya's trickster tendencies, Guruji likes to refer to him as Narada, a famous trouble-making sage in Hindu mythology who plays tricks on the gods, making them angry at one another and causing general mayhem.

Aiya's antics seem to have the opposite effect on temple participants, however; rather than creating dissention, they tend to foster a sense of community. Anthropologist Mary Douglas (1966, 1968) likewise notes how playfulness can function to foster intimacy. She proposes that laughter and joking most fundamentally reveal the arbitrary nature of socially constructed categories. Shared laughter thus can work to suspend hierarchy, level social differences, and challenge the balance of power. With this in mind, it makes sense that ritual playfulness at the Rush temple functions to reflect, underscore, and further validate one of the primary aims of the temple and its founder, that is, to challenge power structures by leveling distinctions having to do with caste, gender, and ethnicity. The fact that ritual playfulness reinforces the temple's aim to bind and level human relations is only a portion of the equation, however. Since the central purpose of temple rituals is to appeal to and create ties with divinity and divine power, reverent playfulness enacted during ritual further underscores its aim toward human-divine intimacy, narrowing more profoundly the breach between the two realms.

Creating intimacy through ritual playfulness in the widest sense, Aiya regularly evokes laughter during rituals by joking in Tamil and English at the expense of participants, both human and divine. This occurs most commonly during *homam* fire rituals, where Aiya often interjects explanations and humorous asides. Drawing more exclusive parameters, he also plays with Sanskrit words, a joke genre lost on nonseasoned chanters, marking a boundary of belonging around those who understand and laugh.

While Aiya is the master joker, others can play the role as well. For instance, a teenage boy named Tharamam used to, when he was younger, add mischievous levity to *homam* fire rituals. According to temple convention, Tharamam would assist *homam*s by walking through the crowds with the tray of offerings bound for the fire, allowing participants to piously touch the tray and its contents. This tradition of passing the homam tray is unique to Rush, performed in defiance of priestly convention by enabling all present to offer sacrifice. Adding his own version of playful deviance to the process, Tharamam would periodically offer the tray to a devotee and snatch it away before she or he could touch it. Eventually contact was made, and Tharamam's mischief was rewarded by warm laughter and tweaks of his chubby cheeks. While the Rush *homam* tradition aims at leveling caste and gender distinction, consequently freeing previously blocked channels between humanity and divinity, teasing and laughter seem to underscore the process by closing the gap between mischief and piety.

While examples of everyday ritual playfulness such as these abound and are significant for their regularity, there are also instances in which levity bursts into ritual space with flourish. A good example of this is the *maha abhishekam* "mud fight" enacted during the Navaratri festival celebration in the fall of 2002. Unlike Saturday *abhishekam*s, where participants carefully douse the three main deities with milk, the hour-long *maha abhishekam* is of a much grander scale, involving bucketloads of various substances.[6] Aparna, an Euro-American devotee, describes the intensity of the ritual itself:

> When you're doing the *abhishekam* rituals on this level it's almost as if the intensity builds because you're drenching Her. It's as if She's going for a water ride or something like that. And I'm sure it's exhausting for Aiya, because it takes a lot of strength. Because he's picking up and lifting over his head buckets for an hour. So that's physical labor.

Figure 5.2. Aiya leads camp counselors in a public *homam* ritual during the summer of 2007. *(photo by author)*

> So you can see that his adrenaline is probably going too, because it takes a lot of physical energy to do that, and spiritual energy. Because it's almost as if, if it stops, it's not going to create the same effect. And so you're building it. And you can feel it.

The mud fight begins to break out during the point at which people perform a gesture common to Rush's Saturday *abhishekam* involving turmeric-colored liquid that is ritually infused with sacred energy and processed around the temple in a metal vessel (*kalasam*). This liquid is then poured on the granite Shri Rajarajeshwari *murti* and contained by a low tile wall surrounding the three main deities. Devotees then rush to put their hands into the liquid, press it to their eyelids, and lightly slap it onto their cheeks and perhaps the cheeks of the person next to them. This sharing of liquid *prasadam* is a loving gesture under normal circumstances, ever so slightly naughty and playful. Aparna describes the transition from the Saturday *abhishekam* gesture to the *maha abhishekam* "mud fight," seemingly inciting hilarity not only in the devotees but in the temple goddess as well:

> Now we escalate that, because now we're in an escalated situation. So it started out like in that simple ritual that we always do, that's familiar to us. So we go to do what's familiar and all you need is for one person to do the next thing. I don't know if it was Aiya or who, but all of a sudden someone put in their forehead and then someone else's arm went in, then somebody else's other arm went in.
>
> The last substance was the sandal paste. And that was what we started getting into a fight with, because that's more like mud. You can actually pick it up and make a shape and throw it. . . . I didn't feel like we were being sacrilegious to the Devi [the Goddess] at that point. She has so much on her, you have to scoop it off. Aiya's pouring it on her, but as Aiya's pouring it on her, other people are there scraping it off, just to scrape it down so that there's more room for him to pour more on. So it starts off as kind of a practical thing. You're part of the worship, you're doing your role, right? So then all you have to do is take one hand that has a little too much on it, and you don't want to put it down, so you put it on someone's arm.
>
> . . . And so Aiya was right there, and I was right at the Devi and there was a lot of it [on my hand] and it just went on [Janani's] arm. And Aiya just looked at me and said, "I saw that!" And then it was like it didn't matter. Even though he said, "I saw that!" as if you were being a naughty kid, you think, "Oh goody, he saw!" So you're almost encouraged and so you take the next one and throw it at him.
>
> And the Devi, y'know normally she's really proper; she has that little apron on and she's basically naked when we do the *abhishekam* except for the little apron, but so much stuff is going on, her clothes are falling off too. So normally people are putting them back up again, but in this situation, we didn't care if her clothes were falling off, we were just going for it. It was this idea that . . . it was just really fun.

Rituals that become play—as described by Aparna, and similarly perceived by other committed Rush devotees of all generations and backgrounds—do not have to leave divinity behind. She can be an active participant, blessing the event by binding the raucous with the sacred, the naughty with the pious. Aiya's mischievous endorsement has a similar effect. Heightened playfulness, rather than being sacrilegious, as posed by Aparna, seems simply to function more effectively in narrowing the divide between humanity and divinity. The *abhishekam* "mud fight" ultimately becomes communal *abhishekam*, bringing Devi into the realm of the human and the human into the divine. For some this may seem sacrilegious, but within the context of Rush temple theology, formed by the Tantric Shrividya tradition, the binding and blurring of the mundane with the sacred, and vice versa, is what ritual is all about. If spontaneous play and laughter help perpetuate and validate this process, then all the better.

Our final example of ritual playfulness involves a mock procession. Although on par with the *abhishekam* event in terms of spontaneity and hilarity, mock processions represent play infused with ritual rather than ritual infused with play. They emerge, on occasion, at the conclusion of large festivals such as Navaratri in the fall or the temple's anniversary celebration (*pratishta*) at the end of May; they take place outside of official sacred festival time when the crowds have dispersed and inner-core members are cleaning up. Opportunities for mock processions most naturally arise when devotees begin to move one of the two temple chariots back into their storage shed.[7] As a small segment of the cleanup crew pulls the chariot from the temple to the shed, Aiya has, on a couple of occasions, laughingly been coerced onto the wooden vehicle for a ride. This gives the cue to the workers to loudly and raucously start chanting, treating Aiya like they would a temple deity. The volume and pitch of the event invariably attract others on the temple grounds who rush to join in. Although the "procession" is imbued with laughter and fun, its seriousness—reflected in the fact that Sanskrit verses are being accurately chanted and the "deity" honored is in the form of an esteemed guru—is difficult to miss.

The first and so far the most raucous mock procession to have materialized at the Rush temple occurred at the conclusion of the first anniversary *pratishta* festival, Memorial Day weekend, 1999. The final real procession had made its rounds, and the crowds had mostly dispersed. Many of the inner-core devotees who had stayed on to help clean up had headed out to the food tent for lunch. As Aiya, on his way to the lunch tent, appeared at the doorway to the temple, a group of young men started shouting "Aro Hara!" and held up a small procession palanquin for him to climb onto. With a sheepish grin on his face, Aiya obliged, and the young men set off around the temple, the palanquin on their shoulders, with irreverent shouts of devotional reverence and laughter.

Waiting around the first bend was a group of young women. Jamuna, Aiya's niece, in her late twenties, held in her hands a hose used earlier for cooling the excruciatingly hot cement. Egged on by the women around her, she sprayed first the palanquin bearers and then Aiya, provoking more shouts and laughter and a small crowd to gather. After he was sufficiently doused, Aiya anxiously motioned for the hose to be passed his way. The young women obliged, and he turned the spray onto the crowd, further heightening the hilarity and drenching those who earlier laughed at his expense. As the procession neared its completion, a group of women hijacked the palanquin from the men and carried Aiya into the final stretch. Once back at the temple door, devotees proceeded to perform perfectly orchestrated *panchapuja* to Aiya, offering the prescribed incense, flowers, fruit, and camphor flame while shouting Sanskrit in unison at the top of their lungs.[8]

By enacting a procession and *puja* mockingly outside of ritual time, yet in a devotionally accurate manner, devotees honored their mischievous yet serious guru who, in all playfulness and reverence, they positioned as a processional deity. With the sacred spilling out into the mundane, the water fight was transformed, by association, into a kind of raucous group *abhishekam*. Laughter, heightened with each new layer of mischief, was affirmed and was furthermore fed by a shared sense of sacrality.

The *maha abhishekam* and mock procession are distinct in that one represents playful ritual and centers on the temple deity while the other enacts ritual-infused play and focuses on the temple guru. Linking laughter with sacrality, both events function to strengthen the bond of intimacy among temple members and between temple members and sources of sacred power and inspiration. Also connecting the two events, fundamental to their hilarity and intimacy, is a communal dousing, one by turmeric and sandalwood paste that dried and crusted over with time and the other by water that quickly evaporated in a late springtime heat wave.

After the raucous *maha abhishekam* event, temple members wandered the grounds in various stages of disarray, the most dramatic display being Ammamma, a special recipient of Aiya's mischief and caked from head to toe with drying sandalwood mud. Ammamma (meaning "grandmother" in Tamil), a woman in her seventies, was Aiya's kindergarten teacher in Sri Lanka. Thus possessing special insight into Aiya's character, she was asked the previous summer to describe him as a little boy. Ammamma responded simply and concisely by mentioning two things. One: he was always teasing the girls and making them mad. Two: he was always looking for his mother.

While these two activities probably bore no connection at the time, they are now—if we may stretch the analogy—inextricable. As reflected by Rush temple rituals and mock rituals, mischief and intimacy with the Mother not only coexist, but they reinforce one another. From the perspective of temple insiders, breaking with convention does not lead devotees dangerously, perhaps laughingly, astray but, rather, offers them a sure-footed path toward divinity. The naughtiness and irreverence of play underscore and are intensified by strains of serious, hard-won devotion.

The interplay of naughty humor with divine intimacy brings back to mind the Kattiyankaran whose irreverent humor, as we have seen, allows him to thumb his nose at social convention and makes way for his self-designated title of *chuttiram*, or "cord" between rudeness and reverence and between humanity and divinity. Earlier in this chapter the Kattiyankaran's humorous defiance of social and religious hierarchies offered insight into dynamics involving nervous laughter from the status quo. Now, after considering temple humor from the perspective of Rush insiders, the Kattiyankaran offers another kind of insight by suggesting that playfulness can provide a "cord" or bridge between heaven and earth. *Chuttiram* also means "artful trick," suggesting the job of linking worlds is not simple or straightforward but requires skillfully supplied mischief. In the Terukuttu street plays, none of the other actors can break barriers in the same way the Kattiyankaran does. The "trick" to the Kattiyankaran's abilities is his exceptional humor and wit, giving him license to perform the otherwise impossible, whether it be knocking tradition or bridging worlds. Likewise, well-honed playfulness at the Rush temple is not simply a pleasant social perk. If the Kattiyankaran has anything to say about it (one side of his mustache pointing up and the other pointing down), mischief and laughter supply the necessary fuel for the Rush temple's "artful trick" of mending the often intimidating divide between ordinary people and priests and, ultimately, between humanity and divinity.

## Notes

This chapter is a product of scholarly and fieldwork collaboration between Corinne Dempsey and Sudharshan Durayappah at the Sri Rajarajeshwari temple between 1998 and 2004. Examples of temple levity also appear in the book that emerges from this period of research (Dempsey 2006). Thanks to Amy Bard, Aparna Hasling, and Selva Raj for their thoughtful reflections and suggestions on an earlier draft of this chapter. Thanks also to Aiya for his patience and generosity throughout the process of research and writing.

1. For a thorough description and history of Shrividya, as well as an explanation of its centuries-long association with the elite Smarta caste within the Brahman fold, see Brooks 1992.

2. The *Chilappadikaram* is a classic Tamil epic attributed to Ilango Adigal, a Jain prince who lived in the third century CE. The *Periya Puranam* is a collection of stories honoring the Tamil Nayanmar saints, devotees of Shiva.

3. See Link 1993 for an analysis of the Kattiyankaran's role as mediator and link between worlds. For a more in-depth treatment of the Terukuttu itself, see Frasca's dissertation dealing with the performance in northeastern Tamil Nadu. Malten's brief account of a Terukuttu performance in the northern part of the state describes the role of the Kattiyankaran as the panegyrist, separate from the *vitushan* from the Sanskrit *vidushaka,* also know as a *kamik,* from the English "comic."

4. This clown phenomena and function can be applied to an array of societies, including our own. Comedians (such as Al Franken, John Stewart, and Jay Leno, to name just a few) often hover somewhere between respectability and the ridiculous; through their liminal state, along with their humor and wit, they seem positioned to critique effectively the status quo in ways that few other public figures are. (Thanks to Selva Raj for pointing this out to us.)

5. See also Turner 1978 for a discussion of this conundrum.

6. There are eleven *maha abhishekam* substances. Each is poured onto Sri Rajarajeshwari, followed by a bucketful of water. In order of appearance, they are: milk, yogurt, ghee (clarified butter), honey, *pancamrit* (five types of chopped fruit mixed with jaggery, sugar crystals, and honey), fruit juice, young coconut milk, turmeric, vibhuti, sandalwood, and rosewater. Also, at some point, water from the creek below the temple, "Kashi," will be poured on the *murti* as well.

7. Traditional Tamil chariots, used for transporting deities in processions, typically fall under two categories. The *chaparam* is a high, conical-shaped chariot, while the *ter* is five-sided and wider in diameter. At the Rush temple, the *chaparam* is used once a year during the May *pratishta* festival celebrating the anniversary of the temple's consecration, and the *ter* is used in the fall during the Navaratri or nine-night festival celebrating and honoring the warrior goddess's defeat of her demon opponents.

8. *Panchapuja* refers to basic *puja* worship in which the priest or officiant offers five elements—incense, flowers, fruit, water, and camphor flame, along with the chanting of mantras—to the deity.

## Works Cited

Brooks, Douglas. 1992. *Auspicious Wisdom: The Texts and Traditions of Śrīvidyā Śākta Tantrism in South India.* Albany: State University of New York Press.

Dempsey, Corinne. 2006. *The Goddess Lives in Upstate New York: Breaking Convention and Making Home at a North American Hindu Temple*. New York: Oxford University Press.

Douglas, Mary. 1966. *Purity and Danger: An Analysis of Conceptions of Pollution and Taboo*. London: Routledge and Kegan Paul.

Douglas, Mary. 1968. "The Social Control of Cognition: Some Factors in Joke Perception." *Man* 3:361: 76.

Frasca, Richard. 1984. "The Terukkuttu: Ritual Theatre of Tamilnadu." Doctoral dissertation, University of California, Berkeley.

Handelman, Don. 1990. *Models and Mirrors: Towards an Anthropology of Public Events*. Cambridge and New York: Cambridge University Press.

Leach, Edmund. 1976. *Culture and Communication*. Cambridge and New York: Cambridge University Press.

Link, Hilde. 1993. "Cord between Heaven and Earth: The Kattiyankaran in the Sacred Theatre of Tamilnadu." *Journal of the Institute of Asian Studies* 11:1: 28–35.

Malten, Thomas. 1981. "Kūttu—Tamil Village Drama." In *South Asian Digest of Regional Writing, vol. 10, Drama in Contemporary South Asia: Varieties and Settings*, ed. Lothar Lutze, 29–37. Heidelberg, Germany: University of Heidelberg, South Asian Institute.

Schulman, David. 1985. *The King and the Clown in South Indian Myth and Poetry*. Princeton, NJ: Princeton University Press.

Turner, Victor. 1978. "Comments and Conclusions." In *The Reversible World: Symbolic Inversion in Art and Society*, dd. Barbara Babcock, 276–96. Ithaca, NY: Cornell University Press.

# Part 2

# Gods and Humans at Play

## *Religious Humor and Divine Intimacy*

# 6

# Friendship, Humor, Levity, and Love in a Hindu Women's Ritual Tradition

Tracy Pintchman

I was sitting in the living room of my research assistant's house one afternoon in 1997 transliterating materials I had recorded earlier at a women's *puja,* or worship ritual, when we hit a particularly dense stretch of tape. Many women were talking at once; there was laughter and the loud clinking of bangles, as happens when women gesticulate vigorously. Unable to sort out the voices myself, I asked my high-caste, male assistant what the women were talking about. He listened to the stretch of tape several times, then screwed up his nose and made a disgusted face. "Just gossip and silliness," he said. He made a sarcastic comment about women's inability to be serious about devotional practice and then proceeded to mock this purported lack of seriousness, caricaturizing the stance of a woman leaning over a religious icon and carelessly tossing *puja* items on it while talking loudly with someone else.

I laughed, but I was uncomfortable. I was back in the city of Benares, North India, to participate for the second time in a particular form of women's devotional practice called Kartik *puja,* a form of ritual worship that takes place daily during the autumn month of Kartik (October–November). I was working on a book on Kartik *puja,* and I had been spending hours sitting with women while they engaged in ritual practice, interviewing them about their devotional practices, and seeking their help in translating stories and songs associated with their ritual performances. These women expended a good deal of time, energy, care, and money to engage in Kartik *puja,* even at the risk of inviting the impatience or even wrath of husbands and other male relatives who, many women reported, sometimes view women's rituals as a waste of time. The women I encountered had memorized numerous ritual songs and stories, sacrificed sleep to rise very early and get the *puja* done before having to return home to prepare food for their families, and scrimped to set aside money to purchase ritual items. This seemingly quick dismissal of women as devotional lightweights did not correspond to my experience *at all*.

When Hindu women gather to perform female-only ritual practices, it is indeed true that they often chat, tease one another, and joke around one another while ritual actions are taking place. Such informal chatting, teasing, joking, and related activities are all behaviors that I consider to constitute "levity" in religious performance. But should we conclude, as my assistant seemed to have, that women who engage in such behaviors are frivolous devotees lacking in seriousness or religious discipline? Does levity in religious practice inherently imply levity in religious commitment? In this chapter I want to explore this issue in relation to Kartik *puja*. I would argue that at least in this tradition, banter, lighthearted and playful interchanges, teasing, and joking around should not be taken as a sign of women's inherent lack of religious *gravitas* or devotional focus—although surely some women, as well as some men, are in fact not serious about religious devotion. Rather, such behaviors serve several purposes. First, they serve to counteract some of the social divisions and hierarchies that tend to characterize everyday life in this part of North India. Second, they help cultivate interpersonal bonding and feelings of friendship among co-worshipers, which participating women tend to see as an essential component of satisfying ritual practice. And third, they serve to humanize God, narrowing the divide between human and deity and fostering a sense of devotional intimacy.

My arguments are grounded in research I conducted on Kartik *puja* traditions in 1995, 1997, and 1998 in Benares.[1] In this city, as in many other parts of India, Kartik is celebrated as a deeply sacred month, and many Benarsis count Kartik among the three or four most religiously important months of the year. The key religious injunction pertaining to the month has to do with the maintenance of the month-long Kartik *vrat*, or votive observance. The central practice associated with this *vrat* is Kartik *snan*, daily ritual bathing throughout the month. In Benares, most Kartik votaries bathe in the Ganges River. Then, after bathing, many female votaries gather on the *ghats*, the stepped platforms that run along the river's bank, to perform the daily *puja*, in which only women participate. Participants use devotional images that they construct out of Ganges clay; forming a circle around the images, they then perform *puja* to them. While many deities are represented and honored, several informants told me that the *puja* itself is really for Krishna, with the other deities called to be present chiefly so that they, too, can participate as devotees.

Most of the participants I formally interviewed indicated that they consider Kartik *puja* to be related to Krishna's *rasa-lila,* which many informants construe as referring to both the famous erotic circle dance of Krishna lore and also the sum total of all events in Krishna's early life in Braj leading up to his departure for Dvaraka.[2] Informants also tended to speak of their role in the *puja* in relation to both these levels of meaning. Like other forms of Krishna worship, Kartik *puja* invites worshipers to envision themselves as participants in Krishna's divine *lila* and assume the role of his original devotees. In this case, it is specifically the *gopis*, the cowherdesses who adored and cared for Krishna during his childhood and later accompanied him in his erotic play, who serve as role models for *puja* participants. The love that the *gopis* lavished on Krishna in ancient times becomes for many *puja* participants the prototype for the love they lavish on him in the *puja* circle. Within Kartik *puja,* however, the nurturing role that devotees assume acquires a progressive character, with participants ritually raising Krishna from infancy to adulthood and, toward the end of the month, arranging and executing his marriage to the plant goddess Tulsi, the auspicious basil plant used in Vaishnava worship.[3]

Figure 6.1. Kartik votaries dancing in anticipation of Krishna's wedding. *(photo by author)*

Krishna is considered to be in child form for about the first twenty days of Kartik *puja*. Toward the end of the month, however, there is a shift. *Puja* participants have a male priest come to their worship circle to perform Krishna's *janeu* or *upanayana*, the ceremony marking his investiture with the sacred thread and designating Krishna's transformation from child to young man. For this occasion, a brass image is used in place of the usual clay one. After the *janeu*, Krishna is no longer thought to be a child, and participants begin to plan his impending marriage to Tulsi. When the time for the marriage arrives several days later, *puja* participants celebrate it with great fanfare.

Participants conclude the daily *puja*, then clear and purify a space for the marriage pavilion. The groom Krishna, represented on this occasion as in the *janeu* by a brass icon instead of a clay one, is brought to the *puja* circle and prepared for the wedding. The bride, a potted Tulsi plant, is also brought to the circle, draped in appropriate red and gold wedding garb and adorned with tinsel, small mirrors, and other decorations. Gifts are placed before the bride and groom and displayed as dowry offerings, and, as in the *janeu*, a male priest is called in briefly to recite appropriate wedding *mantras* and to collect the dowry items as *dan*, donated gifts.

The marriage takes place on Prabhodani Ekadashi, the eleventh day of Kartik's second fortnight, when Vishnu is said to awaken from his annual slumber during the inauspicious four months of the rainy season (the *caturmasa*). Sanskrit texts highlight Vishnu's awakening, and many Benarsis, including many of the women who participate in Kartik *puja*, commemorate it in homes and temples all over the city. Yet Kartik *puja* does not celebrate it at all, stressing instead the marriage of Krishna and Tulsi. Since women control and shape Kartik *puja* traditions, these traditions tend to reflect women's values and concerns. For Hindu women, marriage is a highly significant event. In the *puja* Krishna's marriage thoroughly eclipses the Sanskritic, textually sanctioned observance of Vishnu's awakening.

Inside the worship circle women tend to refer to themselves and each other as *sakhi*, "female friend." In Krishnaite contexts the term *sakhi* is sometimes used interchangeably with the term *gopi*. But apart from its association with Krishna traditions, *sakhi* is also commonly used by women to describe girlfriends, especially their closest girlfriends, and in Kartik *puja* women interpret their role as *sakhi*s in social, as well as devotional, terms. Indeed, when in the course of interviews I asked participants about the meaning of the term *sakhi* as it is used in the *puja*, many of them defined it primarily in terms of human friendship, invoking the term's connection to Krishna mythology only at my prompting. Participating women tended to stress to me the bonds that they share with one another. This is an inherently collective ritual; as one participant noted, "This *puja* cannot be done without *sakhis*." And to worship with other women brings participants pleasure. On several occasions, women highlighted to me the enjoyment they derived from collective female participation in the *puja*.

One of the most basic aspects that women articulated to me about being a *sakhi* in the worship circle involves the sentiment of love, or *prem*, that such a role requires. The *gopis* typically are held to be exemplars of devotional love for Krishna. But in keeping with their understanding of *sakhi* in primarily human terms, when participants spoke about the feelings of love associated with being a *sakhi* in this context they emphasized the term's association not with love for Krishna (although that is certainly important in the *puja*), but with love *for one's co-worshipers*. When I asked one participant why women refer to each other in the *puja* circle by the term *sakhi*, for example, she told me, "*Sakhi* means that there is a lot of love (*prem*) among the *sakhi*s. All of us are going to the Ganges, both younger and older women. Sitting together, talking together, and doing *puja* together, we all become *sakhi*." When participants refer to one another as *sakhi* and speak of love among *sakhis*, they evoke feelings that they associate with human friendship.

Scholars have noted that in an Indian context, love—whether it is between friends, family members, or spouses—tends to connote primarily feelings of interdependence, social attachment, and mutual obligation.[4] However, two particular qualities characteristic of love among *sakhis* in the context of this *puja* came to the fore among the participants with whom I spoke: mutual assistance in conducting the *puja*, and equality. Mutual assistance is promoted most conspicuously by the sharing of *puja* items among participants. Many women bring extra supplies with them to the worship circle, and they pass these supplies, including flowers, rice, *arati* wicks, and so forth, continuously around the worship circle. One participant commented on this practice by noting, "*Sakhis* help each other, and . . . when one of us runs out of something, the others help. In Kartik, if you help someone with the *puja* things, this is considered very auspicious." The emphasis on mutual assistance also has implications about the stance of the "ritual body" in the course of this tradition of worship in a way that reinforces a stress on interpersonal relationships. Catherine Bell notes that ritual actions impress upon bodies values that are fundamental to the ritual situation (Bell 1992, 100). In Kartik *puja*, passing around of worship items throughout the course of the *puja* obligates one to constantly engage other participants both verbally and physically. Indeed, there is a tremendous amount of touching, chatting, laughing, and helping that occurs continually throughout the *puja,* directing one's attention away from the ostensible focus of worship, the icons of Krishna and the other deities who occupy the space at the center of the circle, and toward other worshipers. The constant engagement with other participants reinforces the collective nature of this form of worship and its stress on friendly interaction among fellow participants.

Regarding equality, in the *puja* circle participants are supposed to abandon all ordinary terms of address in favor of the universal use of the term *sakhi*. Ordinarily, women address one another in various ways that signal relational hierarchy. Young women, for example, generally would not address older women by their names, using instead a respectful term of address, often a kinship term such as "older sister" (*didi*) or "paternal grandmother" (*dadi).* In the *puja* circle, participants are supposed to abandon all such terms of address. As one participant noted, "If you call me 'Auntie' or 'Mother' or 'Mother-in-Law,' a mother-daughter relationship entails difference. But *sakhi*s are equal. So if you are my *sakhi,* you will sit next to me and you will be equal to me." This ideal of equality is reflected in the physical construction of the worship space as a circle, which grants all participants equal access to the icons used in worship regardless of their social context. It is also facilitated by a pattern of informal leadership that affords all worshipers the opportunity to participate in construction of the icons and narration of religious stories.

In fact, women did not actually abandon all hierarchy in the worship circle. For example, I did not observe any participation on the part of low-caste or Untouchable women, suggesting that they might not be welcome in the *puja* circle. Among the women who did participate, however, caste and class, two of the most important markers of social hierarchy in daily life, did not figure prominently as important markers of hierarchy within the worship circle; instead, women tended to grant special honor to age, piety, and religious expertise. In particular, older women whom other participants recognized as religiously knowledgeable and highly devout were accorded great respect, and on many occasions I saw other women touch their feet in the widespread Hindu gesture of reverence to a superior. While elements of hierarchy persist, however, the aspiration toward equality that several participants clearly identified as an important dimension of being a *sakhi* in this *puja* remains a central ideal of the tradition.

Chatting informally, helping one another, and fussing over clothes, hair, and *puja* items might appear on first blush to reflect a lack of seriousness in ritual participation. But one might better construe such activities instead in a positive manner as indicating a specific ritual ethic, one that prizes kindness, friendship, and mutual support among devotees as an important component of the ritual tradition itself. Humor functions in a similar way, helping foster feelings of equality and level hierarchies that predominate outside the worship circle. Participating women see joking and teasing to be an important component of the tradition, which is not only a form of devotional worship but is simultaneously considered a form of entertainment (*manoranjan*) or merriment (*maza*). During the three years in which I participated in the *puja,* one story in particular became a vehicle for friendly teasing of other members of the worship circle. In this story, a greedy old lady refuses to share her sweets with God, so to punish her God turns her into a pig.[5] She makes her way back to her own neighborhood, where she starts ferreting around in garbage. On at least two occasions, the storyteller singled out one or more of the women in the circle as the woman-turned-pig, much to the glee and laughter of the other women in the circle. In using the story as a vehicle to tease fellow worshipers, the storyteller amuses everyone and fosters feelings of intimacy and warmth among *puja* participants, feelings associated with friendship.

The fun is sometimes physical as well. At the time of Tulsi's marriage to Krishna, for example, participants offer the deities yogurt sweetened with brown sugar, a mixture traditionally eaten by the bride and groom at the time of their wedding. In both 1997 and 1998, a food fight broke out at the *puja* circle I attended, and participants started chasing each other and smearing the yogurt mixture on one another's faces and limbs, laughing boisterously and clearly enjoying themselves a great deal.

As a foreigner, I functioned as a particularly tempting target for this messy enjoyment, and women from the worship circle in which I had participated delighted in smearing me with sticky yogurt. I experienced these attacks as congenial and good-natured, and for a few moments I enjoyed the feeling, however temporary and incomplete, of having transcended the worlds of difference that tended to separate me from the women I had come to observe. Linguistic, educational, cultural, and economic distinctions mean little in the midst of a gooey food fight.

Since Kartik *puja* focuses on marriage, sexual joking is also prevalent. The occasions of Krishna's *janeu* and wedding in particular invite bawdy humor and teasing. The *janeu* ceremony is known as a "half-marriage," since it marks a boy's transition from childhood to

Figure 6.2. Women having fun smearing each other with yogurt. *(photo by author)*

adulthood; in contemporary India, if a high-caste boy who is getting married has not undergone a *janeu,* then he will often undergo one just before the wedding ceremony. Hence it is associated with marriage and the sexuality that marriage implies. In the ritual *janeu* that I attended in the fall of 1998, while women were passing the brass icon of Krishna around the circle to participate in rubbing it with mustard oil and turmeric—considered cleansing and purifying substances—one participant yelled that we shouldn't rub him too hard or his crotch would be too sore for him to have sex with Tulsi on his wedding night. Another retorted, "No, you're the one who's sore (from having sex)!," and everyone laughed. After the *janeu* ritual itself an older women jumped up and started dancing in a sexually provocative manner, singing a bawdy song that ended with the line, "So slip it to me!," while she gyrated her pelvis. While some participants feigned shock and embarrassment, it was clear that they considered the bawdy behavior funny and did not take any serious offense.

Pauline Kolenda (1990) notes that joking around in Hindu marriages can function to foster equality between unequal parties. Kolenda is referring here specifically to the kin of the bride and groom in the context of a human marriage. But the kind of sexual joking that takes place surrounding Krishna's marriage, too, bypasses everyday social hierarchies, rendering irrelevant issues of caste, class, kinship relation, or age. All of the women gathered around the worship circle are householders, former householders, or daughters of householders, who will themselves (presumably) someday marry. Their bodies are not only devotional but also sexual, and bawdy joking emphasizes their equality in this regard. As "friends," all participants are rendered equals in devotional practice; as sexual females, all participants are rendered equals in embodiment.

Sexual joking also functions to narrow gaps not only between human and human but between human and divinity as well. Krishna can suffer from sore genitals, just as a human groom can, so don't rub him too hard! On the day of Krishna's marriage in 1997, when participants started singing *galli* ("abuse"), the funny and often sexually explicit songs that Hindu women sing at marriages, one participant turned to me and said, "Today God is the groom, so today we abuse (*galli dena*) God." Sexual joking functions to equalize human and deity alike.

Several scholars have noted the role of humor in confronting us with the irrepressible and often disruptive drives that characterize our own embodied nature (e.g., Scott 1966). In his study of Indian humor, Lee Siegel notes that comedy in general celebrates "the victory of the body, with its basic urges and primary impulses, over spirit, will, idea, or feeling" (1987, 17). Sexual humor, like scatological humor, is particularly potent in this regard. Siegel also observes that the merging of sexual and religious domains occurs in both mystical and comic environments, but with different purposes and outcomes (190). Mystical poetry, notes Siegel, sometimes uses erotic language to express religious experience. In a similar vein, the Sanskritic literature associated with Krishna's devotional traditions has tended to understand Krishna's erotic antics as exemplifying religious experience, experience that is sometimes portrayed as available only to a certain religious elite. Comic poetry, on the other hand, may attribute sexual content to purportedly religious or mystical scenes and guises. In Kartik *puja,* joking about Krishna's sore genitals and singing bawdy verses to him render him in human, bodily, sexual terms, and this is funny. God is no longer only a transcendent being: God has a vulnerable and potentially disordered body, just like us.

Participants humanize Krishna in other ways too. During the period between Krishna's *janeu* and his wedding to Tulsi, for example, some participants pretend to be family members of the groom or bride, haggling over dowry and feigning disgust or anger at the way negotiations are going. Krishna and Tulsi are playfully turned into one's own son or daughter, and haggling over dowry becomes a joke, not the very serious and stressful negotiation that it actually is in real life, especially for the parents of the bride. Humorous stories that women narrated at the worship circle also function to humanize Krishna. I will recount here one story, for example, that has to do with the last five days of Kartik—the day of Krishna's marriage to Tulsi and the four days that follow, up to the time of the full moon—which are dedicated to the character Bhishma of the great Hindu epic, the *Mahabharata*. This period is known as the Bhishmapancak, and in Benares enormous images of Bhishma are constructed along the *ghats* out of Ganges clay. Votaries circle the body during these five days, making offerings and worshipping a different part of the body each day (see Pintchman 2005, 33–41). Some Kartik votaries insist that the images represent not Bhishma but Bhima, also called Bhimsen, who is the most physically powerful of the *Mahabharata's* five heroes, the Pandava brothers. Popular belief in Benares maintains that Bhishma/ Bhima seizes the religious merit of any Kartik votary who refrains from performing the ritual bath during these last five days of the month. On two occasions in 1995, Kartik *puja* participants recounted the following story to explain why this is so. I reproduce it here in slightly condensed form. The story revolves around rivalry between Radha, Krishna's consort, and Rukmini, one of his many wives[6]:

> Radha said to Krishna, "Oh Lord! Arrange for me to bathe in the Ganges for the month of Kartik, and stay with me for that whole month." Krishna said, "Ask Rukmini. I can only stay with you for the month of Kartik if Rukmini gives her permission." So Radha went to Rukmini and said, "Oh, Sister, Give me Krishna for one month." Rukmini said, "I will not be apart from Krishna for even one day! How is it that I should give him to you for one month?" So Krishna said, "Please stop fighting! Whoever feeds me early tomorrow morning, whether it is Radha or Rukmini, I will become hers."

Krishna created an illusion (*maya)* so that Rukmini remained asleep while Radha got up early in the morning, cooked and fed all the cowherd boys (*gval-bals*)[7] and God along with cows and cattle. Rukmini woke up and said, "It is too bad that I remained sleeping and Radha did all the work! Now I have to give God to her." So Lord Krishna went off to spend the month of Kartik with Radha.

Krishna would go from ghat to ghat with Radha to do his Kartik bathing and would joke around with the cowherdesses (*sakhis*). Half the month passed in this way. One day while Rukmini was watching her sheep, the birds pecked at them, so she took a stick and chased them away. The birds said, "She is so proud of her sheep that she is chasing us away with a stick, but in Radha's house we peck pearls and jewels." This made Rukmini angry. She said, "If even birds have pearls and jewels to peck at Radha's place, why would Lord Krishna ever return from there?"

When five days were left—the five days of Bhishma-pancak—Rukmini called Bhima and told him to go and spy on Krishna. So he went, and from a distance he saw that Krishna was having fun, laughing, cracking jokes, swinging with some of the women (*sakhis)* in a swing, and really enjoying himself. But when Krishna saw Bhima coming from a distance, he immediately took the form of a leper. When Bhimsen saw him, he asked, "Oh Great King (Maharaj), what happened to you?" Krishna said, "What can I do? If Rukmini had not slept in that day, then I would not have had to go with Radha. You can see what has happened to my body with Radha. I have to do her laundry, clean her saris, massage her, and do all kinds of service to her. You can see that because of this, my health has deteriorated to half of what it used to be." Bhimsen said, "You must be in great pain, Lord!" And Krishna said, "I am just waiting for the month to pass somehow, and then I will go back."

When Bhimsen returned, Rukmini asked, "How is everything there?" Bhimsen said, "What can I say? God has lost weight, he is very skinny, and he is in great pain." The next day, Rukmini asked Bhima again to go and see how Krishna was doing. So when he went there on that day, he saw that God was having great fun doing the circle dance (*rasa-lila*) with the cowherdesses, laughing, and having a great time. Bhimsen suddenly appeared in the middle of

> this activity and said, "Oh Krishna! The other day you were so skinny and in bad shape! How did you become like this today?" So Krishna said, "Please do not tell Rukmini! Don't tell her, 'God is having fun there.' In return, for the five days from Ekadashi (the Eleventh) to the full moon, the merit of all the people who bathe during the month but not during those five days will go to you.

In this amusing story, Krishna is portrayed in terms that are all too human: he wants to play around behind Rukmini's back, but he seems afraid of her, so he uses deception to get what he wants. He isn't clever enough to see Bhima coming the second time around, so he resorts to bribery to keep Rukmini from learning his secret.

Conrad Hyers observes that "Humor has an ethical dimension to it. . . . It delights in humbling the mighty, counterbalancing inequities and reducing conflicts" (Hyers 1981, 34). I would argue that levity, playfulness, and humor function in this way in Kartik *puja*. When participants have fun during the *puja,* talk to and help one another, joke and play around, and tell stories they find amusing, they are leveling hierarchies, both among humans and between human and divine realms.

To what extent might we generalize from this one example to other contexts involving Hindu women's ritual practices? On one level, the Krishnaite nature of this tradition makes playfulness especially appropriate, especially with respect to the human-divine relationship. Krishna is, after all, the god of play (*lila*), and worship of Krishna in other contexts also tends to embrace playfulness and humor. Siegel notes, for example, that Jiva Goswami, a theologian of the Krishnaite Gaudiya Vaishnava movement, collected jokes in Krishna traditions, observing that jokes did not seem to be considered blasphemous in that context (Siegel 1987, 366–67). Those who participate in play, furthermore, always understand it to be provisional; it is a stepping out of "real" life into a temporary sphere of "pretend," a sphere that represents freedom from the structures of ordinary existence (Huizinga 1950, 7–8). But ordinary existence prevails outside of the sphere of play.

With respect to the role of levity and humor in promoting interpersonal bonding and friendship among participating women, however, I would suggest that larger patterns concerning women's values and women's ritualizing practices may come into play. Many scholars of Hinduism have stressed the nature of Indian culture as a "group-oriented" culture in comparison to Western cultures. While Western cultures strive to cultivate selves that are autonomous and independent, so the argument goes, Indian culture tends to cultivate interdependence and what Alan Roland calls "we-ness," a sense of self entailing ego boundaries that "remain much more permeable to constant affective exchanges and emotional connectedness with others" and a "heightened empathic awareness of others" (Roland 1988, 233). Seymour stresses that in Hindu culture, given the orientation toward group membership, there is a persistent, continual tension between the individual's own selfish desires and the interests of the joint family. That is why, she concludes, renunciation of personal desire is culturally lauded (Seymour 1999, 270). Seymour rightly cautions that one should not overemphasize the difference between independent Western selves and collectivist Indian selves. She notes that interdependence-independence might best be understood as a "continuum along which cultures fall according to the particular mixture of collectivist and individualist elements that they exhibit at any one time" (269).

What seems to be largely missing from these discussions, however, is thoughtful engagement with the ways in which girls and boys are socialized differentially toward autonomy and interdependence, both in Western contexts and in India. Carol Gilligan's groundbreaking work on women and morality, for example, argues that for American women, identity tends to be defined less in terms of an autonomous, independent self and more in terms of relationship, where the self is judged by standards of responsibility toward others (Gilligan 1982, 160). American women's selves, according to this analysis, seem to approach the model of the "we-self" that Roland locates in India. Conversely, I have often wondered about the relationship between the alleged empathetic Indian sense of "we-ness" and the emphasis on renunciation of personal desire, as I have watched Benarsi men sit by idly as their wives and daughters scurry around fulfilling their needs and wants, offering tea to family members and guests, caring for children, massaging the bodies of elderly family members, and so forth. While Indian men may indeed value interpersonal bonds, clearly they tend *not* to express this value in the same ways that Indian women do. For Indian women, interdependence and "we-ness," especially in terms of family, manifest themselves in the repetitive, everyday acts of physical care for others that are performed much more frequently by women than by men. In her study of female-dominated religions, Susan Sered notes that in contexts where women's lives are more apt than men's to revolve around caring for others, women's rituals and beliefs tend to reflect the interpersonal orientation of women's familial lives such that "strengthening interpersonal bonds is an important ritual focus of women's religions" (Sered 1994, 121, 138).

The incorporation into formal ritual practice of a stress on friendly interaction and mutual support and playfulness and humor both reflects and promotes an emphasis on the interpersonal realm in Hindu women's lives. This is certainly true in Kartik *puja,* where participants embrace fun to engage ideals pertaining to not only devotion but also feelings of emotional relatedness between and among fellow devotees. The term *sakhi,* as it is deployed in this context, embodies these emphases. Having fun, teasing, joking, chatting, and engaging in small acts of caretaking within the *puja* circle all function as a female idiom for fostering intimacy and parity, both between humanity and divinity and between *sakhi* and *sakhi,* and communicating the relational love, *prem,* among human participants that being a *sakhi* in this tradition requires.

## Notes

1. This chapter is based on my fuller study of Kartik *puja,* presented in Pintchman 2005.
2. John S. Hawley notes in his research on *rasa-lila* performances in Braj that there, too, the term *rasa-lila* is also used to indicate both the *rasa-lila* episode itself and the entire *lila* of Krishna's life enacted in liturgical drama. See Hawley 1981, 1983, chapters 6 and 7.
3. For a more detailed description of Kartik *puja,* see Pintchman 2003, 2005.
4. For example, Seymour 1999, 85; Derne 1995, 73–74.
5. I recount this story in full in chapter 3 of Pintchman 2005.
6. I recount this story also in Pintchman 2005, 39–40.
7. The cowherd boys or *gval-bals* were Krishna's childhood companions and playmates when he was growing up in Braj.

## Works Cited

Bell, Catherine. 1992. *Ritual Theory, Ritual Practice.* New York: Oxford University Press.

Derne, Steve. 1995. *Culture in Action: Family Life, Emotion, and Male Dominance in Banaras, India.* Albany: State University of New York Press.

Gilligan, Carol. 1982. *In A Different Voice.* Cambridge, MA: Harvard University Press.

Hawley, John S. 1981. *At Play With Krishna: Pilgrimage Dramas From Brindavan.* Princeton, NJ: Princeton University Press.

Hawley, John S. 1983. *Krishna, the Butter Thief.* Princeton, NJ: Princeton University Press.

Huizinga, Johan. 1950. *Homo Ludens: A Study of the Play Element in Culture*. London: Routledge and Kegan Paul.

Hyers, Conrad. 1981. *The Comic Vision and the Christian Faith: A Celebration of Life and Laughter*. New York: The Pilgrim Press.

Kolenda, Pauline. 1990. "Untouchable Chuhras through Their Humor: 'Equalizing' Marital Kin through Teasing, Pretence, and Farce." In *Divine Passions: The Social Construction of Emotion*, ed. Owen M. Lynch, 116–53. Berkeley: University of California Press.

Pintchman, Tracy. 2003. "The Month of Kartik and Women's Ritual Devotions to Krishna." In *The Blackwell Companion to Hinduism*, ed. Gavin Flood, 327–42. Oxford: Blackwell.

Pintchman, Tracy. 2005. *Guests at God's Wedding: Celebrating Kartik among the Women of Benares*. Albany: State University of New York Press.

Roland, Alan. 1988. *In Search of Self in India and Japan: Toward a Cross-Cultural Psychology*. Princeton, NJ: Princeton University Press.

Scott, Nathan A. 1966. *The Broken Center: Studies in the Theological Horizon of Modern Literature*. New Haven, CT: Yale University Press.

Sered, Susan Starr. 1994. *Priestess, Mother, Sacred Sister: Religions Dominated by Women*. New York: Oxford University Press.

Seymour, Susan C. 1999. *Women, Family, and Child Care in India: A World in Transition*. Cambridge: Cambridge University Press.

Siegel, Lee. 1987. *Laughing Matters: Comic Tradition in India*. Chicago, IL: University of Chicago Press.

# 7

# Laughing until It Hurts . . . Somebody Else

## *The Pain of a Ritual Joke*

William P. Harman

Levity, in story and ritual, has long been associated with the annual ten-day festival celebration of the Marriage of Shiva (locally known as Chuntarechuvarar) and Parvati (locally known as Meenakshi) in the grand temple of Madurai in southern India. In this chapter I shall focus on one particular event, a portion of a "Journey Festival" understood by most of the population of the Madurai region to be a part of this Hindu marriage festival. This ritual event constitutes a portion of the Journey Festival, and accounts of it evoke varying reactions: amusement and laughter, generally among Hindus, but a sense of offense, annoyance, and embarrassment in the local minority Muslim community. In focusing on this ritual and its interpretation, I want to explore the "bite" of ritual humor, and how it can be used as a put-down for those who are the butt of its humor. Of crucial importance is the fact that this chapter deals with two disparate perspectival interpretations of the same ritual event. The context is layered historically, socially, and ritually, but the event itself is simple, straightforward, and not particularly distinctive unless we begin to investigate its interpretive "overlays" and how those overlays are understood and appropriated by various religious communities.

The event primarily involves a particular deity in the Hindu tradition, Vishnu (known locally as Alakar), and the events that transpire during a ritual procession in which Vishnu's image is carried on a palanquin in the company of a rather large group of his devotees. The procession travels from Vishnu's temple twelve miles north of Madurai down to the Vaigai River, which once formed the northern border of the city.

This event occurs as part of an annual festival, the Journey Festival. Each year, during a rather grueling nonstop procession in the scorching heat of May, temple bearers carry the palanquin of the large metal image of the deity Vishnu into the city of Madurai from the temple in Alagarkoil, a famous pilgrimage center. The reason for the trip has a textual base in the sacred history of Alagarkoil. It focuses on Vishnu's willingness to travel to the city and to visit a certain location there, a visit intended to remove an unfortunate curse incurred by one of Vishnu's devotees.[1] During the two-and-a-half-day journey festival, Vishnu and his retinue repeatedly halt the progress of the procession as it passes before each of many elaborately constructed, but temporary, roadside shrines. At each shrine, a prearranged ritual—some more and some less elaborate—has been planned to honor Vishnu and to acknowledge this auspicious passing of Vishnu through each particular region on the way to Madurai. Sponsors of the pavilions offer special gifts to the priests accompanying Vishnu,

Figure 7.1. The image of the deity Vishnu is carried on a palanquin by worshippers during the Journey Festival. A Brahman priest attends to the deity as they walk along the twelve-mile road from Vishnu's temple into Madurai. *(photo by author)*

Figure 7.2. During the Journey Festival, the image of Vishnu (atop the silver horse) arrives at one of the larger pavilions erected to receive him on the road to Madurai. *(photo by author)*

and the amount of time the deity's party spends at each pavilion, or *mandapam*, is often directly determined by the value of the gifts the local sponsors have offered. Sponsors include wealthy individuals, local village groups, police associations, caste unions, and various temples. Typically, Vishnu's entire retinue will pause a few minutes to receive gifts and worship and then will be off down the road to another of the hundreds of pavilions.

Offering Vishnu this sort of hospitality is both a responsibility and a privilege. By the end of the second night, exhaustion begins to overtake the festive exuberance of this walking pilgrimage-procession. Vishnu's image and his attendants stop for an extended rest and to receive respectful visits from a long string of worshippers at one of the larger Vaishnava shrines in a suburb of the city of Madurai, a community called Vantiyur. The suburb has a relatively large concentration of Muslims, as does Goripalayam, an adjacent section of town with one of the city's largest mosques.

Throughout the procession, the number of lay devotees will "snowball," growing larger and larger as increasing numbers of people join the procession passing through their regions. On the final day, Vishnu emerges from his six-hour rest in the Vantiyur temple on the outskirts of Madurai and continues his journey down to the Vaigai riverbed as tens of thousands gather to witness his auspicious arrival.

With his retinue, he then begins a journey eastward along the riverbed to stop in a pavilion later that night in a Muslim neighborhood.

Distinctive about this stop is the extraordinary account people give regarding what happens during Vishnu's stay for the night in the pavilion adjacent to the predominantly Muslim neighborhood. It is common knowledge among both Muslims and Hindus that a long-established and deeply embedded oral tradition narrates how Vishnu spends that night in divine sexual abandon with a Muslim protégé-courtesan named Tulukka Nacciyar. Nearly all Hindus and Muslims with whom I spoke in Vantiyur are aware of this interpretation of why Vishnu travels to this particular spot on this particular night. It is an interpretation that appears in popular accounts of the festival, in newspaper descriptions that come out annually, and even in printed Christian commentary on the festival that seeks to expose the "moral depravity" of both Muslims and Hindus. While the deity's palanquin is sequestered inside the pavilion, priestly caretakers are far more conscientious than at any other time during the festival about admitting no onlookers or visitors who, presumably, would be present less to seek a sacred audience or *darshan* than to intrude improperly on this

Figure 7.3. Large crowds assemble in the Vaigai Riverbed as Vishnu's procession arrives there. *(photo by author)*

primal scene as voyeurs. Security is strict, I found out, even when the professedly dispassionate academic observer wishes to engage in an objective scholarly investigation of the "bare facts" of the ritual. My concerted attempts to enter the pavilion during the night on two separate occasions in two separate years did not succeed. I can, therefore, attest to no special knowledge about what "really" goes on while Vishnu's image is inside that structure. And so the testament of relatively unanimous sources of reported, oral tradition constitutes my evidence for this allegedly sensuous, if not amorous, encounter.

What I hope to do here is place the interpretation of this ritual—one that evokes laughter from Hindus, anger from Muslims, and bemusement from the rest of us not implicated in this drama—into a context that makes it possible to understand the source of the humor, the discomfort, and the bemusement.

An appreciation of what is going on here requires us to step back a bit to gain perspective. First, it would help to make a few comments about the social structure among the people involved in this festival. The city of Madurai is primarily a Shaiva town, and the prestige of the temple there is associated with the ritual purity and high status accorded to the many priests who serve on the temple staff. Urban Shaivas tend to see themselves as the proud transmitters of a long and noble Shaiva religious tradition. There are Vaishnava temples within the town, but they are fewer and smaller, even though they are also associated with a rigorously pure Brahmanic ritual tradition. What is extraordinary about the followers of Vishnu who follow Vishnu into Madurai on the Journey Festival is that they tend to be, for the most part, uncouth, rural, low-caste folk associated in many cases with the Kallar community, a traditionally meat-eating group of professional cattle rustlers and thieves. They sacrifice animals in preparation for this festival, and they spend many hours of the festival under the influence of intoxicants. The beef-butchering and beef-eating Muslims cast an even darker shadow on the social status landscape. Muslims in Madurai are not simply poorer than many Hindus; they are ritually an abomination to conscientious Hindus. Given these dynamics, we can understand why, in part, both the rural Vaishnavas and the Muslims might become targets for a traditionally deprecatory humor.

We can also place this ritual event into a larger cultural and literary context as well. The context of this particular ritual is that region known as the Madurai District in Tamilnadu, India. Dennis Hudson and I have written elsewhere about the festival of which this ritual is a part, the festival generally called "The Chittirai Festival," after the month in which it is celebrated, or "The Marriage Festival," after the event that provides the narrative backdrop for this ritual and many others.[2] That event is, essentially, a ten-day festival. In its origins, it is a festival that consists of two separate ritual events, but in the seventeenth century the events were rescheduled so as to coincide. Once the two festivals began to be celebrated at nearly the same time and in nearly the same place, they came to be associated intimately with each other. A popular perception of a single ritual event has emerged, and that perception has generated an independent, noncanonical, but widely popular, version of the mythology explaining the dynamics of this festival. Strangely enough, that popular perception has essentially displaced the more esoteric, text-based traditions, whereby the two festivals supposedly have nothing to do with each other.

The result is that we have a fairly stable history of popular interpretation regarding the festival, one that is at least 250 years old, inventive, imaginative, and perhaps, most important of all, synthetic. It seeks to explain the occurrence of two separate ritual events. One is Shaiva and celebrates the marriage of the deity Shiva and Parvati inside the city. The second celebrates the coming to the city of Vishnu for a special curse-removal ritual. But as the two festivals coincide calendrically, the popular interpretation insists that Vishnu is coming to town to attend the wedding because Parvati is his sister, and as the new groom's future brother-in-law, Vishnu must give Parvati away to Shiva in the marriage. It is generally the brother of the bride who gives a woman away in the Tamil marriage ceremony.[3] Normally the ritual should not occur without him; indeed, ritual propriety would provide that there be no wedding until his arrival. But the ritual enactment in Madurai adds an interesting twist to the account that normally would see Shiva and Vishnu participating together in the ritual event. When the image of Vishnu carried on his palanquin nearly reaches the Vaigai riverbed, another form of Vishnu whose temple is inside the city is brought on a palanquin to a prearranged meeting area and there the two separate forms of Vishnu meet. The Vishnu from inside Madurai (named Kudalalakar) reportedly informs the Vishnu who has traveled to Madurai to participate in the wedding that the marriage has already occurred. In other words, Shiva and Parvati have been married without the ritually mandatory presence of her brother Vishnu. Furious at this ritual slight, Vishnu halts his journey and refuses to go into the city, angry that the ceremony was not postponed until his arrival. He storms down the dry riverbed of the Vaigai River and there stops for the night in a privately guarded pavilion owned, it is said, by the Islamic community. Everyone seems to know the score, however: the breach in ritual marriage conduct becomes both prelude and pretext for Vishnu's transgressing a boundary of his own choosing. He spends the night there with a Muslim mistress, Tulukka Nacciyar. His sense of indignant rejection ends in a tryst about which Hindu devotees will giggle if they are asked. Muslims, on the other hand, are generally annoyed by this interpretation of the event.

This popular story that integrates Vishnu into the marriage scenario emphasizes the need and hope for cooperation and good relations between the followers of Shiva and Vishnu. We know, however, that historically there have been tensions between the two traditions, and that followers of Vishnu routinely terrorized and held for ransom Shaivas who attempted to travel on the main trunk road north of Madurai. The popular myth works toward diffusing this enmity as it incorporates, integrates, and seeks to promulgate a sense of community by making the minority, country-bumpkin, generally lower-caste worshippers of Vishnu welcome in the Shaiva city of Madurai, but they are welcome only on Shaiva terms.[4] Still, the integration of the two communities never occurs. The breach of ritual marriage propriety bungles everything. Shortly I will want to suggest that the noncanonical but pervasive subplot about Vishnu and his Muslim mistress functions in much the same way in relation to the Muslim and Hindu communities. Just as the wedding ceremony incorporates followers of Vishnu into the story line of the marriage, so the account of a Muslim mistress incorporates Muslims into the story line of Vishnu's visit to Madurai. But it does so strictly on Hindu terms. To this theme I shall return, but I wish now to consider how both of these stories are consonant with the playfully pious mood that surrounds Hindu religiosity in Madurai.

There is, I suggest, a pervasive mythic context and theme associated with the founding and the history of the great temple of Madurai. It is best reflected in a document traceable to at least the eleventh century entitled the *Tiruvilaiyatarpuranam*.[5] It is usually translated as *The Story of Shiva's Sacred Games*, but "Sacred Games" does not quite capture the whole sense of the mood that this document projects. These are not games with rules. Far from it. Rather, we are talking here about sacred "Shenanigans," "Gags," "Jokes," or even "Tricks" if we understand the document as a recounting of divine escapades that are sometimes funny, sometimes ironic, but nearly always surprising, because they reverse normal expectations. There is a slapstick quality to the way Shiva deals with those devoted to him and with those who need to pay more attention to devotion. Indeed, the stories portray Shiva as a transgressive deity whose actions verge on the outrageously ludic. In 1988, a popular, full-length Tamil film appeared, based on several of the more amusing events in the document. Called, of course, *Tiruvilaiyatarpuranam,* it was a riotous and yet righteous comedy hit.

In the document's famous sixty-four chapters, we find a series of events narrating how the Madurai temple was founded, how Shiva came to Madurai in the first place, and the many miracles he performed there as the city's patron deity. In these stories, the gracious Lord makes pious tomfoolery of religious, royal, and social pretension, and almost always does the shockingly unexpected in order to teach his followers a lesson or two or sixty-four. It sets a mood for the many rituals that are enacted annually with the marriage celebration. *The Story of the Sacred Games* is therefore quite naturally associated with this festival, because so many of its sixty-four chapters are enacted during the festival, including most especially the marriage, which Vishnu actually attends, according to the text.[6]

But Shiva clearly takes center stage in the document. In one instance he becomes a dirty, low-caste, lazy coolie day laborer who plays insolent practical jokes on an arrogant, self-important Pandyan king obsessed with his own power and prestige. In another, he appears as a street merchant, a lecherous seller of bangles, who brazenly and improperly tests the chastity of proud wives of great sages. As a wood merchant he shames the sensibilities of higher-caste merchants in Madurai, and once, when the king out on a hunt heartlessly kills the mother of a brood of piglets, Shiva takes the form of a mother pig and breastfeeds these babies, who eventually grow to become the brilliantly half-divine, pig-headed (literally) ministers of the king. Throughout the document there are clear repetitions of the pattern whereby stiff and insensitive human conventions and foibles are exposed for what they are, and divine contravention of expected norms confounds conventional wisdom about the way things should be. And always, Shiva comes off as the majestic jokester, smirking behind the scenes, sometimes strictly for his own amusement and sometimes for the enlightenment of the human community. He cuts through malicious pride or random tragedy by restoring justice in dumbfounding ways, but he also thwarts justice to demonstrate that religious devotion trumps reason and right. He demonstrates that there is hardly anything he cannot do: when his mother-in-law desperately desires a ritual bath in the sea but is not well enough to make the trip, Shiva horrifies, and then amazes, the assembly by bringing the sea to her. And if there is nothing he cannot do, neither is there anything he will not do. His wedding is full of jokes—he enters the city in such a handsome form that the women riot just to be near him as they fall under the spell of lascivious behaviors and public indiscretions. The thousands of tons of food left over from the wedding Shiva commissions his ravenous dwarf to consume in a few seconds. Effortlessly, astoundingly, and cavalierly he performs miracle after miracle, laughing all the way.

The document, then, reflects an apprehension of divine behavior that is sometimes licentious, sometimes mischievous, sometimes offensive, and always unpredictable. The divine does what the divine damn well pleases, as is suggested by the notion of "play," "games," and even "shenanigans." It seems likely to me that this narrative mood becomes translated into the ritual context, and remains an ever-present backdrop for the festival in which Vishnu is understood to participate. During the annual festival, a Mardi Gras quality emerges in many parts of the city, though not near the main temple. Devotees consume both liquor and cannabis freely; spirit possession (a giving oneself over to less identifiable spirits) can be found on any street corner; and respectable women wandering the streets are likely to have welts, pinches, and bruises all over their bodies to commemorate their encounters with random young male revelers whose concern for the normally puritanical values that govern intergender relations has abandoned them in the face of festivity and celebration. In short, during the festival there is latitude for excess, and people revel in the variety of excesses, not the least of which is the kind of eroticism exalted by the fifth chapter of the temple's official epic history. That chapter describes the celebratory sexual abandon in the city when the stunningly handsome Chuntarechuvarar arrives there for his wedding ceremony.

There are arguably contextual reasons why our story of Vishnu's "night out" resonates with the mood of this festival atmosphere. Specifically, pervasive and popular mythologies seek to interpret into a single account the otherwise disparate ritual events during the Madurai Chittirai festival. They seek to integrate those events into larger contexts that include simultaneous ritual activity and social relations among communities involved in the events. At the same time, a local, associated religious and literary tradition that highlights the ludic, the sometimes silly, the joking and the playful creates a backdrop that helps put into perspective Vishnu's cavorting with a Muslim mistress and explains why the event is silly for some, serious for others. Like Shiva in his Holy Tricks, Vishnu contravenes the norms, goes against accepted and expected moral standards, all for the implied purpose of making a moral point. That point invites his followers to see relations between Muslims and Hindus in new ways.

Let me reprise, and expand upon, some selected specifics of this ritual event as a bit of a review.

Vishnu travels to Madurai during the Chittirai Festival. As he arrives at the city's boundary, millions of worshippers await him. There he meets, they say, another deity, another form of Vishnu from the city's interior Vaishnava temple, a deity named Kudal Alagar. The retinue and the images of both deities dwell under a palanquin for much of the day. But the popular mythology tells us that Vishnu is then and there informed by Kudal Alagar that the wedding has already occurred. He is a day late. Indeed, the ritual events of the marriage are always so timed in the Shiva temple that Vishnu arrives on the outskirts of the city exactly a day late. Hearing the news, Vishnu (worshippers say) feels insulted that they would have celebrated the event without him. Indeed, the popular mythology goes further to suggest that the reason Vishnu is late is because he has been deliberately misinformed about the date of the wedding during his stop a day earlier at a Vaishnava Temple on the road to Madurai, the home of the deity Perumal. Popular piety preserves the oral tradition that Perumal has played a trick on Vishnu because Perumal hopes that Vishnu will stay longer as a guest. So he misinforms Vishnu of the date for the wedding. For this reason, Perumal is known locally as "Lying Perumal," or "Gossip-Mongering Perumal." In any case, the day's events find Vishnu late, angry, disoriented, and annoyed about the misinformation as he enters the city limits. News that they would have celebrated the wedding without him is just too much. He refuses to visit the newlywed pair, relinquishes the gift he has brought for his sister, asking that Kudal Alagar transmit the gift to his sister on his behalf, and then rashly takes off with his retinue along the banks of the Vaigai River toward the Muslim areas of Vantiyur. After making a few stops at minor shrines, he halts for the night to spend it with his Muslim companion.

In the popular myth, then, Vishnu would not have visited the Muslim mistress had he become a rightful guest at the wedding. But a breach in proper ritual conduct, and in family courtesy, becomes the cause of his own breach of normal, respectable ritual conduct. In a sense, Vishnu is empowered to stretch, if not violate, the norms because he has endured a respectable divine host's lie, a gross ritual impropriety, and a sister's insult. And as his image rests inside the pavilion where, supposedly, erotic activity is going on, devotees linger outside all night long. Many camp there, build fires, cook, and talk. Wandering bards stroll among the crowds singing unusually bawdy songs that evoke embarrassed laughter.

Figure 7.4. Devotees of Vishnu dress festively, sing bawdy songs, and playfully squirt water on festival-goers as they proceed with Vishnu's entourage to the Muslim section of the city. *(photo by author)*

At no other place during the twelve-day journey did I encounter such songs. Hindus with whom I spoke were clear about what the night represented. In some of the mildest language I heard, Vishnu was "tying one on." Earlier the victim of a trick, he now participates in turning one. The atmosphere suggests in some ways that at a Tamil wedding, when the newly married couple is privately secluded their first night together, the guests collect outside trading sexual jokes and generally making an auditory nuisance of themselves in an attempt to distract or amuse the newly married couple.

Muslims in the area were much harder to identify and isolate than were their Hindu counterparts. They were fewer in number, but also they were not interested in wearing their identifiable dress, the lungi. Late in the night I managed to track a few down. When I asked why they came to a Hindu festival, they said what I knew to be true. They really could not get away from it. Because the town's population swells to three times its normal size for the festival, and so much is going on, it is impossible to ignore all of the fairs, festivals, parades, concerts, and activity. Buses cease to run, most town services stop, and a general holiday atmosphere prevails. The festival, in other words, comes to them. When I asked them about the Muslim mistress Tulukka Nacciyar, the reactions were mixed. Several were offended, saying it is a malicious, silly story made up by Hindus to associate Muslims with prostitution. But others were less hurt: at least, they said, the story demonstrated how it is okay for Muslims to participate in a Hindu festival. They pointed out that several Muslims did come out to enjoy the crowds and celebration, and that the union of Vishnu and Tulukka Nacciyar showed how that was possible.

Whatever else the story represents, it is a clear statement of rank. The male in India normally associates with a female of lesser status. Of course, here the male is a deity. Clearly, the Muslim party to this relationship is inferior. But it is also true that in other contexts deities do in fact, mate with humans. And when this happens, it becomes a clear step up for the female in the pair. Indeed, this happens on two occasions in the *Tiruvilaiyatarpuranam.* In both cases, becoming a concubine/wife of god is a genuine promotion. So at the same time we have here a statement of Islamic rank in relation to Hindus and of the possibility that the distance between Hindu and Muslim can be bridged. Naturally, minority Muslims associating with majority Hindus are portrayed here as doing themselves a social-status favor by acquiescing to the narrative that Hindus promote.

The story of Vishnu and Tulukka Nacciyar is one of how otherwise disparate but proximate religious elements might, if only for a short period, be integrated into the ritual and social worlds of this festival celebration. The popular myth does exactly the same thing when it comes to the worshippers of Shiva and Vishnu who are united by the common thread of a goddess who is bride to one and sister to the other. It establishes hierarchy, for if Shiva is marrying Vishnu's sister, then Vishnu—in this predominantly Shaiva town—is inferior to Shiva. The rules of female hypogamy dictate that a woman "marry up" in status and a man "marry down." If Parvati is beneath Shiva, then so is her brother Vishnu.

In interpreting ritual, what this popular myth-making process does is establish order, relationships, and hieararchy, and often at the expense of those whose voice is muted. My experience in talking with Hindus about this festival is that if anyone ever brings up the historic origins of this festival before the 1700s, that is, if anyone insists that this is not really one festival but two unrelated ones, then it will be the orthodox Vishnu worshippers. They detest the implicit inferiority that the popular myth assigns them.

Helpful in understanding these dynamics is Huizinga's (1950) book *Homo Ludens: A Study of the Play Element in Culture*. He proposes that ritual and play have much in common. "In myth and ritual," he says, "the great instinctive forces of civilized life have their origin: law and order . . . poetry, wisdom, and science" (Huizinga 1950, 5). "Inside the play-ground an absolute and peculiar order reigns, creates order, *is* order. Into an imperfect world and into the confusion of life it brings a temporary, a limited perfection. Play, like ritual, demands order, absolute and supreme" (10, emphasis in original).

What we have seen here is how an unofficial public creatively and imaginatively has interpreted a ritual in such a way as to bring temporary mythic order to events that otherwise would be disparate, even chaotic. And this process is at work playfully, artfully, as indeed the mood of so much of the festival attests. The same is true with the relationship between Muslims and Hindus. They are separate communities, but for a brief time once a year an attempt is made to align contiguously—if not always harmoniously—their ritual realities. But in the case of the two Hindu communities, as in the case of the Muslim and Hindu communities, there remains the element of resistance and dissent. Again, Huizinga's insights are helpful. He writes cogently of the embedded aspect of tension in ritual and play: "Tension means uncertainty, chanciness; a striving to decide the issue and so end it. The player wants something to 'go,' to 'come off;' he wants to 'succeed' by his own exertions" (11). The ritual of Vishnu's visit to Vantiyur is one in which those involved in the ritual game—and we should be clear that games often are quite serious—seek to establish a social order and a relationship between two groups historically linked by resentment, misunderstanding, and enmity. There is an attempt to deal lightly and humanely with the tension by proposing an attenuated resolution symbolized by a less-than-licit sexual union. Vishnu himself is not adhering to accepted norms of behavior here, and so both the Muslim and Hindu players in this drama are complicit in their departure from the norms. What brings Vishnu and Tulukka Nacciyar, and implicitly Hindus and Muslims, together is the conspiracy of this act, an act that draws its energy from the impertinence of the Shaiva retinue who messed up royally in the celebration of the wedding ritual.

Despite the ritual's eloquent attempt to create community, many Muslims, indeed and most likely, the majority, find the whole event offensive, silly, and irrelevant. They refuse to play the game, to buy into the ritual and its interpretation. I saw no Muslims loudly protesting this event or insisting on its elimination. That would have been an extremely serious breach of ritual and social etiquette. Again, I resort to Huizinga, who observes that in ritual as well as in games,

> . . . as soon as the rules are transgressed the whole play-world collapses. The game is over. . . . The player who trespasses against the rules or ignores them is a "spoil-sport." . . . It is curious to note how much more lenient society is to the cheat than to the spoil-sport. By withdrawing from the game he reveals the relativity and fragility of the play world in which he had temporarily shut himself with others. He robs play of its illusion—a pregnant word which means literally "in play." Therefore he must be cast out, for he threatens the existence of the play community.[11]

Participating in the festival, actively or passively, rather than subversively seeking to disrupt it, becomes for the Muslims a form of acquiescence to the messages that the popular mythology bears. Many will acquiesce freely. Their attachment to the Muslim identity will be minimal, and they will share at least once a year a joke and an event that will bring Muslims and Hindus together. They will have a good time. There is an implicit invitation in these cases for those who are the butt of the joke to laugh along with everyone else. If they can do so, or if they can abide the laughter without taking public offense, without remonstrating or denying the continuity of the "play" in progress, then they are, at least, acquiescing. Indeed, they are facilitating a larger community spirit, but at their own expense. It is important for Madurai Muslims to know their place, and in this case their place is scripted by folkloric humor.

There is a postscript to this ritual bundle that might be worth mentioning. About twenty-four hours after this mildly scandalous event in the pavilion near the Muslim neighborhood, the image of Vishnu, once again mounted on the palanquin, starts the long march back to his temple twelve miles north of Madurai. When the procession finally arrives at the doors of the temple that is Vishnu's home, Vishnu's image is placed in a small pavilion outside, and for several hours it undergoes an elaborate series of purifying ritual and physical ablutions. I was told that the deity cannot reenter his own temple until he has been purified, and purified especially from the contact he has had in Vantiyur with the Muslim woman. Though sex in the Hindu tradition is understood to be polluting, the impression I received was that sex with a Muslim woman would require purifications that are particularly involved and intense. But other participants in Vishnu's cleansing homecoming, in the spirit of the bemusement that Vishnu's peccadillo elicits, claimed that it is Vishnu's wife, Lakshmi, who insists that he cool his holy heels for a while as an act of penance outside the domestic/temple space in punishment for his rather public indiscretion. She will suffer his entrance only when he removes all pollution from this degenerate act.

The mood, then, of this Madurai festival as it occurs north of the Vaigai River is bawdy, rude, derisive, and concerned with inclusiveness among participants. The spirit of the text that is its backdrop reflects that tone. In the text, it is always Shiva who stoops to riotously low levels. In his humorously self-deprecating grandeur, he becomes a lecher, a breastfeeding sow, and a shiftless bum, to name a few. He chooses to be the butt of the humor, because he knows he will also choose the time and place when others suffer a reversed fate of humiliation at his hands, and on his conditions. Shiva always has the last laugh when humans fail to be sufficiently humble, or simply fail to appreciate the subtlety of the workings of divine will. In the ritual as well, both humans *and* deities bear the brunt of humor that cuts as it comes and cuts as it goes. In all of this ritual "acting out," the "out groups," the rural bumpkin Vaishnava contingent and the hapless Muslims, are the subjects of intermittent ridicule. The pecking order reveals a clear hierarchy: Muslims endure Vaishnava abuse, Vaishnavas endure Shaiva abuse, and even Shiva, in narrative terms at least, endures the abuse of innocents who will eventually receive their due.

And so it seems appropriate that at the Journey's end Vishnu should be publicly shamed by his wife, ridiculed and held up as a subject for bemused derision. In a world of divine actors, where ludic ritual and narrative play hold sway, nothing is sacred because everything is.

## Notes

1. The story is summarized in the annual publication printed for devotees as a calendar and explanation for the festival.

2. See Hudson (1971), "Two Citra Festivals in Madurai," and Harman (1989), *The Sacred Marriage of a Hindu Goddess*.

3. For additional information about this particular dynamic, please see Harman (1985), "Kinship Metaphors in the Hindu Pantheon: Shiva as Brother-in-Law and Son-in-Law."

4. In the Madurai region, followers of the form of Vishnu brought to Madurai for the Journey are understood to be far less sophisticated than followers of Shiva. Strict rules pertain about the extent to which Vaishnavas with religious markings that so identify them may participate in worship inside the city at the Madurai temple, the site of the Marriage Festival ceremony. Generally, they are permitted to enter the shrine to Parvati, but not to go any farther. And in Shaiva processions in the city that both precede and follow the marriage celebration, Vaishnavas may not walk ahead of the carts carrying the Shaiva deities.

5. See, for example, the *Tiruvilaiyatarpuranam*. See also my (1987) article, "The Authority of Sanskrit in Tamil Hinduism: A Case Study in Tracing a Text to Its Sources."

6. It is tempting to observe here that scripture often represents a perfect world, while ritual is played out in the imperfections of daily life, and so it involves a tension not necessarily implicit in the polished idealism and poetic realities of narrative.

## Works Cited

Harman, William. 1985. "Kinship Metaphors in the Hindu Pantheon: Shiva as Brother-in-Law and Son-in-Law." *Journal of the American Academy of Religion* 53:3: 411–30.

Harman, William. 1987. "The Authority of Sanskrit in Tamil Hinduism: A Case Study in Tracing a Text to Its Sources." *Mankind Quarterly* 27:3: 295–316.

Harman, William. 1989. *The Sacred Marriage of a Hindu Goddess*. Bloomington: Indiana University Press. 2nd ed. New Delhi: Motilal Banarsidass, 1992.

Hudson, Dennis. 1971. "Two Citra Festivals in Madurai." In *Asian Religions: 1971*, ed. Bardwell Smith, 191–222. Chambersburg: American Academy of Religion.

Huizinga, Johann. 1950. *Homo Ludens: A Study of the Play Element in Culture.* Boston, MA: Beacon Press.

*Tiruvilaiyatarpuranam of Parancotimunivar*. 1927 [1967]. *Commentary Na.Mu. Venkatacamimunivar*. 3 vols. Cennai: Tenintiya Caiva Cittanta Nurpatippu Kalakam.

# 8

# Gods' Play and the Buddha's Way

## *Varieties of Levity in Contemporary Sinhala Practice*

JONATHAN WALTERS

## Introduction

This chapter explores the role of ritual levity among some contemporary Sinhala Buddhists in Sri Lanka. There, as appears to have been the case in Buddhist traditions throughout the Indic world, Buddhist religiosity was and still is characterized by a complex interweaving of distinctly Buddhist elements with originally non-Buddhist elements, a wide range of "Buddhicized" ideas, deities, and rites that were originally Shaiva and Vaishnava (Hindu) forms imported from India as well as indigenous, pre-Buddhist cults of lesser, lower spirits. I distinguish these two basic strands or layers of Sinhala religiosity as "the Buddhist layer" and "the Theist layer," respectively, in order to advance—but also complicate—my thesis that the Theist-layer rituals are veritably characterized by ritual levity, whereas the Buddhist-layer rituals seem almost conspicuously devoid of it or, in other words, these Sinhala Buddhists play with the gods but not with the Buddha.

My approach here is descriptive and anecdotal, focusing upon specific rituals and ritual contexts I have witnessed, heard described by participants, and/or participated in myself, because anecdotes are best suited to the nuances within which, at least in this case, all the fun occurs. These anecdotes are drawn from a rural village near Anuradhapura, in Sri Lanka's North Central Province, where I have worked and lived as a participant-observer on and off since 1984. This village is home to several regionally significant lineages of male "healers" (literally "Vedic Gentlemen") who practice Ayurvedic medicine as well as the Theistic arts collectively called *gurukam* ("Gurus' Practices"), and over the years there I have attended many hundreds of their Theist-layer rituals, including festivals for the gods, protective rites, fortune-telling, exorcism, and the ritualized production of herbal medicines.[1] The Buddhist layer, conversely, is embodied in the village temple, ever being restored and improved through the collective effort of the villagers, and in the village monk. The range of Buddhist-layer rituals and practices that I have experienced over the years is equally wide: offerings of flowers, incense, lamps, betel, or the first serving of daily alms to Buddha images, the stupa (reliquary monument), the *bodhi* tree, and the incumbent monk; almsgiving ceremonies; funeral rites; observance of the Full Moon Day each month, when every villager who can will visit the temple to make offerings, and the pious among them, and sometimes schoolchildren en masse, will adopt the special "Eight Precepts (see text that follows) and a highly regimented quasimonastic lifestyle for the day; rituals associated with monastic ordination and promotion; annual presentation of monastic robes; fund-raising events; pilgrimages; Sunday School ceremonies, and so forth. In my experience, the many different Theist-layer rituals and practices of the healers are full of obviously playful elements, whereas those performed by the monk in the Buddhist layer are characterized instead by a solemnity and sobriety that entails an absence of precisely that playfulness.

These brief introductory comments about ritual levity in the Theist and Buddhist layers of Sinhala Buddhist village religiosity are developed in turn—and problematized—in the following two sections of this chapter. In the conclusion I return to the relationship between these varieties of ritual levity and the implications of this Sinhala case for the larger discussion of ritual levity in South Asian religions.

## Originally Theist Varieties of Ritual Levity

I was living in the village when I received the editors' request for a chapter on ritual levity, and as I sat pondering the category I was paid a visit by a Sinhala Buddhist friend and learned village healer, Dr. Gunatilaka. As he has entered his fifties, and following the deaths of the older generation of village healers, Dr. Gunatilaka has emerged as the premier ritual expert in the village. His father, grandfather, and an unknown lineage of ancestors before them were noted Ayurvedic pediatricians, and he married the daughter of an equally well-known

Ayurvedic ophthalmologist; father and father-in-law both were also in their way officiants in rituals involving play with the gods, especially Vishnu. Dr. Gunatilaka practices a wide range of both medical and Theistic arts, his specialties in those areas being the manufacture of medicinal oils as well as his father's pediatrics and Theistic arts empowered by a deity called Ratu Kambili (but also Vishnu, who used to possess his father), respectively, and he long served, as did his father-in-law before him, as the primary officiant of the Vishnu shrine at the foot of the recumbent Buddha image in the village temple's image house. When anyone in the village has need of formal Theist-layer rituals, Dr. Gunatilaka is invariably asked to participate, whether to officiate or to direct the production of ornate coconut-frond ritual altars and ornamental gateways, the preparation of the ritual area, and the placement of protective diagrams. It is he who gets asked by farmers to perform rituals that protect their fields, most notably the creation of protective boundaries and chanting spells against wild elephants, a persistent problem there; to give advice on astrologically auspicious times and places for New Year's rituals or new house construction; to "recharge" amulets polluted by funerals or first menses rituals; or to exorcise malevolent spirits. Dr. Gunatilaka is also an active supporter of the Buddhist temple, sometimes observes the Eight Precepts on Full Moon Days, is the leader of a local group of men that performs lay chanting of Buddhist protective sermons, and regularly advises the current (2004) temple monk, who is young and somewhat inexperienced, on the ritual activities and procedures of the Buddhist layer. My own ability to speak generally about village rituals is the result of my long association with Dr. Gunatilaka—and his father, father-in-law, and other healers mentioned later—all of whose knowledge of them far exceeds/exceeded my own.

So when Dr. Gunatilaka fortuitously arrived, I asked him about ritual levity. Not yet sure even how to phrase the question in Sinhala, let alone whether it would be a fruitful line of inquiry, I simply explained that I had received an unusual request to contribute to a volume of essays about playing with gods. I chose the ordinary Sinhala verb "to play" (*sellam karanna*), which is—like most everything connected to the gods—derived from Tamil,[2] and I asked whether he thought that to be a significant dimension of the deity-related rituals he performs. "What else?," he immediately replied, laughing, "those folks play a lot!" So does Dr. Gunatilaka, who makes it a point to laugh as often as possible, even in the face of illness or other tragedy ("It purifies the blood," he once explained to me). His animated participation in the ensuing conversation convinced me that ritual levity is an appropriate interpretive lens in the Sinhala Buddhist context, even though I had never previously theorized the case in quite those terms, and because Dr. Gunatilaka usefully laid out a variety of angles on the relationship of play (*sellam*) to the gods, and provided several informative examples, I will dwell on that conversation a bit longer here.

In Dr. Gunatilaka's view, gods are meant to be entertained by the variety of things offered to them, including flowers, food, and drink, scented resin, scented water, oil lamps, betel leaves and areca nuts, money, a mirror and comb (explained as useful to goddesses, who always like to look their best!), fresh fruits, dance, drumming, conch- and horn-playing, *and* objects for play, such as margosa-leaf clubs, a toy bow and arrow, and/or whips. This desire to entertain is even clearer in rituals designed for lesser and malevolent spirits, who are provided with party goods such as meat and fish, tobacco, alcohol, marijuana, and spicy snacks. According to Dr. Gunatilaka, gods and lesser spirits come to ritual altars and occasions for their own fun, and both social etiquette and the dictates of these Theist-layer traditions require that they therefore be given whatever they might enjoy.

Just as every dinner guest need not be served a special feast every time, however, so there are various levels at work in the degree to which the gods or other spirits must be entertained. A simple spell-chanting or lime-cutting ceremony requires no more than betel, areca nuts, flowers, a couple coins, and, of course (in case any goddesses should arrive), a mirror and comb, arranged in a lotus pattern on a tray or plate, whereas an elaborate amulet empowerment, not to mention the annual obligatory festival for a healer's own working deity, will require a long list of special objects that can cost many thousands of rupees and a great deal of time to assemble. On a grander scale still are regional and national festivals and processions of the gods; Dr. Gunatilaka singled out the annual Aesala Perahera of the island's guardian deities and the Buddha's Tooth Relic in Kandy. Similarly, lesser spirits can be tricked into staying away from the routine production of medicinal oils with a few betel leaves rolled into pouches and filled with roasted paddy to resemble meat or chunnam dyed red to resemble blood, which they will follow to an altar in some forlorn place, but exorcising a major spirit who has possessed someone, or employing one to do malevolent deeds such as bewitching or stealing buried treasure, will require that the offering on the altar be a live chicken or even, at least in myth, some number of sacrificed children. Still, according to Dr. Gunatilaka, all of these practices share the same basic motivation of entertaining the gods and spirits. If those beings enjoy themselves, then they will do the bidding of their hosts; if not, even the gods and especially the spirits can be the angriest of slighted guests.

Expanding on this basic stance—that the gods and spirits come to altars to play and that the dance and music, rhythmic chanting of Sinhala-language descriptive paeans dedicated to particular deities, brightly clean new clothes, and the feasting of participants are particularly enjoyable (*vinodayi*) to them—Dr. Gunatilaka proceeded to demonstrate that gods do indeed *like* to play, a theme that is quite obvious in the poetic depictions of them.[3] He pointed out that when they have most fully arrived, that is, possessed the ritual officiant and/or participants, they themselves play. Possessed people, that is, the gods themselves, break into frenzied dance, run and flail about, play with special toys, gutturally grunt and laugh, cross-dress, and otherwise bend genders (I have many times witnessed possessed males playing dress up with their red sashes as saris, holy ash as cosmetics, and the comb and mirror for guidance), playfully teasing or even directly oppressing participants.

Both Dr. Gunatilaka and I were able to recall many colorful examples of that latter sort. I mentioned one of the anyway-always-playful festivals presented annually to his working deity—a lower spirit, Kadavara, who is also called "god" out of deference, but who is famous for his ability to get things done whatever it may take—by another village healer, Dr. Rambanda, wherein the deity (i.e., the possessed healer) danced so long and so furiously that the drummer was sweating and panting to keep the beat. "What's the matter," teased the deity, "too fast for you? Are you getting old? Maybe sleepy?" As we discussed that healer's festival procedure, numerous additional examples of ritual levity poured forth: the attractive altar display and space that he always constructs and the wonderful array of singers of paeans and other musicians who attend; the deity's dress-up play there; the several women whose own spirits invariably come forth/actively possess them in the presence of the deity ("He's their boss, you know," added Dr. Gunatilaka pejoratively), causing them to dance and banter with sexual overtones, which in turn causes the deity to chastise them, ultimately with a real rod and whips; various antics with the chicken as its early-dawn sacrifice draws closer, and then with its blood; the fact that about everyone in the village attends, as do patients of Dr. Rambanda's from further afield, even Colombo and the South, for whom the village is its own form of entertainment, and they so for the villagers; the good time had by all consuming snacks, betel, and tea and punch provided by the host, and/or getting drunk as the evening proceeds. The spectacle is highly entertaining and inevitably recounted with chuckles and smiles for days afterward.

All of these elements, in more or less extreme forms, are found in the rituals and experiences of the other healers too. In this region the most famous whipper of women possessed by spirits was not Dr. Rambanda but the now-deceased officiant of the shrine to god Aiyyanar in a nearby village. When the god possessed him, he would brandish a long stake with seven nail-studded leather whips attached and would take on the whole lot of spirits who came in droves to possess women in the audience. And Dr. Gunatilaka related the village's most famous case of the teasing and ultimately playing out of a healer by a god, the story of why the late Dr. (K. V.) Appuhamy stopped practicing Theistic arts altogether.

Dr. Appuhamy was widely reputed as a practitioner of Ayurvedic medicine until his death, at age ninety-five, in 1992. The repeated warnings I received not to accept tea during my many long visits to his house—lest caught off guard I find myself bewitched!—made clear that he was still feared as a powerful practitioner of the Theistic arts as well, though he denied having uttered so much as a simple spell in forty years. But there had been a time in his life when, as he once put it to me, he "played with gods and spirits all the time." He explained this use of the term "play" (*sellam*) to mean that he got possessed by them and/or sent them off to possess others. The most famous instance of this was invoked by Dr. Gunatilaka in the course of our conversation: a young girl mocked Dr. Appuhamy's nickname "Skeleton" by querying within his earshot, "Skeleton or a stick?," and his response was to sick a spirit on her, which he later released only after her parents brought her to him, stark-raving mad, and begged his forgiveness. He kept one deity, whom he called "my friend," trapped as his personal assistant in a small case of clairvoyant oily goo and "bound up" numerous others, troublemakers, with a combination of enchanted thorns and ropes; he laughed and joked with them, threatened or cajoled them, and hung out with them. But some of them did not like his game, and in the end they forced him out of it.

The basic story of that fateful encounter when his play with the gods and spirits went bad, as told to me by Dr. Gunatilaka during our recent conversation and by Dr. Appuhamy himself in 1985, is this: One day when his sons were still young boys, during the 1950s, Dr. Appuhamy heard that a young man in an adjoining village had become possessed. It sounded simple enough, so he headed out, at night, without even remembering to bring his "friend." When he arrived on the scene, he found the patient exhibiting obvious signs of spirit possession: his hair was disheveled, his sarong was untied, and he was cursing his own mother in foul language, seemingly as mad as that enchanted girl. Without a thought, he began to chant spirit-binding spells—"That was a routine thing for me those days," he told me—but in fact this was a deity in disguise, and that deity was far more powerful than Dr. Appuhamy's spells (or his friend). Suddenly expressing rage at Dr. Appuhamy's audacity to try to bind a deity with spirit spells, which the deity had tricked him into attempting, the deity, that is, the possessed man, commanded him to fetch some chunnam for a betel chew, and Dr. Appuhamy, realizing that he had seriously misjudged the situation, obligingly turned to get it. When he turned back around, the deity had revealed herself in the visage of a beautiful young woman—Dr. Gunatilaka told me it was "Lanka Mari," identified as the Sri Lankan incarnation of the Tamil goddess Mariamman, or the Virgin Mary, or both—who informed him that his days binding spirits were over. Those spirits, it turns out, were Lanka Mari's friends whom his successful binding techniques prevented from coming out to play with her! Dr. Appuhamy "lost his mind," but somehow—he supposed with the help of his "friend"—he stumbled home through the dark and dangerous jungle only to find his treasured palm-leaf manuscripts of spells and magical diagrams literally incinerated, their silver covers a molten mess, and to face, in the coming days, the death of his wife and then of his nephew, who was his favorite young pupil. One of Dr. Appuhamy's teachers intervened to help, tricking yet another healer into tricking his possessing deity into calling off the wrathful Lanka Mari, which was achieved on a promise that Dr. Appuhamy would never practice the Theistic arts again, and, therefore, Dr. Gunatilaka added—for his father was this Dr. Appuhamy's great rival, as Dr. Appuhamy's son is his own—"their medicinal oils don't work, whereas just a drop of mine cures everything."

So there is more to the levity attending these sorts of Theist-layer rituals than the passive enjoyment effected in the gods and humans who participate in them, though that itself, at least in Dr. Gunatilaka's view, constitutes genuine play. The gods and spirits themselves play with the objects on the altar and with the humans at their mercy, and when they possess healers or women in the audience it is they themselves who perform the singing and dancing and unexpected or miraculous things in which everyone there delights. Some of this play is not always harmless, either, as was apparent in Dr. Appuhamy's old eyes while recounting the death of his wife and beloved pupil, and as might have been attested by that spirit-filled little girl, or the women getting the spirits whipped out of them by the god Aiyyanar, though in the latter instance it is said that pain, blood, and/or scarring are the deserved effect on women who were faking it; none of this apparently accompanies the whipping of the genuinely possessed.

## Buddhist Varieties of Ritual Levity

If my conversation with Dr. Gunatilaka affirmed that "ritual levity" provides a valuable angle on Sinhala Buddhist rituals of the Theist layer, and indeed contributed the substance of the preceding section of this chapter, then it also helped articulate and account for the absence of such levity in rituals of the Buddhist layer.

This is not to say that Buddhist rituals lack entertainment value. When I first put the question to him, Dr. Gunatilaka responded, "Oh yes, we also feel happy (*satutuyi*) making offerings to the Buddha or giving alms." We discussed the beautiful arches and pavilions that are sometimes constructed for such rituals, the fragrant flowers that are always piled high on the altars in the temple image house, the festive meal, albeit outside temple premises, that is usually their result, the pleasant association with groups of friends and relatives at the temple. We discussed the thrill of pilgrimage to the Buddha's footprint on Adam's Peak or to the great stupas of Anuradhapura and Mihintale. But when I pressed the point he clarified that the entertainment value is not quite the same in the Buddhist-layer rituals as it is in the Theist-layer rituals. Use of the terms "play" (*sellam*) and "enjoyment" (*vinodaya*) would be inappropriate to the strictly Buddhist/temple context, he conceded, as would be the sorts of merrymaking, joking, dancing and singing, sexual innuendo, and dangerous play that these terms label in the Theist-layer ritual contexts described earlier.

As we discussed this, it became clear that not only temple etiquette—where the norm is respectful and meditative behavior—but also the Buddhist-layer rituals themselves virtually guarantee that the Buddhist context will be different. For example, one conspicuous and popular Buddhist temple ritual is the taking of the Eight Precepts on Full Moon days, during which the pious augment the Five Precepts of ordinary lay Buddhists[4] with a stricter moral discipline that excludes, by definition, all sexuality (the Third Precept's prohibition of adultery is strengthened to include all sexual activity), feasting (the Sixth Precept is restraint from eating at the wrong time, i.e., after noon), the various entertainments of Theist-layer rituals (the Seventh Precept enjoins against watching dance, song, instrumental music or humorous shows, wearing garlands and scents and perfumes, and adorning oneself with cosmetics or ornaments such as bangles), and even being comfortable (the Eighth Precept entails restraint from sitting on an elevated chair or couch). The 227 precepts of the monastic disciplinary code are stricter still; monks ideally undertake to avoid even such playful activities as small talk or smiling in a way that shows the teeth.[5]

I do not want to overemphasize the degree to which these ideals are realized in practice. The austere white attire worn by Eight-Precept holders on Full Moon Days can become its own kind of fashion. I have seen children not join their classmates in this practice only because they lack the *de rigueur* white sarong, white shirt, and white sash, and I have seen even regulars pass on taking the Eight Precepts on an occasional Full Moon Day when theirs somehow did not get washed and ironed in time. I also have heard village purists criticize the treatment of the strings of seeds used for counting chants as though it were jewelry, and the failure (or sometimes inability) of many elderly female Eight-Precept holders to remove their gold ear ornaments for the day. Similarly, the current (2004) incumbent monk has a great sense of humor, and I have seen him smile and laugh many times, both in the temple and out of it, teasing villagers and even cracking small jokes in sermon contexts. And, as mentioned, there is certainly a lot of pleasant association among ordinary Buddhists who also visit the temple on Full Moon Days, though the Eight-Precept holders, conversely, do tend to remain congregated in the preaching hall, silently meditating or studying; while not the norm, drunks, flirting teenagers, unruly children, people having angry arguments, and so forth are sometimes among those congregated for temple rituals.

But even in such instances, the ideal will not be far out of mind: no one would call the special garb "fashion" nor the rosary "jewelry" in a noncritical context. The monk's occasional joke is intended to draw listeners into the always very serious sermon, and he is certainly not doing stand-up comedy when he preaches; his deportment is widely praised as exemplary and sharply contrasted with that of some previous incumbents or contemporaries in other temples who "played around" with creature comforts. At least within the preaching hall on Full Moon Days, even those who have not adopted the special precepts will deport themselves as though they had, and drunks, flirts, overly active children, or quarrelers will certainly be chastised by others and/or asked to leave the temple premises if their inappropriate behavior does not cease. Even in the case of Buddhist pilgrimage, wherein those journeying will likely engage in raucous sing-alongs and even drink, the songs are more likely to be devotional than sexy pop songs,[6] and the drunks are likely to avoid the formal rituals—such as worship at the pilgrimage's goal—altogether. In other words, even in its breach, the ideal for behavior within a temple or another Buddhist sacred site, or during a Buddhist ritual, remains just the opposite of that in the Theist layer: quietude, gentleness, moral restraint, seriousness. That Buddhist atmosphere is preserved through the absence of many of the mainstays of Theist-layer "enjoyment," such as consumables other than betel and tea, music other than ritual drumming on certain occasions, dance, bright lights, funky clothing, possession, exorcism, and sacrificial practices.

The difference is, of course, more fundamental than these external trappings, for the Theist- and Buddhist-layer rituals focus upon different objects of devotion. Interaction with gods and spirits is not just the same as ordinary human interaction, but it is certainly at least analogous to it: gods like and dislike, get angry or are pleased, have wants and needs, give worldly benefits (or not), need cajoling and gratitude and sometimes threats, or, in the case of malevolent spirits, discipline; the gods are here in this worldly reality (*samsara*), actively participating in it. The Buddha, on the other hand, by definition, is not. And even when alive, being Buddha, he rose above the gods in having no needs or wants, no likes or dislikes, no anger or unwholesome pleasure.[7] Since his final passing away, this characterization has of course become absolute.

Nor is it just a matter of these objects of devotion differing; conceptualizations of the power and purpose of Buddhist-layer rituals likewise differ from those that underlie rituals of the Theist layer. The latter, as many scholars have noted, like the gods who empower them, are wrapped up in worldly concerns: curing disease, bringing good fortune, averting divine wrath, obtaining justice, repaying vows. The gods and even the lower spirits are valuable *because* they remain in this conditioned existence (*samsara*) we call "the world," capable of changing it for what is considered by any particular devotee or group of devotees to be the better. The Buddhist-layer rituals, conversely, are soteriological, and hence they are dubbed "religious" (*agamika*), a term that I have never heard used to describe any of the Theist-layer rituals. That is, Buddhist-layer rituals, though they certainly produce worldly benefits too in terms of good feelings, fearlessness in the face of death, good reputation and prestige, and so on, are concerned less with this world than with the next: their purpose is cultivating merit or "good karma" for oneself while alive, and/or availing it to others after they have died. The Buddha, subsequent Buddhist saints, and ordinary monks constitute the most fertile "merit field" or object of devotion for Buddhist-layer rituals, precisely because they are *not* of this world, because in actuality or at least ideally they model the achievement of Nirvana, the goal after which these Buddhist rituals, unlike the Theist-layer ones, strive.

Yet in the months since that conversation with Dr. Gunatilaka, I have regularly returned to his initial response that people also feel happiness (*satuta*) in that specifically Buddhist context. Certainly, however different the external trappings, the Buddhist- and Theist-layer rituals share a basic, perhaps mundane, kind of ritual levity that I characterized earlier as passively being entertained. Probably all rituals, indeed, any number of human activities, involve this sort of levity: the "fun" of getting dressed up, going out, meeting friends, being in the place to be. But as I have clarified with Dr. Gunatilaka and many other Buddhist friends in subsequent conversations, this "happiness" in the Buddhist context is not limited to that passive entertainment any more than dancing and drumming exhaust the "play" and "enjoyment" of the Theist-layer rituals. There, I suggested, the passive entertainment afforded by the spectacle is supplemented by more profound sorts of ritual levity, including active play with, and even of, the gods and spirits. I conclude this section of the chapter by unpacking the "something more," which I have come to see likewise supplements mundane ritual levity in the specifically Buddhist context, however different it may be from the games Sinhala Buddhists sometimes play as deity-possessed spirit-whippers.

Unlike the language of play (*sellam*), which as noted is derived from Tamil and has no firm foundation in classical Sinhala texts, Sinhala literature provides a wonderfully rich vocabulary for the rarefied "happiness" (*satuta*) that ideally is experienced in Buddhist-layer rituals. This vocabulary of happiness consists entirely of old Sinhala and originally Pali or Sanskrit words already in use from the very beginnings of Sinhala Buddhist literature around the tenth century A.D.[8]: *paehaeda/pahada* and *prasada, prasanna, prasan* (all meaning "pleased"); *santosha/santushthita/tutu/tushtha/tushthi/tus* (all synonyms/relatives of *satuta/satutuyi* ["happiness, happy"]); *priti/pina/pinana/pinavum/prina* (all meaning "overjoyed" or "delighted"). And, as is typical of the Sanskritic languages generally, over the centuries and for different literary purposes these have been combined with verbs and compounded with other nouns, and conjugated or declined, prefixed, suffixed, and/or intensified with modifiers that extend this classical lexicon of happiness further still. These terms are the ones that have recurred in my conversations about Buddhist-layer ritual levity, and given that all the early texts that employed them were, like most premodern Sinhala literature, specifically religious (Buddhist) writings, it is correct to say that this rich vocabulary has been developed precisely for discussing that "something more" that supplements the mundane ritual levity of the Buddhist layer. Indeed, some texts (especially *Buddhavamsa* and *Apadana*) of the ancient Indian Theravada Buddhist canon contain an even richer vocabulary of happiness than this, in Pali, which I have argued elsewhere emerged in and for the large-scale Buddhist festivals sponsored by the most powerful emperors of the early-post-Ashokan era.[9]

That one of these terms (*pina*) is also the Sinhala word for a meritorious deed is suggestive of the way that rarefied Buddhist happiness relates to soteriological expectations. The Buddha himself is reported to have declared karma a matter of mental state/intention, and in the *Buddhavamsa* and *Apadana* texts mentioned earlier, the soteriological implication of this equation is explicit: the Buddha and the saints achieved Nirvana, in the end, as a result of "good karma" heaped up in Buddhist rituals performed during previous lives; the operative dimension of those rituals was precisely the mental happiness that their rebirth precursors experienced at those times. So merit is earned when the mind delights in the ritual, a connection also made explicit by Dr. Gunatilaka and others with whom I have discussed this question. They have suggested a number of different ways of conceptualizing this connection: that when performed with "happiness" (*satuta*) or "wholesome pleasure" (*prasanna*), the ritual produces meritorious seeds for future attainments[10]; that these rituals are meritorious because they produce such spiritual states of mind[11]; that there is a cumulative enhancement of happiness to spiritual states more rarefied still, such as faith (*sraddha*), devotion (*bhakti*), loving-kindness (*maitri*), and ultimately the passionless-ness (*upeksha*) that characterizes an enlightened being.[12] But in all of these configurations, it is this Buddhist counterpart to ritual levity, religious joy, that transforms a person in the Path, and paves the way to its culmination in Nirvana.

## Conclusion

As should now be clear, the question of ritual levity in the Sinhala Buddhist case is complicated by the presence there of both Buddhist and originally non-Buddhist ritual forms. Even the most uneducated villagers will articulate the differences between these two categories of ritual, not in the abstract scholarly terms employed here, nor perhaps in the theological and Buddhological terms employed by ritual experts such as Dr. Gunatilaka but, rather, in the thick of the ritual itself: everyone knows not to put salt in the food if it is being cooked to offer to the gods and not to omit salt if it is being cooked to offer to the Buddha (and in either event not to taste the food while cooking it). Everyone knows not to offer to the Buddha the dark red flowers that are *de rigueur* in many Theist-layer rituals; always to burn scented resin for the gods and never for the Buddha; and only to give roasted meat or marijuana to lower beings. Everyone knows, in short, which types of levity are appropriate to which ritual contexts.

Emphasizing these distinctions is not, however, to imply that these "layers" constitute separate religions. Dr. Gunatilaka has witnessed, participated in, and/or officiated at *all* of the different sorts of rituals I have mentioned, Buddhist and originally Theist, bespeaking their integration in his own person. Indeed, the Sinhala Buddhist ritual contexts I have described exhibit this complex overlap of the Buddhist and Theist layers more than I have yet allowed. It is perhaps most evident in the belief that the gods themselves are Buddhist. Both Vishnu and the other deity who usually joins him in Buddhist temples (identified in the North Central Province with god Saman, in the Kandyan area with god Natha, and in both instances with the future Buddha Maitreya)[13] are considered buddhas in the making (*bodhisattvas*). Their shrines are in temples because that is where they themselves want to be, worshipping at the feet of the Buddha. Not only they but all of the gods crave merit, even more than the treats on their altars. The performance of meritorious deeds in which the gods can vicariously participate is the most important "capital" that Sinhala Buddhists such as Dr. Gunatilaka possess in their dealings with them; god Aiyyanar used to start brandishing his spirit-whip against possessed women only after he, in the body of that healer, had personally worshipped the *bodhi* tree near his shrine. Even for the gods, in other words, Buddhist-layer happiness or pleased-ness—religious joy—takes precedence over Theist-layer forms of ritual levity, such as enjoyment as an honored guest and engaging in playful relationships with devotees!

If we understand ritual levity to mean playfulness or joking (literally "lightness") in and as part of ritual contexts, then in this case it appears to be largely restricted to the practices and theologies of what I have dubbed the Theist layer of Sinhala Buddhist religiosity. Given the widespread relevance of ritual levity to actual Indian Theist (Hindu) traditions, as documented in other chapters of this volume, its persistence in the Sinhala Buddhist case is not particularly remarkable;

over the centuries during which these hybrid traditions were being formed, ritual levity was imported from India along with the gods and the rites that could manipulate them. But in at least two ways this Sinhala case is a unique one, important to the general discussion of ritual levity in South Asian religions.

First, the Sinhala Buddhist case presents an interesting anomaly for its ambiguity about ritual levity. The Theist-layer practices in which ritual levity is most obviously present constitute at best subordinated or hierarchically inferior aspects of Sinhala Buddhist religiosity, and, as mentioned, many Sinhala Buddhists would not consider them "religious" at all; "religious" (Buddhist-layer) rituals actively neglect, even proscribe, ritual levity of the Theist sort. This Sinhala case thus presents a challenge to any simple assertion that ritual levity is a necessary or an essential part of South Asian religions. Yet it does not easily argue against such a position either, for as I have suggested, the Buddhist-layer rituals do share with their Theist-layer (and actual Theist) counterparts a certain mundane sort of enjoyableness, as well as rarefied counterparts to ritual levity. And these Sinhala Buddhists did, after all, import and continue to perform rituals that do constitute a place for ritual levity of the Theist sort in their overall practice, however subordinated it may be, which might suggest that ritual levity cannot be done without, no matter how hard one might try.

Second, as many chapters of this volume also make clear, unlike Sinhala Buddhists the various actual Indian Theists from whom these rituals have been imported consider them very much "religious," wrapped up in soteriological and existential expectations of the highest sort, and Theists have treated their forms of ritual levity as extensively and thoughtfully as Buddhists have discoursed on "happiness" and "wholesome pleasure." There is thus a certain harsh edge to Sinhala Buddhist levity *about* Theist rituals, that is, their treatment of Theist rituals as—to invoke modern American usage for a moment—"a joke." Although competition between different religious communities is certainly not always at issue—Dr. Gunatilaka knows no actual Theists (he speaks only limited Tamil) and has never been to India; he reveres and fears the gods even if (or perhaps because) they are merely more advanced co-aspirants to the Buddha's path—yet contemporary Sinhala practice has emerged out of a long history in which Buddhists and actual Theists obviously were interacting closely. That these interactions were sometimes positive or harmonious is evident in the degree to which Theist practices have, indeed, been appropriated by Sinhala Buddhists. But this history has also included more contentious moments. Poking fun at or more seriously attacking Theists, their rituals, and their gods, precisely because of the sorts of levity in which they engage, dates back to the earliest strata of Buddhist literature, and it (as well as rebuttal by Hindus) has been a consistent feature of South Asian religious history since. It may even be the case, as Daud Ali has suggested (see n. 5), that *not* participating in Theist ritual levity was an important factor in giving shape to Buddhist practice and identity. Extending that dialogical understanding farther, it may then be that self-distinction from the Buddhists can help us account for the great degree to which South Asian Theists have not only allowed but actively emphasized ritual levity as an integral dimension of their religious practice.

## Notes

1. Constraints on space prevent an extensive presentation of this complex ethnographic context in the present chapter. For further discussion of it, and of the relationship between Buddhist and originally Theist layers in practices that parallel those discussed here, see Walters 1998, 2003. The sorts of practices described here parallel—though in important ways differ from—the healing traditions of Southern Sri Lanka that have been treated extensively by, among others, Wirz 1954 and Kapferer 1983.

2. See Sorata 1970, II, 1122. Rev. Sorata gives no indication that the word—which he defines as "enjoyment" (*vinodaya*), "activity that produces enjoyment" (*vinodatmaka kriyawa*), or "game" (*kridawa*)—has any witness in the vast number of classical Sinhala texts he consulted to compile this extraordinary Sinhala-Sinhala dictionary.

3. Thus, for example the paean for god Ilandari, working deity of the late Dr. (S.) Appuhamy, addresses him: "You whom we know as Young Man God/are you a prince who was born on a lotus?// . . . Like a lotus afloat and in bloom in a pool/carelessly playing on the golden waves// . . . You walk and play near pools and crossroads/hiding to sicken someone you might see//You sicken the folks coming, going at night/you obliterate your servant's disease, Black God."

4. The Five Precepts entail attempting in the course of day-to-day existence to refrain from taking life, taking what is not given, adultery, false speech, and drunkenness. They are chanted in Pali, in unison, at the beginning of virtually all Buddhist ceremonies; many villagers light incense in front of a Buddha image and chant them every morning after waking to start the day in their moral embrace. The Eight Precepts include the first five (the third being augmented to complete celibacy) but supplement them with three further precepts, described later, which imitate monastic lifestyles. The ritual occasion on which these precepts are formally accepted (in Sinhala, "received" [from the monk]) entails adopting a special monklike dress (a white shirt, sarong, and

sash for men; a white blouse, skirt, and sash for women), the use of special pronouns ordinarily reserved for monks and nuns, and a detailed schedule of religious activities, such as offerings to the Buddha, Bodhi tree, stupa, and monk, and listening to sermons and meditation exercises.

5. Ali 1999 convincingly argues that Buddhist monastic discipline is in fact constituted in intentional opposition to/with the fineries of courtly society, art, and passion, as represented by the *Kama Sutra* literature (the several Pali texts called *Kama Sutta*, conversely, basically say: "Don't!").

6. In older pilgrimage practice there were no songs at all (Buddhist devotional music is a modern phenomenon in Sri Lanka) but rather rhythmic chanting of classical Sinhala poems. For a contemporary Theist-layer contrast, see Holt 2004, 362–65.

7. As I have demonstrated elsewhere (Walters 1990), Theravadins through the ages have taken pains to maintain this characterization even in their discussions of the handful of unpleasant things believed to have befallen Gotama Buddha during his otherwise charmed final existence.

8. For citations to early uses in the preserved literature, see the entries on each of the following terms in Sorata 1970; the earliest are from *Dharmapradipikawa*, which is the earliest extant Sinhala text.

9. See Walters 1997. On the soteriological significance of this happiness as portrayed in these texts, cf. below.

10. This connection is not magical nor in the Buddhist view supernatural; rather, when performed with a happy heart, these practices constitute a sort of low-level or initiatory training in what those later attainments will entail. Thus taking pleasure in refraining from laughing too loudly in the temple confines is meritorious, because in the future one will be able to refrain from showing the teeth, gladly refraining from eating anything there that will enable one later to take up the monastic training of no food after noon; willingly refraining from bawdiness or drunkenness, lying or harsh speech, excessive pleasure, and so on, which will similarly magnify until the perfection of morality (*sila-paramita*) is achieved. It can be easily understood that the absence of happy-mindedness would undermine the efficacy of these trainings: if one feels resentment or impatience or dislike for them, thinking "I wish I were elsewhere so I could tell this bawdy joke," or (as the Sinhala has it), "I'm so hungry I could eat a spirit," then one can become a foundation for movement in the opposite direction on the Path.

11. Thus for example meditating on Full Moon Days or chanting particular verses when making offerings to the Buddha is meritorious because it cultivates loving-kindness, detachment from one's own body and life, or other Buddhist virtues.

12. In fact, asking Sinhala Buddhist friends and colleagues questions about the role of happiness in Buddhist-layer rituals has generated quite a discourse on how these mental states relate to each other, their relative hierarchy in terms of spiritual self-cultivation, and so on, but it is enough to recognize here that all of them constitute what can be identified as Buddhist parallels to

"ritual levity," even if by their very definition they stand in contradistinction to the types of levity found in Theist-layer (and actual Theist) rituals.

13. For an extensive treatment of this deity/bodhisattva and related motifs, see Holt 1991. Maitreya-to-be is already so advanced that he reposes in Tushita ("Happiness") heaven, temporarily otiose from the human perspective; Vishnu, having farther to go in his quest for Buddhahood, still condescends to answer the petitions of devotees in exchange for merit (cf. Holt 2004).

## Works Cited

Ali, Daud. 1999. "Technology of the Self: Courtly Artifice and Monastic Discipline in Early India." *Journal of the Economic and Social History of the Orient* 41:2: 159–84.

Holt, John C. 1991. *Buddha in the Crown: Avalokitesvara in the Buddhist Traditions of Sri Lanka*. New York: Oxford University Press.

Holt, John C. 2004. *The Buddhist Vishnu: Religious Transformation, Politics, Culture*. New York: Columbia University Press

Kapferer, Bruce. 1983. *A Celebration of Spirits: Exorcism and the Aesthetics of Healing in Sri Lanka*. Bloomington: Indiana University Press.

Sorata, Ven. Pandit W. 1970. *Sri Sumangala Sabdakoshaya.* Mt. Lavinia, Ceylon: Abhaya.

Walters, Jonathan S. 1990. "The Buddha's Bad Karma: A Problem in the History of Theravada Buddhism." *Numen* 37:1: 70–95.

Walters, Jonathan S. 1997. "Stupa, Story and Empire: Constructions of the Buddha Biography in Early Post-Ashokan India." In *Sacred Biography in the Buddhist Traditions of South and Southeast Asia,* ed. Juliane Schober, 160–92. Honolulu: University of Hawai'i Press.

Walters, Jonathan S. 1998. *Buried Treasure in Sri Lankan History*. Colombo: Social Scientists Association.

Walters, Jonathan S. 2003. "Deanimating and Reanimating the Dead in Sri Lanka." In *The Living and the Dead: Social Dimensions of Death in South Asia,* ed. Liz Wilson, 113–26. Albany: State University of New York Press.

Wirz, Paul, 1954. *Exorcism and the Art of Healing in Ceylon*. Leiden: Brill.

# Part 3

# Playing to Win

*Edging Out the Competition*

9

# Playing with Durga in Bengal

RACHEL FELL MCDERMOTT

## Setting the Scene

This chapter is about a public Hindu festival that I am choosing to examine and interpret, reflexively, through the lens of ritual levity. In other words, can the festival be illuminated through a discussion of ritual play? And can theories of play be informed by adding this festival to their interpretive repertoires? Before beginning, it is important to note that there are many ways of investigating and explicating this particular festival; I emphasize play here partly because I find it interesting to consider to what degree public rituals slide back and forth between the serious and the lighthearted, and partly because I myself, in my years of attending this festival, look forward to it as a time of "fun."

Durga Puja is *the* religious, national festival for Hindus in Bengal. At its center is the goddess Durga, whose coming in the autumnal season after the rains have ended brings renewal, revelry, and a much-anticipated chance to worship her. In each city and town of Bengal, temporary images of Durga and her family are fashioned out of straw, clay, paint, and decorations. This goddess is a combination of the classical Mahishasuramardini—the warrior goddess who slays a buffalo demon (*asura*) named Mahisa—and the gentle daughter Uma, who returns home to her parents once a year, accompanied by her four children, Ganesha, Karttikeya, Sarasvati, and Lakshmi. Sculpting these images takes weeks, and the finished products are masterpieces of skill. The day before the four-day festival begins, the images are brought from the artisans' districts to localities throughout each city, where they are installed in makeshift *pandal*s, or temporary dwellings, built from bamboo poles, colored cloth, and many accessories; to herald her arrival and to entertain the public, the *pandal*s are surrounded by intricate lighting displays assembled by trained electricians.

These *pandal*s, ranging in shape from small templelike structures to huge buildings, are crowded by building specialists into every nook and cranny of the city landscape. In 2000, there were 1,300 of them in Kolkata. Inside there is a platform for the goddesses and in front a large space for visitors to take *darshan*. Once the festivals begin, the goddesses are worshiped according to scriptural injunctions by priests hired to tend to their ritual needs. Most people spend little time bothering about priests, however. This is an occasion for revelry, and people mill about in the thousands, especially at night, when the lighting is visible and the mood electric.[1] Durga Puja, which lasts four to six days, affords ample time for *darshan* seekers to roam the city, visiting as many *pandal*s as possible, showing off new clothes, and delighting in the carnivalesque quality of the religious holiday.

Such Puja celebrations are called *sarbajanin* Pujas, or public Pujas for people regardless of background. They are financed by neighborhood associations and civic groups that band together, collect subscriptions, and arrange for the Goddess, the *pandal* design, and the lighting displays. One of the biggest motivators in their decisions is the prospect of garnering status and prestige through winning prizes. In 1985, Asian Paints began this tradition with one prize; the mania for competition has been so successful and stimulating that now it gives money and trophies in several categories—best image, best *pandal*, best lighting, and best overall. These, plus several other, more recently established awards, provide impetus for both creativity and rivalry among Puja organizers.[2]

At last the festivals conclude. The priests invite the Goddess to leave her clay casings, and once the life is removed, the images must be ceremoniously immersed in a body of water. Goddesses are processed through the streets and carried (or trucked) to the nearest river. *Pandal*s and lighting displays, too, are dismantled, their creators taking with them as much as can be reused for the next festival or the next year. People are sad. The Goddess brings joy, a chance to relax and be merry, an occasion to reunite with loved ones home for the holidays.

People feel many things at Puja time—anticipation, nostalgia, anxiety, devotional fervor, disdain, and a host of other emotions. Overall, however, Durga Puja is widely perceived to be fun (*moja*). In a manner akin to Christmas in Western societies, people send each

Figure 9.1 Nighttime illuminations at Ekdaliya, South Kolkata, Durga Puja, September 9, 1998. *(photo by author)*

other Puja cards and give each other Puja gifts; merchandise is aggressively advertised using the festival as a buying incentive; offices and schools adjourn for a two-week Puja holiday, affording families the opportunity to come together; and once the Goddess arrives in the *pandal*s, people flock in droves, all day but especially at night, when the illuminations light up the sky, to see the creativity of the artisans and to enjoy an outing with family and friends (see Figure 9.1).

This festival is open to all types of people; Bengalis work together, jostle together, to fete the Goddess.[3]

## The Dazzling Spectacle: Imitation, Satire, and Entertainment

Every year, the *pandal*s get more and more imaginative and expensive, the urge for novelty fueled by the lure of prizes and the taste for competition. Conceived and paid for by neighborhood associations and clubs, these temporary structures for housing the Goddess range over a wide variety of subjects. To be sure, Durga and her children are often installed inside *pandals*, which look like temples or shrines, and the associated lighting displays frequently depict scenes from religious texts. One can see woodcuts, paintings, or lighting shows depicting Durga's *akal bodhan*, or untimely awakening, when Rama entreated her help in autumn before his war with Ravana, or scenes portraying her war with Mahisha. Religious scenes are not confined solely to the goddess-worshipping public, however. Equally popular are depictions of Krishna's play with Radha and illustrations from the *Ramayana*. Most temple-*pandal*s are what is called *kalpanik*, or imaginary, but some are copies of actual temples. Especially popular are models of Kolkata's famous temples, such as Kalighat and Daksinesvar, and terra-cotta temples from Bishnupur, but one also finds replicas of the Jagannath, Amarnath, Tirupati, and Konark temples, as well as even Buddhist and Christian places of worship[4]—all magically transported to the streets and alleyways of Bengali towns. Similar sorts of *pandal*s are those that simulate some natural environment, such as a Bengali village, complete with real rice and a tiny river; Ajanta Caves; or a Rajasthani desert and two camels shipped in especially for the occasion.

Many *pandal*s are built to replicate civic buildings. These can be locally important, such as Kolkata's Victoria Memorial or houses of historic zamindar families, or they can resemble distinguished buildings in other parts of South Asia, such as the assembly building in Mysore and palaces from Jodhpur and Bhutan. Interesting to the foreign observer are eminent sites in Europe or America, such as Buckingham Palace, the Eiffel Tower, Harvard University, constructed in Howrah in 1999 to honor Bengali Nobel Laureate Amartya Sen, Chicago's Parliament of Religions, and a London metro station.

But such religiously and secularly oriented "homes" for the Goddess are only half the story. Just as prominent—and, in fact, more attention-grabbing and prize-prone—are *pandal*s and lighting shows illustrating current events.

Disasters, accidents, and social problems are popular themes for *pandal* designers and electricians. A group in Kolkata made the floods of 2000 in West Bengal the center of its *pandal*, depicting homelessness, lack of clean water, and the threat of flood-borne poisonous snakes. Too, the hijacked Indian Airlines plane at Kandahar in 2000 became a shelter for Durga and her family, who were—like the actual trapped passengers—unable to see outside during their confinement. Other themes of this ilk are the 1999 sinking of the Russian submarine Kursk; the bus-train collision at Jadavpur in South Kolkata in 1999; and the crash of the Concorde in Paris in 2000. Mother Teresa and Princess Diana died all over again in the lighting shows of 1998, and several organizations have used the festivities as an occasion to raise consciousness about women—in particular, dowry abuses, child marriages, and bride burning.[5] Other *pandal*s advertise the necessity of wildlife preservation (one 2000 *pandal* depicted Durga as a tree, crying), the problem of political corruption, and the fight against disease.[6] Two of my favorite reflections of popular culture are lighting shows, one from 1995, in which a fat Ganesha drinks milk, and another from 1999, in which Bill and Monica carry on. I have even heard of, but never seen, a Durga whose face was Monica's.[7]

And then there are the nationalistic and patriotic *pandal*s and lighted scenes. In 1991, these depicted the Gulf War and the assassination of Rajiv Gandhi; in 1995, the skirmishes between India and Pakistan in the Siachen heights; and in 1999, Kargil. For those wanting to experience the battles on Tiger Hill, one only had to go to Shealdah Athletic Club in Kolkata, where Bofors guns sounded in the background and Indian soldiers resisted Pakistani shelling, or to visit Santosh Mitra Square to see a replica—160 feet high, 140 feet long, and 80 feet wide—of the INS Vikrant, India's aircraft carrier, equipped with an MiG fighter plane and a Chetak helicopter. The Goddess can also be depicted more symbolically—as Bharatmata, as a map of India, or as residing inside a map, with India at its center. In these exhibitions, the best way to indicate one's "enemy" is to give Mahisha, the demon killed by Durga, his likeness. Demons of recent years have been Nawaz Sharif, the dacoit Veerappan, Fiji's George Speight, and even Bill Clinton and Tony Blair.

Not all is serious, however. Also added to the Puja mix are *pandal*s designed to evoke a smile: a computer (Figure 9.2), a structure made up entirely of playing cards, a capsize-proof version of the Titanic, which was all the rage in 1998 after the release of the blockbuster movie, with every Bengali city of any size boasting at least one ocean liner in its precincts,[8] and dinosaurs (Figure 9.3).

For three nights running, when people mill about by the thousands in electrified excitement, the air of enjoyment is palpable; the atmosphere is akin to that of a fairground, with amusements, stalls selling food and drink, and plenty to astonish the eye. Favorite topics for neon lighting vary with the whims of the time. Children can enjoy Humpty Dumpty, Mickey Mouse, Godzilla, and vampires. Larger children and adults can enjoy the Hindi version of "Who Wants to be a Millionaire?," famed cricket players, and the Olympics. Even on the last day, when the Goddess is taken out of her *pandal*s and processed to the river for immersion, a mood of gaiety prevails: women have a special ritual known as *sindur-khela*, or playing with vermillion, during which they douse the Goddess, and then each other, with red

Figure 9.2. A *pandal* in the shape of a computer, Moran Road, Chandannagar, Jagaddhatri Puja, November 4, 2000. *(photo by author)*

Figure 9.3. A dinosaur opposite the Kalighat Temple, Kolkata, Kali Puja, October 19, 1998. *(photo by author)*

powder, and on the road to the riverbank, men and boys—who are often inebriated by this time—dance, laugh, and yell obscenities at each other as they gyrate along the way.

## Understanding Durga's Play

Even since I began working on the Bengali Durga Puja in 1994 I have wondered how to characterize the festival. It is certainly "fun," and people look forward to it all year. However, as seen earlier, the Pujas do not always, or even often, embody the comic, or produce belly laughs.[9] So how can one understand the enjoyment, the "fun," the playfulness? Should one approach it through humor's first cousin, theological reflection? For as Jonathan Z. Smith reminds us, the distance between humor and religious experience is minimal. Both play upon the juxtaposition or incongruity between expectation and actuality; "the normal expectation has been suspended and the unexpected intrudes[,] relativizing all previous modes of thought."[10] Indeed, what is the Goddess, the Creator and Savior of the world, doing inside a computer? Or astride a dinosaur? Such seeming collisions in the mind "play" on devotees, just as the Goddess is claimed to do. They goad, perplex, and taunt one into reconsidering frozen conceptions of divinity. Should one therefore understand the revelry and make-believe quality of the Puja *pandal*s as an expression of Durga's *maya*, her illusory power, or *ananda*, her blissful nature, or *lila*, her cosmic proclivity for unbounded, unpurposeful fun? Scholars from the great eighth-century Indian philosopher Shankara to modern Western interpreters such as C. Mackenzie Brown, John Stratton Hawley, David Kinsley, and William Sax have used the idea of the playfulness of God—whether Brahma, Kali, or Krishna—to interpret the divine creation of our world with all of its vagaries. Perhaps one should, as Lee Siegel puts it, see the Goddess as the "the archcomedienne, ever-laughing, . . . the source of the macabre tricks and sinister pranks that are her *maya*."[11] Another hermeneutical key might be found in the description of Durga from the famed *Devi Mahatmya* stories, where she is said to bestow both *bhukti* (earthly enjoyment) and *mukti* (liberation). However one reconciles the disjunctures between "sacred" and "secular" in the Puja *pandal*s, Jonathan Z. Smith and D. W. Winnicott remind us that play of any sort, theological or otherwise, necessitates trust and a sense of ease with the tradition. Hence those who embrace and celebrate the imaginative effervescence of the festival as nothing other than an expression of the Goddess's divine character—in essence, attributing the creativity to Durga and feeling comfortable with the incongruities presented by her festal tableaux—are experiencing the "cuddly," comfortable side of levity.[12] Put in such terms, there is no reason why the savior of the world cannot display her glory from inside a model Titanic.[13]

Tantalizing though these interpretations are, I wonder about them; I have never heard or read in Bengal of any overarching theology associated with the Puja, save the assertion that the Goddess is pleased by its performance, and Durga herself is treated with the utmost reverence. She may be placed inside a satirical or humorous *pandal*, and she may be dressed or depicted in such a way as to satirize the evils of society. However, she herself is never a joke, a caricature, a misfit, or an occasion for laughter. She is always beautiful, a magnet for devotion. Moreover, she is a Goddess who must be worshipped meticulously over four days by Brahmin priests. Her tableau illustrates her puissance over evil, which is serious, solemn business. Her protection, as mother of her people, can assume nationalistic or militaristic proportions, and, in a rite many Bengalis consider fearsome, she is frequently offered the blood of goats and buffalos. If there is laughter heard at the festival, then it is due to the revelry of the occasion and the joy of one's companions, not necessarily to what one sees.

Indeed, many Bengalis are deeply critical of what they perceive to be the frivolous, facetious nature of the Pujas—even while conceding that the mania for prizes has helped uphold a high standard of artistic excellence. The year 1998 was one of many celebrities, from soccer stars to blockbuster movies. But not everyone approved of the effect of such media icons on the Pujas. "Don't expect the *asura* at *our pandal* to have muscles like Ronaldo!" challenged representatives of Ultadanga's Yubo Brinda Club in Kolkata.[14] And journalist Balarko Gooptu, in his review of the Titanic birthed in a field in Salt Lake, north of the city, asserted that it was "inappropriate" for a ship to house the Mother: "Devotion, anyone?"[15] In 2000, another *sarbajanin* club, the Young Star Club of Uttarpara, had the audacity to reject the prize it won for its *pandal*, claiming that prizes go against the spirit of the festival.[16] This critique of the Puja craze for novelty and glitz is aptly summed up in a cartoon spoof from 1999: the Goddess herself laments that she does not know what the priest is doing or saying, cannot hear the devotees' prayers for the cacophony of blaring film songs, and judges that *bhakti* fled from the land long ago if this is how the gods are treated.[17] Hence those who do the most theologizing about the Pujas appear to be its critics, those who decry the irreverence of the displays. The creativity evidenced at the Pujas is, according to this view, human silliness and folly, not reflective in any meaningful way of the Goddess's desire or approval. In an ironic twist, it may be her foreign, Western, non-Hindu "devotees" who are most apt to interpret the experience of the Pujas from a positive theological perspective; heir to a Protestant Reformation through which thrift and industry have been emphasized at the expense of laughter, excess, play, burlesque, and lampoonery (Bastien 1987, 526–29), they may find assertions about *maya*, *ananda*, and *lila* theologically stimulating.

If the Pujas are, in general, neither back-slappingly funny nor an occasion for theologizing, then in what sense can they be considered "play"? Ever since Johan Huizinga's magisterial book, *Homo Ludens: A Study of the Play Element in Culture*, it has been acknowledged that while play is pervasive in human culture, including in religious myth and ritual, it does not necessarily involve laughter (Huizinga 1938 [1955]).[18] Ritual play, or ritual levity, connotes lightness, effervescence, juissance, and the opposite of gravity and solemnity. For both Huizinga and his greatest interlocutor, Roger Caillois, play is also free, voluntary, enjoyable, limited, and separated out from "reality" in terms of time and space, unproductive of real-life wants and aspirations, and either regulated by rules (as in a game of chess) or given over to make-believe (as in a child's game with her dolls) (Caillois 1958 [2001]).[19]

Caillois further divides play into four types, two of which Huizinga had previously discussed and which are especially apropos for our example of Durga Puja. The first kind of play is the *agon*, or competition; the second is *alea*, or the game of chance; the third is mimicry, through theater or spectacle; and the last is surrender to induced intoxication, or vertigo. Regarding the first, the competitive urge, Huizinga claims that it is intimately connected to play; "the ludic function" is "inherent" in the *agon* (Huizinga 1938 [1955], 90). Rivals display their skills in arenas bounded by geography, rules, and audience members[20] and enjoy testing themselves for prizes, status, and recognition. Although too much pressure can destroy a game, combatants typically relish the tension that derives from the pleasure of risk taking (compare Caillois 1958 [2001], 173, and Huizinga 1938 [1955], 47–52). And even if the contest may involve aspects that look like real fighting, game playing is never "to the kill," because there is no pursuit or conflict outside of the space delimited for the competition (Caillois 1958 [2001], 16).[21] Both Huizinga and Caillois also note the degree to which the competitive game and the game of imitation (Caillois's first and third types) complement and overlap each other. This is particularly true when the goal of the competition is to represent something or to fascinate the spectator with its ability to "show forth" its "pretense" of reality, through ostentatious elements of mimicry (Driver 1991, 156).

It is in this context that one can consider the analog of carnival, a temporary suspension of normal life on account of the season for sacred play (Huizinga 1938 [1955], 12–13). Carnival celebrations in Spain, Brazil, Mexico, and Trinidad are strikingly similar to Durga Puja. They are (1) public, (2) voluntary, (3) enjoyable, (4) galvanize almost all of society, and (5) act as markers of national identity. Regarding this last point, consider Brazil. After 1935, when Carnival was made official, the samba schools, or rival associations for the creation of popular floats, songs, and dances, were required to enact national and heroic themes, idealizing Brazil as a generous mother country in which all peoples could live harmoniously. Since the 1960s, the festival has been taken over by the urban lower and middle classes, who have transformed it into a genuine expression of the popular national character (Goldwasser 1987, 103). Peter Mason, in his recent book on carnival in Trinidad, noted the following themes in the costumes, floats, and lyrics composed for the occasion in the mid-1990s: fantasy, outer space, insects, ghosts, vampires, government ineptitude, male/female relationships, West Indian unity, problems with the national highway, the lottery, and even haircut trends (Mason 1999).

A sixth component of carnival is the emphasis on the individual innovator, who, in association with other creative individuals over wide sections of the population, has the responsibility for organizing and paying for the masquerades, calypso, and music. According to the famed theorist of ritual, Victor Turner, anti-structure, or *communitas,* which one experiences in festival situations, is the liberation of the human capacities of cognition, volition, and creativity from normative social restraints (Turner 1974, 75). Indeed, carnival cultures are known for their participants' fierce rivalries for coveted prizes through flexing their creative muscles; thematic novelty, in which contemporary life is incorporated into the art forms created for the celebrations each year, is the key to success.

A seventh element of carnival fits less well with the Bengali case, and this is the "tension alleviation" aspect of the festival. Expressed most famously by Mikhail Bakhtin, this interpretation characterizes carnival as the resistance to official serious culture by a playful suspension of social barriers (Bakhtin 1968); theorists of carnival since Bakhtin have therefore tended to emphasize its stress-releasing function, including sexual license, role reversals, and burlesque (Driver 1991, 155; Goldwasser 1987, 103). While it is true that the Puja is loved by people in all walks of life, role reversals are rare. The organization of the Pujas is serious business, and the public, dressed in their best new clothes, is made by the police to walk in orderly lines to see the *pandal*s. Festivals of the last two centuries in rural areas are reported to have been bawdier, but now they have been largely taken over by a respectable middle-class sensibility.[22] And, although Puja committees are permitted to lampoon deplorable social conditions and even political parties, they are barred by the government from portraying anything with even the remotest potential for inflaming communal passions. For example, during the 2001 Puja season, one might have suspected that the bombing of the World Trade Center and the Pentagon in the United States would have provided ample scope for both lighting displays and creative transformations of the demon that Durga kills into bin Laden. However, such was not tolerated by the Communist state government, the CPI(M), whose cadres expressly prohibited Puja committees and artisans from creating any representation of the disaster that might stir up communal discord in the state. The implication of such proscriptions appears to be that Pujas may reflect delights, concerns, or problems common to all, but that Muslim feelings must be protected from perceived slight. This rule is also reflected in the use, or lack thereof, of explicitly Muslim symbols in Puja *pandal*s and lighting shows; I have never seen, and only once read about, an attempt to put Durga in a fabricated mosque.[23]

Yet carnival "works" as an analog insofar as it, like the Puja, is a festival ritual that acts as a field for levity and play, involving elements of both *agon*, or competition, and mimicry, or ostentatious, imitative shows of talent. Such a view of play corresponds exactly to what happens at the Puja, where the language of war pervades all aspects of the festivities. *Sarbajanin* Puja organizers freely admit that they want to clobber their competitors, and many of them employ "think tanks" to come up with new ideas. Novelty, size, the ability to confer notoriety—these are the coveted values. Organizers approach artisans and lighting experts who have won prizes in the past. They invite celebrities—politicians, authors, sportsmen, and even national figures such as Phoolan Devi and Mother Teresa—to inaugurate their Pujas. Multinationals such as Bata, Coke, Goodridge, Heinz, Hindustan Lever, Maruti, Pepsi, Phillips, Proctor & Gamble, and Whirlpool donate money to particular *pandal*s with the stipulation that they advertise their products near the gates or in recorded songs played on a loudspeaker. In the struggle to garner such company sponsorships, Puja committees defame one another, and during the celebrations they anxiously watch the papers. Who is drawing the biggest crowds? Who is giving most to charity? Who pays the biggest electric bills?

When a Puja committee wins a prize, its members proudly proceed through the streets with the trophy and then display it in the *pandal* for all to see (Figure 9.4).

To me, the most interesting type of sparring—some of it deadly—is political. After being in power uninterruptedly for nearly a quarter century, in the years just before and just after 2000 the CPI(M) was challenged by Mamata Banerjee's Trinamul Congress, or Grassroots Congress. The political rivalry was not polite and involved physical brutalities. In early 2000, for example, mutual violence, property destruction, and evictions occurred in the districts, particularly in Midnapur.

This antagonism affected the Pujas. Reacting to what she termed the "red terror," Mamata directed her Trinamul workers to aid homeless victims of the Communist backlash in Midnapur by sponsoring Pujas. And she got then Prime Minister Vajpayee to reprimand Jyoti Basu, at the time Chief Minister of the State, for the disturbances. In order to give the appearance that all was back to normal, CPI(M) cadres apparently "forced" villages under their control to hold Puja celebrations.[24]

In Kolkata, where there was posturing but little violence between Communists and Trinamul workers, *pandal*s organized by Trinamul

Figure 9.4. Prizes on display at the Tas Bospukur *pandal* at Kasba, Kolkata, Durga Puja, October 7, 2000. *(photo by author)*

members sported pictures of their leader, sold her literature, and festooned their displays with political slogans. Some of the big-budget Pujas were backed by politicians close to Mamata. They not only rivaled one another but enjoyed attempting to humiliate the "Congress Pujas"—the Congress Party being the third, and weakest, claimant for power in the state.[25]

It is noteworthy that there is no Communist Puja, no *pandal* allied with a name in the state government. This is because, strictly speaking, the Communist ideology does not permit an acknowledgment of religion, devotion, or grandiose spectacles of piety funded by the elite.[26] In the past, Communist Party members have even been publicly admonished for taking part in the Pujas. After the mid-1990s, perhaps because Jyoti Basu was nearing retirement, valued pragmatism, or desired to combat Mamata Banerjee on her own turf, he began practicing lenience and even indulgence toward the Goddess. Since 1995, I have seen newspaper articles and even photos of CPI(M) chiefs inaugurating *pandal*s, offering flowers to the Goddess, and wandering the streets of their neighborhoods, enjoying the season's delights. This is in addition to the over 4,500 seasonal book stalls, strategically placed since 1964 throughout the city, for the spread of Marxist teachings. While the new breed of liberal Communist justifies his or her behavior by claiming that the Goddess is the *shakti* of Communist rule, or that Durga Puja is a form of "social communism,[27] many others censure what they perceive to be a sellout of the party to hypocrisy, opportunism, and social pressure.[28]

The point is that Bengali goddess worship is inextricably bound up with competition, be it artistic, social, or political. Said an astute observer in 1924, noting that even Indian Christians and Brahmo Samaj reformers were moved by the festivities, "You cannot underestimate the power of Durga Puja on a Bengali!"[29]

I think, then, that one can view Durga Puja as a preeminent example of ritual levity, if one is able to retain, in "levity," an appreciation for (1) the lightheartedness and effervescent quality of the festival, as well as a recognition of (2) the seriousness and even awe-inspiring character of the Brahmanic ritual actions focused on the Goddess, and (3) the determined gravity of the fight-to-win attitude on the part of Puja *pandal* organizers. There is enjoyment, for them and their spectators, in the fray. In this sense the Bengali Pujas are well encapsulated by Caillois's descriptions of play as competition and spectacle and provide a not-perfect but close analog to the European and American phenomena of carnival.

Thus from whatever vantage point one experiences the Pujas, Durga can be said to play. For the devotee who revels in the festivities, she endorses and enables the fun, in the context of an exuberant, competitive, but only occasionally funny, spectacle. For the devoted critic of the Pujas, who feels that the Goddess's honor must be protected, the joke is on her misguided devotees, who are misled by her *maya* to think that she can be encapsulated by coarse displays of human creativity. In both of these cases, as also with the outside observer, the juxtapositions inherent in her festival play inventively on the mind.

## Notes

I am grateful to the participants and audience members of the panel on "Ritual Levity," held at the annual conference of the American Academy of Religion in Toronto, November 24, 2002, and to members of the Columbia University Seminar on Religion, on February 4, 2003, for their valuable feedback on earlier drafts of this chapter.

1. In 2000, three of Kolkata's big-budget Durga Pujas—at Sribhumi Sporting Club, Singhi Park, and Shealdah Athletic Club—each attracted 25,000 visitors per night (*Anandabajar Patrika*, October 7, 2000, p. 1).

2. Other coveted prizes are the Sarad-Siromani, the Ananda-Snosem, and a host of newcomers sponsored by big companies such as Priya Food Products or Mother Dairy, Internet groups, newspapers, and even high schools. The ordinary man or woman on the street can also be a winner—of Puja quizzes, photography contests, and Internet lotteries.

3. Although Durga Puja is the major Shakta holiday of the festival year, Pujas to Kali and Jagaddhatri follow soon after and are modeled on Durga Puja in all respects.

4. Buddhist and Christian places of worship are rare, but not unknown. In Kolkata, a replica of a Geneva church went up at Ekdaliya in 1990 and of a Goan church at Taltola in 1995; in 2000, a French Roman Catholic church was erected in Candranagar.

5. One lighting display I saw in more than one city during the 2000 Puja season depicted a little girl whose father married her to a dog earlier in the year, for fear of the bad luck in her destiny. For additional examples, in 1991, the Ramkrsna Sebak Committee bound its image of Durga in chains to symbolize the exploitation of women, and the Hari Ghos Street Puja members organized the exhibition "Take No Dowry, Give No Dowry." See *The Statesman*, October 17, 1991, p. 11, for descriptions of both.

6. In 1994, Ganesha's rat was often absent from the divine tableau because of the association of rats with the recent plague in Surat (Laxmi Prasuram, personal communication, October 11, 1994).

7. See *India Today*, October 12, 1998, pp. 66–68.

8. The following newspaper reports contain accounts and photographs of various Titanic models, at both Durga and Kali Pujas, and in areas all over

Bengal. "Jela-Saharer Pujo," in *Saptahik Bartaman*, September 26, 1998, pp. 16–19; *The Statesman*, September 30, 1998, p. 3; *Ajkal*, October 18, 1998, p. 5; *Anandabajar Patrika*, October 3, 2000, p. 12.

9. Lee Siegel summarizes the comic *rasa*, or artistic flavor, as based on incongruity and the savoring of bad taste. What makes us laugh is the hideous or deformed, the wearing of the wrong clothes, and excessive desire, audacity, trickery, lying, and criticism of others. In comedy, nothing "fits" properly (Siegel 1987, 9, 13, 29, 32).

10. See Smith 1978, 301. Smith is building here upon the classic work of Arthur Koestler, *The Act of Creation*, who explains that humor is triggered by the discovery of hidden similarities, the "sudden clash of incomparable matricies" (1964, 42).

11. Siegel 1987, 96. Siegel here is actually referring to Kali, a multiform or sister goddess of Durga. For Shankara on play, see his commentary on *Brahmasutra Bhasya* II.1.32–36. Other resources for play in the Hindu tradition are discussed by Brown 1983, Hawley 1981, Kinsley 1979, and Sax 1995.

12. See Winnicott 1971, 51–52. Jonathan Z. Smith made similar comments in his response to the session on Ritual Levity at the American Academy of Religion, November 24, 2002.

13. The Christian parallel to this theological approach to the Pujas may be the "Theology of Play" movement, according to which work done playfully is a sign of grace, where the freedom of festivity helps us reshape our image of divinity and get a foretaste of the kingdom of heaven; see Driver 1991 and Moltmann 1972. Johnston (1983, 64–71) critiques this interpretation as turning Christian play into a form of work; in general, he claims, Protestants legitimate play only insofar as it is purposeful for something beyond itself.

14. *Asian Age*, September 23, 1998, p. 20.

15. "Puja Promenade," in *The Telegraph*, September 28, 1998, p. 16.

16. *Times of India*, October 5, 2000, p. 4.

17. *Sunday Statesman*, insert "Impressions," October 31, 1999, p. 2. Other critiques are equally interesting: see the appraisal of the Kamdahari *pandal* and its demonization of Clinton and Blair (*Ajkal*, September 18, 2000, pp. 1, 5, and *Anandabajar Patrika*, October 1, 2000, p. 1); a photo of a Durga who has doves, not weapons, in her hands (*Yugantar*, October 3, 1995, p. 3); and a depiction of Durga in front of a nuclear explosion. The demon she is killing is a politician (*The Telegraph*, October 15, 1999, p. 17).

18. Ritual is a "matter of shows, representations, dramatic performances, imaginative actualizations of a vicarious nature" (Huizinga 1938 [1955], 15). A psychological perspective, not explored here, also affirms the universality of and necessity for human play; according to D. W. Winnicott (1971, 41), it is a therapist's job to bring the patient to a state of being able to play, for play enables group relationships and communication.

19. Caillois distinguishes between what he calls the *paidia*, or active, tumultuous, exuberant, and spontaneous element of play, and the *ludus*, or calculated, contrived, and rule-oriented element. Yet even within a game, he says, there is always freedom to act *within* the rules (1958 [2001], 27–35).

20. All four of Caillois's play types presuppose not solitude but human company, in the form of either an audience or a rival.

21. Gregory Bateson (1972, 177–93) makes the same point about playful behavior, that the actions of play look like those of "not play" in the context of his behavioral studies with primates.

22. Maria Goldwasser (1987, 100–101) makes this same point about restrictions of the European carnival after the Middle Ages, when, she says "the trend everywhere was to discipline Carnival, restricting the extremes of its licentiousness and violence, while encouraging its artistic aspects." As a result of the Romantic movement, the following centuries saw a beautification of Carnival, with carriages, parades, floats, and fancy-dress balls taking center stage. For a similar argument about the demise of humor, satire, and earthy farce in Western religious contexts, due in part to the Protestant Reformation, see Cox 1969.

23. This was the Vivekananda Sporting Club of north Kolkata, which in 1991 desired to promote communal harmony by designing its pandal as a three-in-one (church, temple, and mosque).

24. See *Bartaman*, September 14, 2000, p. 3, and *Anandabajar Patrika*, October 7, 2000, p. 7.

25. For overview articles on the contests between these *pandal*s and their organizers, see *Pratidin*, September 12, 2000, p. 3; Wednesday, September 13, 2000, p. 3; September 24, 2000, p. 3.

26. Arun Shourie (1998) surveys Bengali public school textbooks expressing the Communist opinion of religion as an instrument of the ruling class to perpetuate its hegemony. For example, on p. 73 he cites *Itihas o Bhugal*, Pt. II (West Bengal Bidyalay Siksa Adhikar, 1975), pp. 25-26, meant for class IV students, where Pujas are criticized for their inception by kings and landlords; on p. 157 he quotes D. N. Jha, *Ancient India, An Introductory Outline* (New Delhi: Manohar, 1977, 1997), p. xviii, who says, "*bhakti* is just the reflection of the complete dependence of the serfs or tenants on the landowners in the context of Indian feudal society."

27. See *Anandabajar Patrika*, October 3, 1995, pp. 1, 3, and *The Statesman*, September 30, 1998, p. 3, respectively.

28. For two sarcastic and plaintive laments on the departure of current Communist ideology from its origins, refer to Raghab Bandyopadhyay, "Bangla Mahisamardini Banam Marks-bahini," in *Des* 65:24 (September 19, 1998): 59–62; Partha Mukhopadhyay in an article for *Pratidin*, October 27, 2000, p. 3.

29. *The Bengalee*, October 5, 1924, p. 6.

## Works Cited

Bakhtin, Mikhail. 1968. *Rabelais and His World*. Translated by Helene Iswolsky. Cambridge, MA: M. I. T. Press.

Bastien, Joseph W. 1987. "Humor and Satire." In *The Encyclopedia of Religion*, ed. Mircea Eliade, 6: 526–29. 16 vols. New York: Macmillan.

Bateson, Gregory. 1972. "A Theory of Play and Fantasy." In *Steps to an Ecology of Mind*, 177–93. New York: Ballantine Books.

Brown, C. Mackenzie. 1983. "Kali, the Mad Mother." In *The Book of the Goddess, Past and Present: An Introduction to Her Religion*, ed. Carl Olson, 110–23. New York: Crossroad.

Caillois, Roger. 1958 [2001]. *Man, Play and Games*. Translated by Meyer Barash. Urbana: University of Illinois Press.

Cox, Harvey. 1969. *The Feast of Fools: A Theological Essay on Feast and Fantasy*. Cambridge, MA: Harvard University Press.

Driver, Tom E. 1991. *The Magic of Ritual: Our Need for Liberating Rites that Transform Our Lives and Our Communities*. San Francisco: Harper San Francisco.

Goldwasser, Maria Julia. 1987. "Carnival." In *The Encyclopedia of Religion*, ed. Mircea Eliade, 3: 98–104. 16 vols. New York: Macmillan.

Hawley, John Stratton, with Shrivatsa Goswami. 1981. *At Play with Krishna: Pilgrimage Dramas from Brindavan*. Princeton, NJ: Princeton University Press.

Huizinga, Johan. 1938 [1955]. *Homo Ludens: A Study of the Play Element in Culture*. Boston, MA: Beacon Press.

Johnston, Robert K. 1983. *The Christian at Play*. Grand Rapids, MI: William B. Eerdmans.

Kinsley, David R. 1979. *Divine Player: A Study of Krsna Lila*. Delhi: Motilal Banarsidass.

Koestler, Arthur. 1964. *The Act of Creation*. New York: Macmillan.

Mason, Peter. 1999. *Bacchanal! The Carnival Culture of Trinidad*. Philadelphia, PA: Temple University Press.

Moltmann, Jurgen. 1972. *Theology of Play*. Translated by Reinhard Ulrich. New York: Harper & Row.

Sax, William Sturman, ed. 1995. *Gods at Play: Lila in South Asia*. New York: Oxford University Press.

Shourie, Arun. 1998. *Eminent Historians: Their Technology, Their Line, Their Fraud*. New Delhi: ASA.

Siegel, Lee. 1987. *Laughing Matters: The Comic Tradition in India*. Chicago, IL: University of Chicago Press.

Smith, Jonathan Z. 1978. *Map Is Not Territory: Studies in the History of Religions*. Chicago, IL: University of Chicago Press.

Turner, Victor. 1974. "Liminal to Liminoid, in Play, Flow, and Ritual: An Essay in Comparative Symbology." In *The Anthropological Study of Human Play*, ed. Edward Norbeck, 53–92. Houston, TX: William March Rice University.

Winnicott, D. W. 1971. *Playing and Reality*. London and New York: Routledge.

# 10

# Turning Karbala Inside Out

## *Humor and Ritual Critique in South Asian Muharram Rites*

Amy C. Bard

In recent years, I have been pursuing an interest in how religious rituals encode and construct emotional complexity. I have found the notion of "emotional texture," the ways "intricate contours [of varying emotions over time] . . . are experienced by a variety of actors," to be particularly useful for thinking about both the choreography and the complexity of ritual as it is lived on the ground.[1] Here I use the idea of emotional texture to launch an inquiry into levity in popular South Asian Shi'ism. As in many ritual settings, joking and play amidst Shi'i commemorations of Imam Husain's martyrdom at Karbala in 680 C.E./61 A.H. can both signal and diffuse social friction among gender, language, and sectarian groups.[2] What is of special interest in these Shi'i rites, known as *Muharram* (also the name of a month), is that levity also points up powerful values and lessons that are more overtly linked to impassioned expressions of grief and mourning. This chapter focuses on how levity—particularly as expressed by women—dramatizes representations and experiences of tragedy, whether in the Shi'i mourning assembly (known as the *majlis e 'aza* or *majlis*), in informal oral commentaries on the *majlis*, or in interactions among different religious groups around broader *Muharram* observances.[3] The range of contexts explored, from internally or domestically oriented settings to more diverse, public ones, reveals ritual structures that guide communal action but allow considerable scope for individual navigation of emotional expression.

Critiques offered through play and joking can shape a community's understanding of (and their debates over) fundamental ritual effectiveness. A successful mourning assembly, for example, allows the mourner to touch or communicate with the Prophet's family (the *ahl-e bait*), and to earn merit (*savab*) through weeping, but not all *majlis*-goers will agree on the mix of components that brings about these goals. Joking—or even mocking—related to the quality of *majlis* performances can illuminate the varying ways in which participants assess mourning rituals. Standards for aesthetics, textual authority, the perceived authenticity of local tradition, or social/political relations in rituals can also be addressed through humor. Finally, the festive *jashn*s (celebrations) that follow the mourning season, with their overtly ludic elements, their abrupt inversion of mourning proprieties, form a sort of postscript, a final commentary on the long period of austerity that the pious observe. Humorous acts associated with *Muharram* mourning, then, are frequently linked to processes of ritual assessment and ritual criticism.

The Shi'i mourning assemblies held in India and Pakistan during *Muharram* are best known for the tears that participants shed over Imam Husain, a grandson of the Prophet Muhammad. Intense devotion to Husain and other spiritual leaders of the Prophet's lineage (*imam*s), notably Husain's father, Ali, marks a significant difference between Shi'i Muslims and Sunni Muslims (who are by far the majority in South Asia and in the world). The division between Sunnis and Shiahs harkens back to the early days of Islam when factions of Muslims supported either the first Caliph, Abu Bakr, or Ali, the Prophet's son-in-law and cousin, as leader after the Prophet's demise in 632 C.E./13 A.H. The actual emergence of Shi'i and Sunni sects was a gradual process, during which followers of various *imam*s, all descendants of Ali and the Prophet's daughter, Fatimah, also branched off from the main group of partisans ("Shiah") of Ali. Sunnis hold Abu Bakr, Umar, and Usman, the first three Caliphs and close companions of the Prophet, in extremely high esteem. Shiahs, in contrast, revere Ali, the first *imam*, and his descendants as legitimate and divinely guided successors to the Prophet who may wield intercessory powers on behalf of the devout. These sacrosanct personages are seen by Shiahs as having been denied their rightful role by the three Caliphs, their supporters, and other enemies within the Muslim community over the centuries.

Remembrance of Ali, Ali's son, Imam Husain, and his family, and the other *imam*s dominates Shi'i religious life. This is so on the levels of everyday observances (e.g., weekly mourning assemblies, pleas to the *imams* to protect travelers) and of major ritual events, namely, *Muharram majlis*es and processions. The implications of Shi'i devotion to "the people of the household," the Prophet's family, are hardly minor, and their mourning practices, surnames, or tendency to wear particular gemstones can render Shiahs readily identifiable. Despite Shi'i-Sunni antagonism (including a Sunni tendency to read Shi'i reverence for the imams as a sinful equation of humans with Allah) and the exacerbation of religious differences in politically tense environments, however, the two communities share a great deal as Muslims. This generally extends to a deep respect for Husain and his submission to God. The emphatic, artistic elaboration of Husain's story has, for the most part, been the province of Shiahs.

*Majlis* poetry, sermons, and relics all memorialize Husain's unwavering sacrifices: the *imam* forfeited his life, the lives of his dearest kin, and his women's dignified seclusion when he might have been spared by pledging fealty to the Ummayad Caliph Yazid. Yazid, as portrayed in Shi'i sources, was the ultimate usurper (his father had displaced Husain's brother Hasan), cruel despot, and impious Muslim. The Husain-Yazid conflict, in the Shi'i view, is far more than a battle over temporal power; it marks a timeless struggle in which *Husainiyat*, or Husain-ness, signifies all that is truly Islamic and virtuous, in opposition to the evil, hypocritical force of *Yazidiyat*.

Despite Imam Husain's foreknowledge of the tragic fate that awaited him, he heeded the call of Muslims who opposed Yazid to confer with them in Kufah, setting out from Medinah with his family and fewer than 100 men. He halted in Mecca, whence he is said to have departed on the eighth of the month of Zilhaj in 680 C.E./60 A.H. Within a month, Yazid's army had ambushed the small party en route to Kufah, denying them access to the Euphrates. A selection from a marsiyah, one of the poetic forms recited in the mourning assembly, recounts how the *imam* watched in agony as blistering heat and thirst tormented his women and children, among them six-month-old Asghar and five-year-old Sakinah:

> But the bird of fortune above the most blessed of men
> had limp, dejected wings
> For him there was no grain and no water—save tears—to
> be found
> Sakinah and Asghar were both reduced by thirst to the
> same pitiful state
> Their countenances jaundiced, lips bluish, tongues dry,
> and eyes red

He cried "milk, milk" through his weeping and gesturing
She cried out for "water, water" to Zahra's darling[4]

As if this were not enough to suffer, Husain then mourned each of the sons, nephews, and friends slain after valiant battles against the massive enemy forces. Once Husain himself was killed, his single surviving son, an invalid, and his unveiled, distraught womenfolk marched as captives to Damascus. At the front of this sorry procession of the now-ragged progeny of the Prophet, and ever in their view, was the *imam*'s decapitated head, borne aloft on a pike.

On one level, then, *Muharram*'s public processional rites reenact Karbala's own processions of fighters (before the battle) and of captives (after it). Non-Shi'i observers are generally less familiar with mourning assemblies than with such processions. *Majlis*es are conducted in Shi'i homes or in halls dedicated to the memory of the *imam*s and members of the Prophet's family (*imambarah*s), while processions, with their largely male participants, engage spectators with the pageantry of glittering tomb replicas, blood-stained and riderless horses, and penitents in chains. Dashes of acerbic humor emerge sharply in the comparatively private, gender-segregated realm of women's rituals, which are social as well as religious high points of the year.[5] Spontaneous laughter, subtle jokes that drive home lessons, competitive, comical parodies, and mocking play, though not prominent, are part and parcel of commemorations themselves, while outside of the ritual forum, participants may at times engage in joking about Muharram rites.

Highly structured mourning assemblies for Husain take place for over sixty days during the months of Muharram, Safar, and Rabi 'ul awwal. The most intense days are those leading up to and including the tenth of Muharram, the date Husain was slain while he paused on the battlefield for prayers. Shi'i women in South Asia initiate their assemblies by reciting Quranic verses and traditions about the crucial guiding role of the Prophet's family, after which a succession of reciters expresses tribute and lament in *soz*, *salam*, and *marsiyah* poetry. Variants of this poetry have been recited in India, probably first in the Deccan region, since at least the sixteenth century C.E., but the genres reached their literary peak in the Shi'i-ruled kingdom of Avadh (especially in Faizabad and Lucknow) in the nineteenth century. In a sermon that follows the poetry, a female lay preacher (*zakirah*, *hadiskhvan*) develops a theme such as the importance of a specific revered figure (for example, Fatimah the Prophet's daughter), or the implications of a term such as "action" (*'amal*), in Islamic living.

Lessons about righteous living and Islamic authority, many of them applicable to Muslims generally, pervade the mourning assembly, but the event culminates with orations that appeal to Shi'i beliefs in particular. Toward the end of the sermon, for instance, the preacher generally summons listeners to Husain's death site, the desert battlefield of Karbala, moving them to wails and sobs by recalling a specific hero or heroine and the particular atrocities visited upon them. She may draw on any of hundreds of episodes: the sobbing Husain carrying the bloodied but still beauteous bodies of his sons back to the women's tent, or the *imam*'s sister exhorting her two sons to fight to the death, though their hands are too small to grasp the battle standard they long to carry for Husain. Or the preacher might instead dwell on the bonds and shackles chafing the limbs of this same sister, Zainab, when she is a captive, or on the vicious enemy soldier who slaps Husain's five-year-old daughter and bloodies her ears by yanking the ornaments from them.

Metrical dirges called *nauhah*s follow the sermon and are accompanied by breast-beating and impassioned cries of "Ya Husain!" A symbolic visitation to the martyrs through a *ziyarat* chant, prayers, and the recitation of the Quranic *Surah-e Fatiha* closes the assembly.[6] *Majlis*es differ somewhat from region to region, but this basic format holds for the assemblies of most Urdu speakers. The events are also, excepting small household observances for family members, gender segregated. Women may generally listen to and perhaps watch men's *majlis*es from the upper floors of an *imambarah*, or from curtained areas, but boys under age seven or eight accompanying their female relatives are the only males permitted into a women's (*zenani*) *majlis*.

A vignette from a Karachi *majlis* sermon will give an indication of how mourning for Husain—and participants' identification with (female) mourners in the Karbala narrative—is the crux of an assembly. Aliya Imam, the erudite, educated preacher, describes Imam Husain's sister Zainab, bereft at Karbala, while on the battlefield lie the blood-soaked corpses of fine young men, all her beloved kin:

> Oh, mourners (for Husain), I beg another minute of your indulgence. A dead silence has shrouded the battlefield of Karbala. Now, when Zainab had called out, when the caravan left Medinah, then the whole group was together. But today we're at a place, we're at a point where when Zainab calls out, alone, no one is about. Mourners, it's human nature to seek out support when terror grasps the heart, but . . . 'Abbas [Zainab's brother, the army standard-bearer] is nowhere,

> Husain is nowhere, Ali Akbar [Husain's son, raised by Zainab], Aun and Muhammad [Zainab's own young sons] are nowhere to be seen.[7]

Dr. Imam's trembling, stricken sobs and plaintive gestures at this concluding point in the *majlis* contrast sharply with her composure and authoritative bearing during the earlier, lecturelike portion of her sermon. In fact, the orator's demeanor as she progresses through the sermon recalls both the stately defiance and the haunted desperation of Zainab herself during the Karbala tragedy. Zainab ultimately survives her horror and grief largely because of the leadership role she must take on. The very isolation that desolates her instills in her the toughness to defend the other female survivors, act as regent for Husain's ailing son, the next *imam*, and carry the history of Karbala: she is the only one left to lead.

Given this scene, part of the "torments" (*masa'ib*) of the Karbala heroes and heroines, it is obvious why most literature on *Muharram* does not dwell on humor. Within the *majlis* itself, open, extended merriment is of course frowned upon, since the main criterion for a successful assembly is the eliciting of salvific tears, but low-key humor can spontaneously surface now and again. If a child, quivering with enthusiasm, unexpectedly cries out "*N'arah-e Haidari*!"—a prompt hailing the Prophet's son-in-law that requires all assembled to respond "*Ya Ali!*"—no one bothers to smother her indulgent chuckles. The timing may be awkward, but such avidity on the part of a young girl signifies the imitation of her elders' pious behavior.

Actions or utterances meant to be somber that strike a participant as humorous, however, can make for intense discomfort in the usually cramped confines of the *majlis*. Kulsum, a young mother from Hyderabad, India, remembered how shortly after she married into a prominent Lucknow family she found herself forced to hurriedly exit a *majlis*: the unfamiliar Lucknow-style poetry recitations moved her to helpless laughter instead of tears. Although *majlis*es everywhere share the Karbala narrative with its resonant themes of oppression, temporal defeat, moral victory, and sacrifice and devotion to family and Allah, many women have a tale or two about painful attempts to restrain laughter and maintain propriety in assemblies with customs and aesthetic tones that are regionally or linguistically foreign to them.

Calculated uses of levity by preachers, in contrast, can relax the assembly's properly solemn mood only to build it up again. Sometimes the preacher will use a half-joking tone to chide her listeners; one Lahore preacher, Dr. Musavi, argued that executing five daily prayers should come as naturally as breathing, and that the ability to perform them is a gift from God. "But," she said, "you all say to me, 'Oh madam, I strike my head on the ground five times a day!' as if you're doing God the favor!" She interspersed such comments throughout: "I'm not one to name names, but someone here complained that to me that *I* make Islam 'too difficult' for her with my answers to her questions about right and wrong. Well, don't forget, I'm in the same boat as you are."[8]

A preacher can also manipulate anticipation, emotional highs and lows, and sudden transitions by concluding a complicated, serious lesson with a brisk punch line that confirms the infallibility of the *imams*. Short selections of poetry that employ multivalent symbols or wordplay to praise the Prophet's family also serve as a medium for such lessons, or for proclaiming Shi'i difference and pride with a tinge of sarcasm at the expense of Sunnis.[9] For example, in a May 1997 sermon, a theatrical young Pakistani preacher whom I will call "Zahra" moved almost without pause from a poem reaffirming the declaration of faith that all Muslims share to this one that points up the tensions between orthodox Sunnis and Shiahs, with their special devotion to the Prophet and his family:

> Should someone ask "Who is Muhammad?" what shall I say by way of explanation?
> Should someone ask—
> "Who is Muhammad?" what shall I say by way of explanation?
> My intellect is stunned; God knows what I should say
> If I say, "God," I'll be afraid of being a heretic[10]
> And I'll have misgivings about being an infidel if I declare him apart from God

This last line could also be rendered in English as "And I'll have misgivings about being an infidel if I say that which is other than the truth." In Urdu, the two possibilities spice up the quatrain so that it delivers a key message about the unique status of the Prophet with a clever, just slightly amusing touch. It also manages to retain enough ambiguity while doing so to avoid making a blatantly unorthodox statement.

This strategic space for humor and virtuosity in the earlier portions of the sermon invigorates the *majlis*'s allusions and analogies, formulaic narrative tropes, and transitions between all-too-human and divine levels. It also serves to set up and set apart the recounting of

Husain's torments and the intensely focused mourning at the end of the *majlis*. But such rhetorical strategies are not merely gently funny diversions that retain the passive attention of a *majlis* "audience"; more than listeners, *majlis* attendees are participants, willing to (and expected to) chime in to complete lines of poetry, augment the preacher's words with slogans and praise of the *imams*, and respond audibly and visibly to her testimony.

*Majlis*-goers also react to the sermon and the assembly outside of the formal *majlis* context. Informal conversations held in between the several assemblies a day that many Shi'i women attend show how strongly notions of ritual effectiveness are influenced by language, class, and gender. A number of women, for example, expressed wonderment that *majlis*es conducted in a language or regional style other than their own could stimulate any mourning at all. Rahat of Lahore forbade me from going to attend a *Saraiki*-language *majlis,* because "you could listen for hours and never shed a tear!"[11] Sufiya, a professional poetry reciter in Lucknow, laughed that Hyderbadi *majlis* performers were skilled but recited far too quickly and stridently to elicit tears. Many younger *majlis*-goers, in their turn, found Sufiya's traditional Lucknow-style recitation to be old-fashioned, retained more for its nostalgic value than for its aesthetic appeal. This style features a wailing melismatic chant by a group or by a main reciter supported by vocal accompanists who produce a drone and then chime in on certain verse lines. In Pakistan, too, the younger generation takes far more interest in the short, lively *nauhah* poems at the end of the assembly than in the *marsiyah*. The generation of migrants that brought Lucknow-style recitation to Pakistan after Partition in 1947, exemplified by the late Kajjan Begam (a well-known classical singer, and reportedly a relative of Sufiya's), is passing away.

Two teenage sisters of my acquaintance in Lahore's old city, though they take the Karbala tragedy deeply to heart, also enjoy delivering campy interpretations of Lucknow-style *majlis* poetry. The girls find the drone produced by the vocal accompanists—a technique referred to with the verb *as lagana*—especially peculiar and unconducive to mourning. "Is that what you mean by *as lagana*?" they asked me, after a few minutes of mimicry and uncontrollable giggling. "That's what the *bhaiyya log* [people whose families emigrated to Pakistan from Uttar Pradesh, India, at Partition] do." The girls' send-up left no doubt that *bhaiyya log* are insular and out of date, and also hinted at how the dominance of the Lucknow idiom in *majlis* performances can irk Shiahs from elsewhere in the subcontinent. Many residents of Lahore and Multan in Pakistan and Hyderabad in India suggested that the attention given to Lucknow poets and reciters tended to obscure other distinctive regional traditions of poetry.

The *majlis* sermon, too, with its intense, emotional content and rhetorical flourishes, can provide fodder for mockery. The preacher's success hinges on an impressive recall of scripture, poetry, and popular religious anecdotes, on her acting ability, charisma, and skill at building a complex and cohesive sermon. Her performance incorporates the tensions of artistic pleasure, goals to be accomplished (educating the audience and moving them to tears), and, arguably, like competitive play, "a testing of the player's prowess . . . courage, tenacity, resources and last but not least, spiritual powers."[12] Most orators sprinkle their sermons with formulaic statements of humility, dedicating and attributing their power to move listeners to Allah, but mobilize charisma and pride to meet their performative goals, and they can thus be drawn into competition with other preachers. Just as listeners dissect sermons after a *majlis*, preachers themselves are often very eager to hear listeners' impressions of other preachers. When I lived in a lay preacher's home in Lucknow, she regularly asked me to rate the abilities of other speakers from far and near and to compare their orations with her own.

In assessments of sermons, then, and in the lectures themselves, competition gives an edge to the drama of playacting and other joking "play." When women evaluate sermons, tensions can emerge around how the preacher portrays Husain and his supporters; is it best to employ restrained, "historically believable" descriptions or imaginative, moving portraits of Husain's small children thirsting to death or being beaten by Yazid's henchmen? Urban Shiahs of both sexes often urged me to listen to sermons prepared by "qualified" male preachers (*zakir*s), for fear that uneducated speakers, and women especially, might embarrassingly represent the community with "sentimentalized" renderings of questionable propriety.

Parodies of *majlis* lectures provide entertainment and comic relief but also underline that Shi'i women hardly share one view of what constitutes a good or proper sermon. Some reform-minded *majlis*-goers feel that they can most responsibly conduct a *majlis* by reading lectures from pamphlets prepared by famous male clerics. Outside of the assembly, these women sometimes invoke the model of men's more edifying sermons by parodying presumptuous, arrogant female preachers with little formal religious knowledge. A charismatic, up-and-coming female orator in Lahore, for example, was caustically mocked on occasion by older, conservative women for her exuberance and the license she took with popular anecdotes about the *imam*s and other revered personages.

In direct contrast, others see in the exclusively female preserve of the *majlis* an opportunity to enjoy an authoritative, but accessible, sermon and to creatively address topics such as requirements for veiling and seclusion (*pardah*), the importance of revered female figures, including Hazrat Fatimah and Hazrat Zainab, and women's educational goals. These *majlis* participants may in turn complexify the idealization of male authority in their commentaries by spoofing preachers who parrot male role models. And preachers who develop a distinct oratorical—at times almost conversational—style for female constituencies may be among the first to criticize other lay preachers who adopt the hectoring tone or thundering delivery of male preachers. One Lucknow orator told me that this latter style was an unfortunate Pakistani contagion that had caught on in some quarters of Lucknow. This woman based a wickedly funny parody of a sermon on her rival's affectation of a "male" style that seemed pompous and inauthentic in the women's *majlis*.

The combination of Karbala's tragic and salvific force with very circumscribed subject matter seems to contribute to competition among those who relate the narrative, and also to debates over the proper balance of humility and orators' pride in their skill, and to the play of humor and sobriety in versions of the tale. Chelkowski and Dabashi, among others, have pointed out that the Karbala tragedy, with its basic opposition of good and evil, has a broad explanatory power that extends beyond the actual ritual space.[13] A righteous, doomed hero can be associated with Husain, a heartless tyrant with Yazid, and the more intimate one's knowledge of their encounter, the more potent and textured the Karbala symbology. The mourning assembly's passionate renderings of struggle against tremendous odds certainly captured the political imagination of Indian nationalists in the 1930s and 1940s, for example, and of Iranian revolutionaries in the 1970s.[14]

Within households, though, the stark opposition between Husain and Yazid can be invoked in decidedly pedestrian ways. I once heard Sadaf, a female college student from Lahore, respond to a frenetic male cousin's incessant interruptions with a half-exasperated, half-amused cry of "Stop harassing me—you, you, Yazid, you!!!" Wielding the names of the revered Karbala figures so casually and humorously might seem to run the risk of trivializing a great moral lesson, but the practice indicates just how deep their associations run in everyday life.

As a preface to broadening the scope of our discussion to examine the role of humor and performative play in interactions between Shiahs and other religious communities, I note that flagellants' processions, mourning assemblies, and the display and burial of *taziyah*s (elaborate replicas, usually paper or wooden, of Husain's tomb) have acted as catalysts for both multi-community participation and communal polarization during *Muharram*.[15] Scholars have extensively documented Hindu, Buddhist, and Sunni Muslim participation in processions for Husain and related rites in locations as far-flung as Ladakh, Bangladesh, and Trinidad.[16] Just as prominent, however, are Shi'i-Sunni Muslim tensions that erupt, during *Muharram*, into sectarian massacres in Pakistan, and lengthy curfews in Lucknow. Observers from the nineteenth-century diarists Fanny Parkes and Mrs. Meer Hassan Ali to Rudyard Kipling, as well as present-day journalists, have made much of the perceived potential of *Muharram* processions, with their bloody self-flagellation, to ignite a volatile mix of religious tensions and "mob mentality."[17] Since the colonial period, sites as disparate as Lucknow, Hyderabad (India), Udaipur, Lahore, and Karachi have seen bloodshed during Muharram, whether the violence exploits Muslim on Muslim (that is, Shi'i versus Sunni) or Hindu versus Muslim antagonism. Practices that are felt to represent the Indianization or Hinduization of *Muharram* rites—including petitionary prayers before *taziyah*s, drumming, and the celebratory trappings of the pre-battle wedding of one of the Karbala martyrs—have also become problematic for those Shiahs who might rather look to much earlier, less flamboyant commemorations, or to contemporary Iran, for "reformist" cultural models.

One phenonenon that emerges against this backdrop is joking commentary that highlights certain aspects of *Muharram* as entertainingly exotic. In many cases Shiahs and non-Shiahs alike can graphically detail the distinctive practices of physical mourning, or *matam*, practiced by specific classes and communities. This is especially true in cases where more elaborate public *Muharram* observances have faded away over the last several decades but are remembered fondly by the older generation. Residents of Lucknow's old city now in their sixties recalled with a mixture of amusement and admiration the dramatic self-flagellation practiced by lower-class groups such as sweeperesses and Afro-Indians. Some of today's forms of *matam* maintain this capability to simultaneously awe and entertain: in *tyublit ka matam* ("tubelight *matam*"), for example, mourners in procession crack fluorescent lights over their heads. Given such practices, it is hardly surprising that a gullible Lucknow resident would believe a prankster's report that in a faraway corner of town Shi'i cooks beat themselves with bunches of spinach in a rite called *sag ka matam*. (Part of the entertainment value of this false rite's description lies in its verbal echo of a real custom, *ag ka matam*, in which participants walk on burning coals but experience no pain because of their devotion to the *imam*.)

Yet in many areas *Muharram* practices are also felt to be so familiar to members of all religious communities that they are intrinsically woven into the fabric of Indian and Pakistani life. Karbalas, the locations where *taziyah*s are buried each year, take their name from Husain's death site, and many non-Shiahs know just where their town "Karbala" is, even if they are hazy on the actual events of the tragedy. A gentleman named Manoj in the North Indian hill town of Almora reported in 1998 that *Muharram* was observed because the Shiahs' beloved king was killed by Muhammad, and when asked if he knew where the event had taken place, he replied, gesturing toward the neighborhood *taziyah* burial ground, "Yeah, it's right over there."

Such locally rooted understandings of *Muharram* trouble some in the Shi'i community, even as they laugh at them. Other pious Shiahs simply say that if outsiders revere Husain's suffering and ultimate moral victory, then the details are of minor import. Also, the notion that "Karbala is right here in my town" might be taken in the spirit of an oft-repeated saying of the sixth imam, "Every day is 'Ashura' (the day of Husain's death), and every land is Karbala."[18] The slogan invokes the moral importance of Husain's tragedy in daily life, challenging listeners to behave righteously, unlike some of Husain's early supporters, who abandoned him.

Much of the interaction between Sunnis and Shiahs related to public *Muharram* rites, or to the *majlis*, has, as noted, a more bitter flavor, even when it is tinged with humor. The celebrations that mark the end of *Muharram* mourning on the ninth of *Rabi 'ul awwal*—which are not by any means endorsed by all Shiahs—bring both laughter and communal conflict to the fore and incorporate play more directly than do verbal humor in the *majlis*, parodies, or jokes about *Muharram*. The most overtly ludic dimension of *Muharram*, these festivities (*jashn*s) bring a period of somber privation to a tempestuous end, but their volatility reaps censure from reform-minded Shiahs, as well as from outsiders.

Ninth of *Rabi 'ul awwal* celebrations follow *majlis*es for the martyrdom of the eleventh Shi'i *imam*, Hasan Askari, on the previous day. The origin of these rites, now sometimes known as *Eid-e Zahra*, or *Eid-e Shuja*, and the historical process of their elaboration, are harder to document than are those for specific martyrdom commemorations during the actual *Muharram* observances.[19] Certainly the date signals the closure of a long mourning season during which bright clothes, extravagant purchases, music, and overt celebrations are all inappropriate.[20] Pious Shiahs now resume their less restricted lifestyles, following a tradition that holds that the Prophet's family itself shed its mourning garb on the ninth. The transition from *Muharram* in Lucknow, with entire streets draped in black, to a burst of festive red and orange outfits, feasting, fireworks, and mockery is an emotional and a sudden one that virtually explodes in neighborhoods such as the one I'll call "Mahaganj."[21] Some attribute the celebratory significance of the ninth of *Rabi 'ul awwal* to the enthronement of the twelfth and final *imam* after the death of his father Hasan Askari on the eighth. The special quality of this twelfth leader, the *imam e-zaman* ("the *imam* of the age"), is that he will reappear on earth as the savior (*Mahdi*), signaling a new and glorious era for true believers.

The carnivalesque mood of these celebrations has a particular edge, though, because of a belief that holds that Umar, the second Muslim Caliph, reviled by Shiahs for his treatment of Husain's father Ali, died on the ninth of *Rabi 'ul awwal*. The day's events feature rather coarse poems that often share melodic settings with the shorter genres of *majlis* poetry but have the express purposes of denouncing Umar and reveling in his death. These bits of doggerel that label the Caliph a "thief" and an "animal" reap condemnation from many Shiahs, not to mention Sunnis who revere Umar. Debates over their crudity probably account in some part for the relatively limited information about the celebration given by Shi'i religious organizations.[22] In Lucknow, residents from a number of heavily Shi'i enclaves (such as the part of Ghazi Mandi in the old city where I resided) pointedly avoid these festivities, or observe a toned-down version of them very quietly. Social class affiliations (or aspirations) mold the distaste some have for the trappings of the most lavish *jashn*s, which are replete with dancing girls, music, and makeup, while others may simply find the cursing of Umar and the accompanying ribaldry unnecessarily inflammatory. The preacher in whose home I lived thought it important for me to witness the events of the ninth in Mahaganj but refused to attend herself.[23]

A final fillip to the drama and distinctively South Asian character of this observance is its culmination with the burning of a towering, oafish image of "Umar." In Mahaganj, this effigy or "puppet" (*putla*) was seven or eight stories high and took half the day to make. It resembled closely the images of Ravana, the demon enemy slain by the Hindu Lord Rama, which are filled with firecrackers so as to erupt into flame to celebrate the victory of good over evil during Hindu festivals in the autumn.

The giant, bearded monstrosity is a clear focal point for emotional energy directed against the enemies of Ali and Husain, an energy forceful enough, paradoxically, to encompass several anti-Shi'i figures. This leaves a little ambiguity about the exact identity of the evil effigy.

Many might say the *putla* to be set alight was not Umar the Caliph but 'Umr Ibn Sa'd, the enemy general who orchestrated the Karbala encounter. Several of those preparing for the Mahaganj celebration in 1998 reported that the image represented Shimr (a warrior from Yazid's forces popularly believed to be responsible for administering the deathblow to Husain) or a conglomeration of Shimr and Caliph Umar. The poems and commentary of the *jashn* and the people who had the most long-standing, direct involvement with its organization, though, tended to confirm that it was Caliph Umar (and thus, for Sunnis, a more troubling target for symbolic violence).

Some families who did not attend the mass celebration built small-scale Umar effigies from old cans, wire, and paper behind the walls of their residences. These comical, almost robotlike figures burned within a few minutes, while the public destruction of the massive Mahaganj Umar took only slightly longer but occasioned clapping, cheering, and hilarity from the teeming crowd packed into an enclosed space just off of the streets. The profusion of firecrackers and color naturally proved exciting entertainment for the many young children on the scene.

At the center of the frenetic fun, which built gradually throughout the day, was a group dressed as bride, groom, and members of a marriage party. A local woman gleefully commented to me that the next day's paper would read, "Yesterday, Caliph Umar was killed at a wedding." This convergence of death and themes of marriages, fertility, and auspiciousness startlingly inverts similar pairings that occur throughout *Muharram* commemorations. In the martyrological poetry of Karbala, the hero's death (as in the *'urs* of a Sufi saint or in some medieval Hindu devotional poetry) marks his union with the divine and so can be dubbed a "wedding." Husain's nephew Qasim, "the bridegroom of Karbala," dies trampled and bloodied on the battlefield in his red celebratory garb, wedding the divine the day after his earthly marriage. In the festivities of the ninth too (Umar's) death is a "celebration," but, lacking the intermixture of mourning and joy that points up the valor and virtue of the Karbala heroes, it becomes an emphatically playful celebration.[24] Here death is *cause* for celebration, and the play is deadly serious, one might say.

The revelry of the ninth, the processions and counter-processions on particular days during which Shiahs curse the first three Caliphs while Sunnis honor them, and the initial days of *majlis*es and *Muharram* processions are all potential sectarian flashpoints that punctuate the lengthy mourning season. In Lahore in 1997 (and during a number of years since), and in Lucknow throughout the late 1970s, 1980s, and 1990s, Shi'i-Sunni *Muharram* confrontations spilled over into ongoing conflicts, with the predictable response of curfews and restrictions on processions imposed by local and state authorities. Despite so much insecurity and acrimony, Shiahs often acknowledge, in a good-natured way, outsiders' stereotypes about the intensity (or sometimes the inauthenticity) of feeling invested in mourning practices. Even zealous *majlis*-goers may laugh at their own fervor, at the inability of others to comprehend it, and at the whole situation.

This tolerant amusement is evident even during the worst of years, and it again problematizes popular (and scholarly) assumptions that Shi'i participants find everything related to *Muharram* unremittingly lachrymose, or that sectarian hatred is relentless and unyielding. For example, Sayyid Baqir Ahmad Shamsi of Lahore, an elderly Shiah with a vast store of religious knowledge, repeated a joke about *Muharram* that I most often heard from non-Shiahs:

> A *Muharram* procession is taking place, and two foreigners, caught unawares, are watching the hysterical weeping, the men beating themselves with chains and knives, with great interest and alarm. They turn to someone on the street and ask, "What happened? Why are they so upset?!"
>
> Came the reply, "One of their great leaders died, almost 1,400 years ago now."
>
> The foreigners asked in even greater perplexity, "And they just found out about it now?"

A friend I will call Sakinah, a dedicated *majlis*-goer, recalled a more original narrative that she and a friend scripted during their college days in the 1950s. Launching from a litany of Husain's torments, the girls detailed their own sufferings when they went to take an exam without having studied. This parody differs from my earlier examples related to sermons in that the perpetrators had in their imaginations a generic or stereotypical *Muharram* lecture, not the style or skill of a particular preacher, nor the spiritual quality of an actual *majlis* space or congregation. In the sort of sermon the women would have used as their model, though, a preacher might relate tearfully how Husain makes camp at Karbala when his horse refuses to travel any farther. When his brother and sister plead with him not to halt at the forsaken spot, Husain replies that it is God's will for them to undergo suffering and death there.[25] It is impossible to recreate here Sakinah's delivery of her parody, but one can imagine the dramatic possibilities:

> Sakinah advances towards the examination room . . . this is the test that will make all the difference for her future,

> her career. She has to sit the exam, but . . . what horror, what calamity; SHE HASN'T STUDIED!!! Sakinah stumbles towards the door, sweat beading her brow, her stomach churning. Her life is over, she will FAIL!!

Entertaining spoofs of the sermon's fevered pitch and its themes of relentless oppression are especially tempting for the young, whether Shiahs or non-Shiahs, much as mimicry of hellfire-and-brimstone Christian fundamentalist monologues might be. I would assert that more leeway may also exist for this sort of humor within Shi'i women's circles; since women's sermons are so often characterized as intellectually limited or less than orthodox in any case, it is arguable that they have relatively little to lose when exploring the comical side of their intense devotions.

An appraisal of the ludic, celebratory, and humorous subtexts of South Asian Shi'i mourning overall suggests that historically there has been some scope in *Muharram* rites to celebrate Husain's ultimate moral victory despite his earthly defeat. Drumming in processions, the famed "tiger dance" of the Deccan, including Hyderabad, and Sunni participation in processions and other public observances have been part of commemorations for centuries. Yet most of these features are now contested. In general, festive, carnivalesque, or lightly comical dimensions of *Muharram* observances have been increasingly problematized by Shi'i reformers over the last fifty or so years. Over the last several generations, since the 1940s or 1950s, the emphasis on men's—or male-dominated—*Muharram* rites being held up as direct models for female mourners, on textual authority, and on dolor, from which the musical and the festive have been expunged, has intensified.[26]

In Lahore, for instance, some Shiahs in the old city refused to believe that their co-religionists in nearby Multan still performed drumming during *Muharram*, seeing this as a problematic, potentially "festive," "Sunni" dilution of mourning practices. The Shi'i drummers, however, along with a number of older *Muharram* descriptions, suggest that drumming expresses martial pride, symbolizes Husain's own martial procession, or simply draws an audience to the *Muharram* procession itself. Sunnis in a number of areas in South Asia, meanwhile, have been discouraged by their religious leaders from participating in *Muharram* rites, including the processions that have been as often occasions for Shi'i-Sunni collaboration as of communal tension. Salim, an Urdu-speaking Sunni Muslim from South India's Nilgiri hills, ruefully told me of how *Muharram* processions and instrument playing had been forbidden in his town, although his own father had proudly taken a central role in organizing the events and playing music, a tradition Salim would have liked to maintain.

Subtexts of humor and play in *Muharram*, then, are less easily "classified," or hierarchized, than are the dominant themes of mourning, in part because of anxieties about their propriety in a South Asian environment impacted by religious reform and increasing sectarian tension. Sorrow in *Muharram* is central and consciously systematized within the Shi'i community; participants in mourning assemblies assert a deeply internalized grief for Husain through individual response, communal physical actions, and, to follow William Reddy, verbal emotional "claims."[27] There are explicit discourses about religious justifications and rewards for weeping, "proper" ways to express grief, and rhetorical arts that facilitate meritorious mourning.

Yet perhaps the very trend of a "narrowing" spectrum of approved sentiment and emotion can contribute to our understanding of the various kinds and degrees of *majlis* levity at the turn of the twenty-first century.[28] Within the *majlis* itself, there is scope for controlled, verbally based humor that reveals the greatness of the *imams* and Karbala characters or provides a contrast and prelude to the profound grief that concludes the assembly. Poetic recitation and sermon styles, as well as cherished regional customs, also within the assembly, provide fodder for comparing *majlis*es and assessing their aesthetic and religious effectiveness. With this process of assessment or evaluation, which can easily become one of parody or mockery with a strong competitive element, we move into "commentaries" on ritual and ritual effectiveness and slightly away from the very structured, usually enclosed surroundings of the *majlis* itself.

The movement from "inside" the *majlis* to an "outside" that gradually becomes more public and varied, less uniformly Shi'i, is a multileveled one. The acknowledgment and expression of sorrow in an *imambarah* by dozens of black-clad women emphasize the proximity of the beloved figures of Karbala. Commemorations of Husain's greatness and suffering that are more visible to the "outside world" still offer religious merit and intercession but have a clear testimonial dimension. Movement outward from a Shi'i neighborhood, *imambarah*, or sacred space in public procession also mirrors Husain's journey from a respected, protected position to an open and a vulnerable one. And with this movement, the possible range of types of humor that interplay with grief and pride, or the implications of one sort of humor, can shift. The same couplets and jokes that bring a smile to the lips of elderly ladies in the confines of the *majlis* might turn contentious or provocative if recited in the presence of Sunnis. Imitations or mockery of sermons, or the sort of lighthearted invocation of Yazid as a classic "bad guy" that is permissible outside of the *majlis*, but within Shi'i homes, would take on a different tone in the mouths of outsiders who might simply be making fun of Shi'i practices.

Certainly some humor that plays on religious difference can be enjoyed broadly outside the Shi'i ritual space. In particular, the sort of formulaic, narrative, widely told "joke" that sends up bemusement or misunderstanding on the part of spectators or non-Shiahs as much as it does Shi'i practices seems to meet with very wide acceptance and occasion little offense. In India, with its considerable religious diversity, such little tales tend to situate *Muharram* as one of innumerable Indian religious observances and, as such, a profoundly Indian feature of the landscape, even if it is at the exotic end of the spectrum. In my experience, such classic, canned humor makes its presence less felt today than other more creative, but potentially contentious, forms of levity and play. Among these are the comparative, competitive mimicry that encodes ritual assessment among Shiahs, sarcastic or caustic jokes ("Did you hear the one about the Sunni/Shiah who invited her neighbor of the other sect to a household ritual and spit in the tea before serving it to her?"), "humorously" offensive descriptions of the other sect's customs, or the provocative play of the ninth of *Rabi 'ul awwal* celebrations.

In addition to incorporating a range of humor that alters in valence and type with movement outward from Shi'i assemblies or religious sites, playful commentaries within and upon *Muharram*'s solemn rites have several other broad characteristics. They capitalize on a highly charged atmosphere with already pronounced affective mixtures, and they actively probe a tension between universality *and* local rootedness in Shi'i mourning practices, ultimately reinforcing the simple fact that jokes in many situations, in many cultures, hinge on the idea that "difference" is funny. As in many other ethnic or sectarian encounters, however, the all-too-visible underside of difference that entertains is the looming possibility of riots, of attackers who make the very religious rites that commemorate valorous death into sites of contemporary massacre and martyrdom, or simply of the denigration of those who are different. It is all too true in these contexts that sometimes one has to laugh so as not to cry.

## Notes

1. Richard K. Wolf and I have explored the implications of mixed affects in poetry, music, and rituals in a variety of regions and communities. Wolf

theorizes emotional texture and contour as representations of how the affective character of a ceremony changes as its constituent rituals unfold. "Emotional contours," he says, "might be envisioned as a series of imaginary graphs, tracking the changing degree of intensity that an individual may experience over time during a ritual" (Wolf 2001, 381). Also see Wolf 2000, 81–116, 2003, 95–112. My own work in this area includes Bard 2000a, 2001, and 2002.

2. See, for example, Harman's chapter in this book on the marriage of Cundaresvarar and Meenakshi in Madurai, South India.

3. The fieldwork for this project was conducted between 1996 and 1999 in Lahore and Karachi, Pakistan, and in India, especially Lucknow and Hyderabad.

4. This is verse 9 of the marsiyah "Paidah shu'ah-e mahr se miqraz jab hui" by the great classical marsiyah poet Mirza Salamat Ali Dabir (Dabir 1980). "Zahra's darling" is an epithet for Imam Husain, which invokes his mother's affection for him (Zahra is another name for Fatimah). The translation is by the author.

5. Some of the following discussion, though, may apply equally well to men's parallel religious observances.

6. *Al-Fatihah* is the first verse of the Quran, often referred to as the essence of the Quran. The *Fatihah* is recited in memory of the dead, and, as Pickthall notes, "It is an essential part of all Muslim worship, public and private, and no solemn contract or transaction is complete unless it is recited" (Pickthall 1977, 2).

The *ziyarat*, chanted by one woman in a singsong mode, is a compulsory series of blessings, benedictions, and praises in Arabic addressed to the Karbala martyrs and to Muhammad, Fatimah, and the twelve *imams*. It signals the closure of the *majlis* and functions as a sort of communal "visitation" to the martyrs. The word *ziyarat* in popular Shi'ism also applies to small replicas of the *imams*' tombs (usually metal) to which *majlis*-goers pay homage, and to pilgrimages to the main Shi'i holy places, mostly located in present-day Iraq.

7. Sermon by Aliya Imam, May 28, 1997. P. E. C. H. S. Imambarah, Karachi, Pakistan. The translation is by the author.

8. Sermon by Shaguftah Musavi, May 10, 1997. The translation is by the author.

9. I thank my friend and resource person, "Sakinah" (who does not wish her real name to be used), for providing additional examples of such poetry, including several famous *ruba'is* (quatrains).

10. Specifically, one who elevates another person or being to the status of God (*mushrik*).

11. Saraiki is spoken in an area of Pakistan's Panjab state, and Saraiki speakers are one of a number of linguistic groups in urban Lahore. There is an active debate concerning whether Saraiki is a "language" or a particularly individuated, vibrant dialect of Panjabi, but whichever the case, Saraiki speakers have a strong group identity based on the language and its expressive and musical traditions. Some activists have even advocated for a separate state based on this language affiliation.

12. See Huizinga 1955, 11.

13. See Chelkowski and Dabashi 1999. Also see Hyder 2001, 339-62.

14. See, for example, Mottahedeh 2000, 14.

15. See Hjortshoj 1977; Raz.a 1966; Hasan 1997.

16. See, for example, Korom 2003; Dunham 1997; Pinault 2001.

17. See Kipling 1899, 133–73; Parlby 1975 [1850]; Ali 1974 [1832]. In Kipling's story, *Muharram* indexes the puzzle of "irrational," religiously based "mob frenzy" in the subcontinent. Ali ( 1974 [1832], 52–53) explicitly mentions bloody Shi'i-Sunni encounters at the *taziyah* burial ground. Recent newspaper accounts from Lucknow and Lahore not only cover the tense encounters between Shiahs and Sunnis (though sometimes they are elusive about naming the affiliations of those hurt or murdered to avoid fanning the flames further) but carry photographs of *Muharram* processions, and sometimes of the bloodiest participants—those who, for example, strike their heads with swords (*shamshir ka matam*).

18. Kullo yawm'in Ashura, kullo ardh'in Karbala.

19. The terms *Eid-e Zahra* and *Eid-e Shuja* have come into use comparatively recently and most noticeably in the diaspora community. Shi'i organizations in the United States and United Kingdom employ these names in their publications, calendars, and event announcements, but many immigrants from South Asia say that while growing up in India or Pakistan, they never heard of Eid-e Zahra or Eid-e Shuja.

20. With the gradual understanding over the last 200 years that "Muharram" commemorations should extend until the eighth of *Rabi 'ul awwal*, the majlis season grew to encompass two months (by the Islamic calendar) and eight days. In the Lucknow area, observances must have lengthened to such an extent only in the latter part of the nineteenth century, for an initial extension of mourning until forty days after Husain's death date (on the tenth of *Muharram*) took place in the late 1820s (and encountered resistance from non-Shiahs). Badshah Begam, a prominent woman in the ruling family of Avadh State, took the initiative to formally shift the burial of *taziyah*s from the tenth of *Muharram* to this forty-day anniversary (*chihlum*). See Cole 1997, 86.

21. Those with a good knowledge of Lucknow and its *Muharram* tradition will likely know of the actual locality to which I allude here, but the level of controversy surrounding the *jashn*s is such that I have been advised to alter the name. When I include information on these festivities, I have no intention of suggesting that these are standard Shi'i practices or of casting Shiahs in a "bad light." As this chapter suggests repeatedly, Shi'i communities are far from monolithic; just as some of those who disapprove of any "festivity" or "music" in *Muharram* customs will refuse to acknowledge that Shiahs participate in such customs, some will deny the existence of ritual cursing of the Caliphs or the more extreme elements of the *jashn*.

22. Whereas a number of educational Web sites maintained by Shi'i organizations or individuals (see, for example, http://www.hometown.aol.com/shabz36/ and http://www.shiaism.2ya.com/) explain in detail the martyrdom-related events commemorated on specific dates during the

*Muharram* cycle, such exegesis is notably absent for the events of the ninth of *Rabi 'ul awwal*.

23. My general description of this celebration is based on interviews concerning several sites in India, but the details of the Lucknow scene come from my field notes from Mahaganj, Lucknow, in the summer of 1998.

24. For a comparative perspective on death as celebration, see Metcalf and Huntington 1991.

25. This scene is a familiar one in sermons and martyrological poetry. In a majlis I attended in Lahore, the preacher began the "torments" portion of the assembly with this episode, which I have translated and paraphrased from a tape of the assembly. The speaker was "Zahra," who delivered the sermon in question on May 11, 1997.

26. See Bard 2002 and Wolf 2003.

27. See, for example, Reddy 2001.

28. See Wolf 2003 for a discussion of this narrowing or "flattening" of emotional spectrum in two very different religious and cultural contexts within South Asia.

## Works Cited

### *Books and Articles*

Ali, Meer Hassan. 1974 [1832]. *Observations on the Mussalmauns of India*. Karachi: Oxford University Press.

Bard, Amy. 1996. "From Elegiac Lament to Heroic Masterpiece: The Urdu Marsiyah Re-examined." M.A. essay, Columbia University.

Bard, Amy. 2000a. "Form, Function, and Feeling in 'Women's Songs' as Poetic Genres of the Shi'i Mourning Assembly." Paper delivered at the annual meetings, Society for Ethnomusicology, Toronto.

Bard, Amy. 2000b. "Value and Vitality in a Literary Tradition: Female Poets and the Urdu Marsiyah." *Annual of Urdu Studies* 15: 323–35.

Bard, Amy. 2001. " 'He Made Me Light Up the Gathering': Pride and Piety in Shi'i Women's Majlis." Paper delivered at the University of North Carolina (Chapel Hill) workshop on "The Aesthetics of Texts and Performance in Islamicate South Asia," April.

Bard, Amy. 2002. "Desolate Victory: Shi 'i Women and the Marsiyah Texts of Lucknow." Dissertation, Columbia University.

Chelkowski, Peter, ed. 1979. *Ta'ziyeh: Ritual and Drama in Iran*. New York: New York University Press.

Chelkowski, Peter, and Frank Korom. "Community Process and the Performance of Muharram Observances in Trinidad." *The Drama Review* 38:2: 150–75.

Chelkowski, Peter, and Hamid Dabashi. 1999. *Staging a Revolution: The Art of Persuasion in the Islamic Republic of Iran*. New York: New York University Press.

Cole, Juan R. I. 1997. "Shi'ite Noblewomen and Religious Innovation in Awadh." In *Lucknow: Memories of a City*, ed. Violette Graff, 83–90. Delhi: Oxford University Press.

Dabīr, Salāmat 'Alī. 1980. *Intkhāb-e marā\Osī-e Mirzā Dabīr*. Edited by Akbar Haiderī Kashmīrī. Lucknow: Uttar Pradesh Urdū Akadmī.

Dunham, Mary Frances. 1997. *Jarigan: The Muslim Folk Epic of East Bengal*. Dacca: Oxford University Press.

Graff, Violette, ed. 1997. *Lucknow: Memories of a City*. Delhi: Oxford University Press.

Harman, William P. 2010. "Laughing until It Hurts . . . Somebody Else: The Pain of a Ritual Joke." In *Sacred Play: Ritual Levity and Humor in South Asian Religions*, ed. Selva J. Raj and Corinne G. Dempsey. Albany: State University of New York Press.

Hasan, Mushirul. 1997. "Traditional Rites and Contested Meanings: Sectarian Strife in Colonial Lucknow." *Lucknow: Memories of a City*, ed. Violette Graff, 114–35. Delhi: Oxford University Press.

Hjortshoj, Keith Guy. 1977. "Kerbala in Context: A Study of Muharram in Lucknow, India." Dissertation, Cornell University.

Huizinga, Johan. 1955. *Homo Ludens: A Study of the Play Element in Culture*. Boston, MA: Beacon Press.

Hyder, Syed Akbar. 2000. "To Die and Yet Live." Dissertation, Harvard University.

Hyder, Syed Akbar. 2001. "Iqbal and Karbala: Re-reading the Episteme of Martyrdom for a Poetics of Appropriation." *Cultural Dynamics* 13:3: 339–62.

Kipling, Rudyard. 1899. "On the City Wall." *In Black and White*, 133–73. New York: R. F. Fenno & Co.

Korom, Frank J. 2003. *Hosay Trinidad: Muharram Performances in an Indo-Carribean Diaspora*. Philadelphia: University of Pennsylvania Press.

Korom, Frank J., and John Bishop, producers. 1999. *Hosay Trinidad* (Video). Watertown, MA: Documentary Educational Resources.

Metcalf, Peter, and Richard Huntington, eds. 1991. *Celebrations of Death: The Anthropology of Mortuary Ritual*. Cambridge: Cambridge University Press.

Mottahedeh, Roy. 2000. *The Mantle of the Prophet: Religion and Politics in Iran*. Oxford: Oneworld.

Parlby, Fanny Parks. 1975 [1850]. *Wanderings of a Pilgrim in Search of the Picturesque*. 2 vols. Karachi: Oxford University Press.

Pickthall, M. M., trans. 1977. *The Glorious Qur'ān*. New York: Muslim World League.

Pinault, David. 2001. *Horse of Karbala*. New York: Palgrave.

Razā, Rahī Mās'ūm. 1966. *Ādhā Gāñv*. Delhi: Akshar Prakashan Private Ltd.

Reddy, William M. 2001. *The Navigation of Feeling: A Framework for the History of Emotions*. New York: Cambridge University Press.

Wolf, R. K. 2000. "Embodiment, Multivalence, and Ambivalence: Emotion and Meaning in Mūsīqī: A Preliminary Case Study in South Asian Muharram Drumming." *Yearbook for Traditional Music* 32: 81–116.

Wolf, R. K. 2001. "Emotional Dimensions of Ritual Music among the Kotas, a South Indian Tribe." *Ethnomusicology* 45:3: 381.

Wolf, R. K. 2003. "Return to Tears: Musical Mourning, Emotion, and Religious Reform in Two South Asian Minority Communities." In *The Living and the Dead: Social Dimensions of Death in South Asian Religions*, ed. Elizabeth Wilson, 95–112. Albany: State University of New York Press.

### *Lectures, Sermons, and Personal Communication*

Imam, Aliya. 1997. Urdu Sermon, May 28. P. E. C. H. S. Imambarah, Karachi, Pakistan.

Musavi, Shaguftah. 1997. Urdu Sermon, May 10. Qasr-e Batul, Lahore.

"Zahrah." 1997. Urdu Sermon, May 11. Qasr-e Zainab, Lahore.

11

# A Catholic Charismatic Healer at Play in North India

MATHEW N. SCHMALZ

## I. Levity

If levity is understood as "humor" or "jocularity," then Jude most certainly would not have used the term to describe his work. After all, what he was doing was deadly serious. Indeed, as a Catholic charismatic healer, Jude's work was about nothing less than eternal life (see Schmalz 2001, 2002a; Schmalz and Gottschalk forthcoming). Jude was born into a Catholic family in Kerala and led what he would often call an "evil" and a "godless" life of carousing until his discharge from the Indian Air Force. After his family moved to Varanasi, where his wife had found work as a nurse, Jude became involved in the Catholic charismatic movement. After several conversion experiences, Jude claimed that he had the power not only to heal but also to read the hearts of those who sought his assistance. This reputed ability made Jude a healer who was much in demand, and his family's small flat in Varanasi would often be an important destination for not a small number of Catholics and Hindus who sought healing in this most sacred Indian city. Given that many who showed up on his doorstep had exhausted all other options, levity was certainly not the dominant mood.

Jude, however, would be the first to admit that any study of human behavior must probe beyond and underneath appearance. And it is precisely beyond and underneath superficial appearances that we find "levity" insinuating itself into Jude's healing ministrations and shaping his understandings of what it meant to be a healed and redeemed person. Take, for example, a conversation Jude and I had one night in Varanasi over a decade ago. We were strolling to the railway station from the Varanasi Cathedral. We stopped at an intersection where we saw a naked man lying unconscious in the middle of the road. Jude said, "He's mad, you know, so we can't take him to the sisters at the Cathedral. Sometimes all we can do is pray." Jude extended his hands in charismatic fashion and repeated in Hindi, "Praise you Jesus, thank you Jesus," before slipping into glossolalia, the prayer of tongues. We then walked through the railway tracks to the station, which was bathed in a yellow glow from the surrounding streetlights. I followed Jude, as he was carelessly crossing the tracks behind the station, and he began to speak of someone he had met at a charismatic retreat. Jude reflected, "He laughed so much, you know I became suspicious. He seemed too happy. I think that his sins were crushing him so much that all he could do was laugh because he had to convince himself he was all right." I asked him then whether charismatic healing was like that sometimes. Jude said, "Oh yes, it can be."

In responding to my rather oblique query, Jude seemed to acknowledge that charismatic healing can be a form of play somehow connected to the levity that masks human pain and suffering. In certain healing contexts, inappropriate levity could be a sign that a supplicant is either unwilling or unable to confront the reality of sin. But if levity can sometimes constitute pathology to be remedied, then the overall goal of charismatic healing is "levity" in its most literal sense of "lightness," for sin has a crushing weight that can be relieved once a healer has revealed its presence to a supplicant. The levity of charismatic healing can be a feeling of freedom, the result of playing or "acting as if." But charismatic healing can also be play in the sense of contest in which levity and freedom are premised on the exercise of power.

The ludic character of charismatic religiosity has been the subject of a number of studies that have focused upon the joyful play of charismatic healing (for example, see Boudewijnse, Droogers, and Kamsteeg 1998). In this chapter, however, I would like to probe the variety of forms of play in Jude's healing ministry in part to move beyond idealized interpretations of play as an unproblematic expression of levity and freedom. But play as levity and freedom is precisely where our discussion will begin as we will first examine Jude's understanding of glossolalia and the process of charismatic healing. Drawing upon Johan Huizinga's *Homo Ludens* (1950), we can see how the joy and levity of charismatic healing seeks to represent or embody the redemption Christ offers to sinners. It will be Huizinga's work as well that will lead us to considering how contest and improvisational freedom also form part of Jude's particular form of Catholic charismatic healing. Yet the play in which Jude is engaged is not "disinterested," to refer to Huizinga's characterization of pure play (9). Instead, for Jude, the play of charismatic healing involves power and domination, just as it does the final inevitability of human pain and suffering.

### *Freedom*

In *Homo Ludens,* Huizinga argues that play is the generative element of culture itself. In a remarkably broad-ranging discussion, Huizinga positions "the play instinct" (*spielement*) as a crucial element in the development of any number of cultural forms, including law, warfare, art, and religion. In its patterns and flow, play allows not only rhythm and harmony but also alternation, climax, and change (75). For Huizinga, the foundation of play is freedom, for true play must be a voluntary activity and never a "task" (7–8). Freedom is also at the foundation of Jude's charismatic healing, for it is in play of glossolalia that he receives divine messages that allow him to discern a supplicant's sins. The acknowledgment of sin, in turn, then produces a special kind of levity that expresses the freedom found in the forgiving love of Jesus Christ.

### *"Ohshallalala, Ohshallalala"*

In a small room behind the main altar of the cathedral, the charismatic team of the Varanasi diocese gathered to pray before a Eucharistic host set in a large sun-burst monstrance. The primary purpose of those sequestered in the prayer room was to receive divine messages for a prayer service that drew approximately 2,000 Catholics and Hindus to the lawn in front of the cathedral. The "messages," as they were always called, usually concerned afflictions or healings among the participants in the prayer service. These messages were regularly announced to the crowd as prophecies about the healings being accomplished by the Holy Spirit. When I walked into the prayer room, Jude was sitting on the ledge bordering the room by the window, his head in his hands. He then began to pray aloud. He prayed in English, "We surrender you (*sic*), we surrender you, we surrender you, we surrender you," then, "sanctify us, sanctify us, sanctify us, sanctify us." Then came ejaculative prayers in both Hindi and English: "Give me your voice," and "I give myself to you." Next there came the prayers of adoration, largely in English: "We love you Jesus, we love you Jesus, we love you Jesus." At this point, Jude moved from his sitting position to his knees. His eyes were open, fixed upon the Eucharist, and filling with tears. Then he prayed for his gift in Hindi, "Give power, give force." The prayer grew faster and faster and then declined in intensity until there was only silence. In these silences, Jude received his messages. After he received a message, he recited his standard prayer of thanks, "Thank you Jesus, thank you Jesus, we love you Jesus, I love you Jesus." This often moved to his prayer of tongues, "ohshallalala, ohshallalala." Next Jude prayed for power, first in English, "give voice, give power," and then in Hindi, "*swar dede, shakti dede*." Then there was silence again and the messages came.

Jude's pattern of prayer conforms well to Huizinga's delineation of the fundamental structure of play. Huizinga (10–11) observes that there are often two fundamental prerequisites of play: space and rules. Play is conducted on a special space demarcated for the purpose, whether it is a field, a court, or the "turf" agreed upon by the players. The separateness of the space for play emphasizes how play itself takes place in "a temporary world" (10) that simultaneously lies within and beyond the ordinary and mundane. Play is also governed by rules that are necessary representations of this different realm of "absolute and peculiar order" (10). Most obviously, the prayer room at the Varanasi Cathedral was a special space, since its sanctity came from the exposed Host, and only specially designated charismatic healers were allowed admittance. Jude began by surrendering his will to Jesus and prayed for God's sanctifying power. He next shifted from a prayer of petition to a prayer of adoration. Then, in the silence that followed, Jude received "the messages." There thus is a paradigmatically charismatic renunciation of will as an opening to grace, the reception of a particular charismatic gift, and an expression of thanksgiving. Initially, then, prayer becomes a way of internalizing a particular theological grammar, or a set of "rules," in which the prayer assumes a structure drawn from the themes emphasized by the movement.

But of course the grammar of the prayer is not its only feature. Perhaps the most distinguishing characteristic of charismatic prayer is speaking in tongues or glossolalia, long a focus of investigation in the study of religion. Emile Lombard (see also Lombard 1907; for an overview of glossolalia research, see Maloney and Lovekin 1985), in 1910, developed a typology of glossolalia with the categories of *phonatons frustes* or rough sounds, pseudo-language, and verbal fabrication. May (1967) extended this typology to include six categories: the language of spirits, sacerdotal language, the language of animals, xenoglossia (speaking in foreign languages), and ermeneglossia (interpreting tongues). Pattison (1968) proposed a more general distinction between "playful" and "serious" glossolalia. Playful glossolalia is produced volitionally and is rapid and fluid. Serious glossolalia, however, is automatic and unintentional, and is marked by a variable and dramatic intonation pattern (76). Considering Jude's form of glossolalia, for example, what is interesting about the phrase "ohshallalala, ohshallalala" is that Jude did not understand it to be a foreign or divine language. Instead, it constituted a playful or volitional kind of glossolalia, and Jude confirmed this by telling me that "ohshallalala" is "only a word." Elaborating his thoughts more fully, he remarked that speaking in tongues is really the language of children, like words of love spoken by infants to their father. The outstretched arms that are characteristic of the charismatic posture of prayer then symbolize this childlike desire for comfort and succor.

Especially striking about Jude's interpretation of speaking in tongues was how it echoed a prominent interpretation of glossolalia as regression in the service of the ego (Maloney and Lovekin 1985, 54–62; see also Kris and Kaplan 1953; Alland 1962; Brende and Risley 1979). According to this view, the ego voluntarily withdraws its investment or cathexis in reality to explore other creative pursuits. Interestingly, Lombard (1910, 260) also maintained that those who spoke in tongues would return to their childhood precisely because their speech sounded childlike. Regardless of whether or not it is appropriate to apply Western psychoanalytic concepts such as "the ego" or "regression," certainly Jude was pointing to how speaking in tongues allows a freedom of symbolic association that moves beyond the structure of most charismatic prayer. For him, to speak in tongues was to withdraw the will and to release a torrent of emotion. Indeed, it was precisely by giving up his will to God and speaking in tongues that Jude received the divine "messages" for which he was known. And so the structure of charismatic prayer initially relies upon rules that bridge the division between the human and divine worlds. Indeed, the rapturous play of glossolalia allows a particularly expansive freedom found in the feeling of transcending ordinary time and space.

## *A Body of Glory*

Central to Jude's healing ministry was what he called "charismatic counseling." During what would usually be a private meeting with a supplicant, Jude would discern the effect of a particular sin upon a supplicant. During one of our tape-recorded interview sessions, Jude related to me the story of a middle-age Hindu woman who came to him for counseling while he was at a charismatic convention in Lucknow. She was married to a military man, and she came and knelt before Jude, who began to pray over her. What follows is Jude's account of the encounter.

> When I prayed, I got something lacking [in her]. When I prayed I got an inspiration to ask her that when she was at the age of ten or twelve she was raped by her father. I got the message and asked Jesus "Should I say this?" I was confident because Jesus will never make me [make] a mistake. I am representing God at that time. Whatever are my words I believe that it is (*sic*) the word of God. If any one has beaten me because of anything that will be a blow against Him [i.e., any one who strikes Jude will be striking Jesus]. So I said "Sister, may I ask you whether your first sin was committed with your Father." She said "Yes, really, yes. . . ." Then she began to cry.

After his message was confirmed, Jude says that she confessed everything to him. From the day her father raped her, relatives and servants all "used her." Soon she became possessed by a devil. She would sense a "bad smell" around her, lose control completely, and would want sex with anyone. Her husband and three children knew about this and were suffering terribly. When Jude heard her confession, he recalled that he prayed to God, "Give me the courage to take her soul to you."

Jude spoke to the woman, "I am going to Calvary, are you ready to come?" He next said that she must separate herself from her body. When he said this, according to Jude, she became limp and he took her hand. He asked her, "Where are you now?" She replied, "I am in a tunnel, I feel very light . . . I am seeing a light . . . I see a mountain. I see three crosses there." Jude then asked, "Do you know the cross of Jesus?" "Yes," she said. "Then go there," Jude softly ordered.

In this meditation, Jude took the supplicant to the foot of the cross. He asked, "Can you see your body?" "Yes, it is lying there." "Where is it?" he probed further. "It is on a bed." "All right, now we are with the soul only," Jude observed to himself. In Jude's interpretation of this exchange, he had separated the woman's soul from her body. He told her "to ask pardon from her body" and asked her to call her father. Jude then said, "Embrace him; forgive him." Jude recalled that she then started laughing and clapping her hands. Jude gently inquired, "What is your father doing?" "He is crying," she replied. "Give him a sweet kiss. Tell him: 'I forgot everything you have committed against me. You are my father, I trust you my father, I love you my father.' " He finally led her back into her body and she opened her eyes and said, "Really I was flying. I was weightless."

In this meditation, Jude unified many of the themes that structured his healing ministry. His paradoxical, and perhaps disturbing, inquiry about his supplicant's first "sin" reflects the charismatic belief that those who have been sinned against often become sinners themselves (for comparison, see Schmalz 2002a, 179–81). Jude asked his supplicant "to ask pardon" from her body, because she had so abused it in her sexual encounters. Throughout the meditation, Jude emphasized a radical demand for forgiveness as he asks his supplicant to forgive the father who raped her. His supplicant's vision of passing through a tunnel before coming to Golgotha obviously reflects the idea of rebirth so central to the charismatic movement and Jude's own personal belief in the power of confession and conversion. We also find the distinction between the soul and the body as well as the emphasis upon how the flesh sins while the spirit remains pure.

Yet there is more than a simple dualism here, for Jude finally reunites the supplicant with her body. Indeed, what seems to be rejection of the body is but a first step to offering the body to the spirit. In the meditation Jude developed for his supplicant, she dies to her body of sin only to be reborn into another body. This rebirth takes places on Golgotha and thus links the symbolic death and rebirth of Jude's supplicant to the Crucifixion and Resurrection of Jesus. Just as Christ's body was raised and glorified by God, so too will the body of Jude's supplicant if she can only die to her body of sin. By purifying his supplicant's body and soul, Jude thus aimed to produce what could be called "a body of glory" that will rise on the last day. Not only did the woman's body itself become "light," her laughter reflected the "levity" offered by the forgiveness of sin.

Huizinga argues that play always is a representation of something (1950, 13). As he expands this fundamental point, he brings together an almost encyclopedic range of examples, from games such as chess to religious and social rituals such as the potlatch. For Huizinga, play is an embodiment, a performance, "a stepping out of common reality into a higher order" (13). For Jude, the play of charismatic healing, from glossolalia and prophetic discernment to the joy of healing, represents or incarnates what it is to be a redeemed person. The literal lightness or levity that one feels upon healing is a freedom from the constraints of mundane human existence: constraints that are the result of the weight of sin.

## II. Power

While maintaining that play is necessarily a representation, Huizinga also argues that it is a contest for something (1950, 13). In his discussion of play's generative power, he often focuses upon its central role in "agonistic" cultures such as Greece and China. For example, Huizinga argues that Hellenistic culture celebrated "the contest," the "supreme life principle" (73) that unified all Hellas at Olympia, Delphi, and Nemea. While Huizinga argues that play is fundamentally agonistic, he nonetheless maintains that it lies outside of normal wants and appetites (49). Indeed, the prize of play is often simply winning itself. Anything concerned with worldly wants, such as money or other materialistic forms of prestige, is not properly play.

But as Clifford Geertz (1973, 412–53) reminds us in "Deep Play: Notes on a Javanese Cockfight," the prestige that victory brings is intimately connected to various forms of social positioning and advancement. The Javanese male, Geertz observes with rather ribald double entendre, has a deep psychological relationship with his "cock" (417). Because of this, the Javanese cockfight involves the representation or contestation of numerous facets of Javanese life. When a man puts his "cock" on the line, he not only stakes his prestige but becomes involved in an elaborate drama that is intimately connected to very real social issues. For Jude as well, the play of healing elicited what were for him pressing issues of religious and social concern: the vindication of the power of Jesus and of Christianity itself. Moreover, through his particular form of healing and prophetic play, Jude also asserted his own superiority over rival Catholic charismatic healers. But if earlier we found that charismatic play was about a freedom gained by playing within the rules, for Jude it was also about the power gained by breaking them.

### *The Recalcitrant Demoniac*

On the last day of a charismatic healing service at the Varanasi Cathedral, most of the participants had departed. Jude and a North Indian Catholic healer named Jagamba were together walking away when screams could be heard coming from the foot of the stage where speakers had led the audience in prayer. Below a garlanded portrait of Jesus sitting in the full lotus position, there was a woman writhing upon the grass. Jagamba and a group of young charismatics ran to her and began to pray. Their voices rose to glossolalia almost immediately as they extended their hands over her. Jagamba stepped forward and began to shake his Bible in the face of the demoniac, only to have her screams rise in intensity (for another description of this scene, see Schmalz and Gottschalk forthcoming).

Suddenly an opening appeared in the circle of charismatics, and Jude stepped forward.

"Look," he said in Hindi. "Look? Look at what?" the woman said as she stopped her screams. Raising her eyes toward Jude, she said in Bhojpuri, "You don't understand me." "Do you understand 'our' (*hamara*)?" Jude inquired forcefully. "I don't understand what he's saying," she said, continuing to speak in Bhojpuri, looking toward the other charismatics who had faded into the background. Jude bent down, looking at her in the eyes: "Do you understand 'my' (*mera*)? Jude pointed at himself. "Jesus," the woman replied. "Jesus!" Jude said startled, "I'm Jesus?" "Well, yes, no, that's Jesus," she said pointing to the picture of Christ on the stage. "Who am I?" Jude demanded, and he pointed at himself again. "You're his representative" (*adhikari*), the woman announced in Hindi. To Jude, this response seemed sarcastic, and he asserted with the utmost seriousness, "I am his slave (*das*), not his representative, his slave!" The woman had difficulty understanding this distinction and replied, "Oh, whatever—He knows," as she

Figure 11.2. Suddenly an opening appeared in the circle of charismatics; Jude stepped forward and knelt to look her in the eyes. *(photo by Peter Gottschalk)*

gestured once again toward the portrait of Christ on the stage. She then began screaming about her family, her husband. Jude pressed her by saying that he was Jesus' slave, that she needed to recognize the power of Christ. The woman continued to scream and to roll around on the grass. Jude laid his hands upon her, talked with her, and threatened to hit her, all to no avail. After ten minutes, he simply left, saying, "It's nothing, it's nothing at all."

When he said, "Do you understand 'our' (*hamara*)?" Jude was in the heat of battle trying to speak Hindi, a language that he had yet to master. What he really wanted to say was, "Do you understand who I am?" But he was only able to make the meaning of his Hindi clear by pointing to himself when the demoniac looked at him. She, in turn, was speaking Bhojpuri and her fusillade of words was only intelligible to native speakers, and then only if they were listening very carefully. At certain moments, when Jude's verb and pronoun forms were recognizable, he was able to communicate with the possessed woman. But, for the most part, their encounter was characterized by its lack of semantic understanding and coherence. The demoniac was

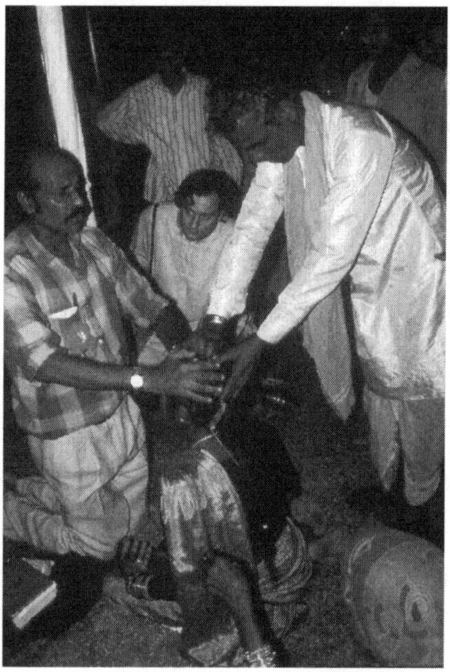

Figure 11.2. Jude laid his hands upon her with the other charismatics. *(photo by Peter Gottschalk)*

screaming about her family, about Jesus, and about the Bible, but not about Jude, the healer, except for one brief moment when their eyes met. Because of this apparent discrepancy in explicit communication, both Jude and the demoniac were seemingly able to act out key portions of their own personal narratives.

Jude, however, was not simply engaged in an idiosyncratic charismatic pantomime. Instead, he was performing, or playing, for the audience surrounding him. Huizinga argues that drama and play are intimately linked in what he calls a "*methetic*" process by which something is not just represented, but enacted (1950, 14–15). When Jude said, "It's nothing, it's nothing," he was actually acknowledging the severity of the possession—the demon was attempting to draw attention to itself, and Jude denied it the recognition it craved. Most crucially, the demoniac was a Hindu as was the demon that possessed her. She and the demon were resisting Jude's power and thus the authority of Christ. As Robert Stirrat (1992) also observed in his study of Roman Catholicism in Sri Lanka, the drama of Catholic charismatic healing has a subtext of contestation with the dominant religion. To vanquish a Hindu deity or spirit, a demon in the Catholic charismatic worldview, would be to assert the dominion of Christ. What Jude understood as ridicule coming from the demoniac was akin to the ridicule he and many other charismatic healers believe they receive from a culture they understand to be hostile to Christian presence. Jude focused the attention of the other Christian healers upon the Hindu woman, intensifying the conflict by drawing in observers in a manner not dissimilar to a Greek drama, which, as Huizinga observes, involved spectators in the reality enacted by the drama itself. And so when taunted, Jude left the demoniac to suffer, perhaps as God will let suffer those who refuse to hear his name.

### *South versus North*

Within the Catholic charismatic movement, there are other points of potential conflict besides that between Christian and Hindu. For example, the Catholic charismatic movement is dominated by South Indians. Potta, Kerala, is the center of the Indian charismatic movement, and even in North India, a vast majority of the prominent Catholic charismatic healers are Syrian rite Catholics from Kerala, like Jude. But North Indian Catholics are Dalits ("crushed"), untouchables from the Chamar caste of tanners. Caste is still very much an issue in Indian Catholicism: Dalits are considered "other" by many Syrian rite South Indians, and Syrian rite South Indians, for their part, are often viewed as "other" by Latin rite North Indian Dalit Catholics. These issues came into sharp relief when I attended a charismatic retreat with Jude and a young catechist who hailed from a village in the Ballia District, about 100 miles north of Varanasi. I observed a small group session that Jude began by narrating the story of his life, from his early infidelities and alcoholism to his final conversion to Christ and the gradual unfolding of his divine gift of healing and prophecy. Attention then turned to the young catechist who spoke about his own life. Holding a Hindi biography of St. Pius X, he recalled that he could have been a teacher or professor but instead had to settle on being a catechist and traveling dusty roads to neighboring villages to gather Catholics together for mass or to inform them of special functions at the mission. He confessed that he often would lose his temper with his wife and sometimes would fly into a rage and strike his children. He concluded, nonetheless, that he remained happy with his job and that he had a rich and fulfilling prayer life.

Upon hearing this, Jude immediately sat up in his chair and turned his eyes toward the young catechist. He said in Hindi, "No, you're not happy with your job. And, what is more—you have an 'ego.'" The word "ego," which Jude did not translate into Hindi, confused the catechist and momentarily brought the exchange to a standstill. To break the silence, Jude then reached into his shirt pocket and took out a cross of gold-plated metal and black enamel. Looking at the catechist intently, he fingered the cross as he placed it on the Bible resting upon his lap. He asked in Hindi, "Do you see my cross? It's a special cross; it gives me a lot of power, [and] it helps me reveal the truth." He then closed his eyes and said, "There's a woman in your past—she's wearing a green sari and calling you. Has there been anything like that in your life?"

The catechist sat silently throughout Jude's attempt to read his heart. When Jude finished, the catechist responded, stiffly and formally, that there was no such person in his past. Jude continued to press the issue, only to hear the catechist respond, "No sir" (*ji nahin*) to each of his inquiries. He finally looked at the catechist quizzically and said, "Well, this [is] something you should look into." The conversation ended there, with the catechist giving the distinct impression that Jude had failed in his attempt to discern his past. Jude, however, believed that the young catechist had not been fully honest, especially since there seemed to be so many unresolved issues in the catechist's life.

The play between Jude and the catechist was initially a simple game of attack and defend. Jude moved aggressively, making bold pronouncements about the catechist's life. When his overt discernment failed, Jude attempted to use his cross to elicit an emotional resonance that would have perhaps overcome the young catechist's resistance. Both Jude and the catechist tried to shame each other in front of the audience that witnessed their exchange. Other North Indian Dalits at the charismatic retreat, who very much resented the dominant South Indian presence, had even talked about setting Jude up for failure by feeding him misinformation about their pasts, or by forcing him to guess about specific past events, such as the date of someone's birth. For some Dalits, playing with Jude, in the sense of humiliating him, was part of a larger conflict about status and power, not dissimilar to the cockfighting Javanese so suggestively discussed by Geertz. For Jude, charismatic healing was a contest in which he sought to gain from his supplicants an admission to the effect that they had, or should have, been playing his game all along. While the young catechist resisted Jude during their first session, at the end of the charismatic retreat, he rose to say how Jude had revealed to him much about his past life—an admission that vindicated Jude's power and also pleased his fellow South Indian charismatics who presided over that last gathering of the retreat.

### *The Battle of the Healers*

During his many journeys as part of his healing ministry, Jude would carry with him a notebook in which his supplicants would record their testimonies. Occasionally, Jude would also write testimonies himself—about the visions he received or about the visions other healers had about him. One of Jude's colleagues on the diocesan charismatic healing team was a "Madam" Swaminathan, a Tamilian who worked as a servant on a military cantonment in Varanasi (on Madam Swaminathan, see also Schmalz forthcoming). Madam Swaminathan also had a large following, and she would often volunteer various prophetic discernments about Jude and his healing ministry. In one notation is his notebook, with the annotation "2:00 a.m." Jude recorded one particularly "disturbing" revelation that Madam Swaminathan had made about him at a recent retreat. The "message" was this: "candle not in proper possition (*sic*)." Jude interpreted this to mean that, in Madam Swaminathan's purportedly divinely illuminated opinion, his inspiration was not appropriately centered.

While meditating about this, Jude discerned a message from God to look at verse six, line fourteen, of what is called in Hindi *Preritra Chatritra*, or *The Acts of the Apostles*: "We have heard him say that he will destroy this place and all the traditions that have come down since the time of Moses. All the representatives from the assembly (i.e., the Sanhedrin) looked at Stephen with great attention."

In likening himself to Stephen before the Sanhedrin, Jude positioned himself in a prophetic role vis-à-vis Madam Swaminathan, whom he placed within what he considered a corrupt clerical class. Notations in Jude's notebook following that entry often make explicit Mrs. Swaminathan's inability to discern or heal the afflictions of supplicants, supplicants who would then make clear that they found respite with Jude. Such written testimonies are the primary currency in the charismatic movement, for they are narratives of the power of the Holy Sprit working through the healer. The disparate testimonies, drawn from diverse supplicants, separated in time and space, show the pervading and unifying power of the Holy Spirit. In collecting and cataloguing testimonies to their healing prowess, neither Jude nor Mrs. Swaminathan were competing for money. Jude, for example, would always refuse the offering (*dakshina*) presented by grateful supplicants. Perhaps then the contest between Jude and Mrs. Swaminathan does correspond to Huizinga's rather romantic description of play as a contest whose "stake" is often victory itself (1950, 50). But the contest between Jude and Mrs. Swaminathan was something more than a competition over who had the greater healing prowess. If with the young catechist there was an underlying dynamic of North versus South and high caste versus Dalit, in Jude's relationship with Mrs. Swaminathan there were also crucial points of contestation: male versus female, Malayali versus Tamilian, Syrian Rite versus Latin Rite. When Jude began to divine messages that Mrs. Swaminathan was a false healer and prophet, it was clear that the play between them was a deadly serious contest of power framed in terms of good versus evil.

### *Healing Play as Liberation*

One Saturday afternoon I was standing outside of Jude's counseling room in a Christian ashram maintained by a Catholic religious order outside of Varanasi, when a man about thirty years old came to me to ask whether Jude was free. For the purposes of anonymity, we will call him by the pseudonym "Bhim," and he was a Hindu and member of a Dalit caste. He had returned from Dubai, where he worked as a driver, on his yearly journey to visit his wife and family. He told me that people in his village had told him of the Catholic ashram in Varanasi as a place of healing. When he arrived, he learned of "Mr. Jude," a healer of power. For the last three years, Bhim had been troubled by a back problem, at times so serious that he could not even bend over fully. He had come to see if Jude could heal him, since the condition of his back had only worsened, and it was difficult for him to imagine returning to his job in Dubai in such pain.

I next saw Bhim during the final healing ceremony at the ashram. I asked him whether he had received any relief from his ailment. He motioned with his hands and said to me in Hindi, "Only a little bit" (*kuch*). Jude, however, had a different recollection of events. Jude told me that he had prayed over Bhim and received the message that he should get up and run around the ashram compound with him. This, Jude says, he did while asking Bhim at various intervals to bend over and touch the ground. Slowly Jude recalled, Bhim's back began to relax—he could touch his feet and then the ground. Jude said that Bhim was on the way to being healed—he only needed to keep praying.

I next saw Bhim two weeks later, at a Friday night healing service at the Varanasi Cathedral. He had with him about fifteen women from his village. Bhim told them that Jude had cured him of his back ailment, and that they too could be healed. Jude prayed over each and every one of them that night. With his cross in his right hand he prayed over women who suffered from everything from gastrointestinal disorders to childlessness. This pattern continued for the next several weeks, with Bhim bringing ever-greater numbers of women to the prayer meeting. After two weeks of this, Jude himself tried to explain to Bhim that he simply did not have time to pray over all of these people—he should bring them to the ashram or to another healer.

On yet another Friday evening, I was waiting for Jude on the steps of the Varanasi Cathedral. Bhim suddenly appeared and came toward me with a very grave look on his face. He handed me a medical report: he had just had his semen tested. The report read "some dead sperm found" and then ended with the conclusion "0% infertile." While I was trying to make sense out of the document, Jude ran up to me and seized the report from my hands, "Come," he said, "we must talk to Father and place this before the Holy Eucharist." Jude could not find the parish priest, and so he decided simply to pray over Bhim near the exposed host. Afterwards, Bhim said that he was preparing to return to Dubai and that he would like me to record his testimony (*gavahi*).

> At this time I am living in Dubai. I have been there for four years and have been suffering for four years. I've been to a lot of doctors but I wasn't satisfied with them. I went from

> private doctors to government hospitals; for ten to fifteen days I was going back and forth. But I didn't get any relief. But then I came into the court (*darbar*) of Lord Jesus. There I got sixty-five percent relief. After that, from coming to the court regularly, I've received comfort and relief.

Bhim's story reflects how much North Indian themes and practices had risen to prominence in Jude's healing ministry. No confession of sins accompanied Bhim's testimony, nor did he dedicate himself exclusively to Jesus. Although he did acknowledge Christ's power, Bhim referred to entering the Church and meeting Jude as coming into the *darbar*, or court, of Jesus. This is a typical North Indian image, and the paradigm is that of seeing and beseeching the deity as royal potentate. Bhim approached Jesus through his *adhikari*, his faithful representative Jude. To ask Christ for healing was essentially to ask for a boon. Yet instead of sacrificing to make oneself worthy of such a divine gift, Bhim requested the favor first, so that the deity would not be placed in debt. As for Jude, he relied upon a divine healing power channeled through his cross and the monstrance containing the Holy Eucharist. Jude's cross now had an even greater power, because he had touched it to the body of his spiritual advisor, Father Ranvir, who had recently passed away. The Holy Eucharist, Jude said, exuded a purifying heat, and simply being in proximity to it would be enough to cure. Like a renunciant who purifies himself by intensifying his internal *tapas*, like an *ayurvedic* coction made efficacious through the application of flame, Bhim's back pain could be transformed by heat. The image of healing then is not that of confession purging the soul and unifying the spirit but of the body and its fluids being transformed by an infusion of divine energy and heat.

The Catholic charismatic movement stands in strong and vocal opposition to traditional or popular forms of Hinduism. *Mantras* are labeled "black magic" (*jadu*), and "idol worship" (*murti puja*) is always explicitly condemned in public pronouncements made at charismatic retreats and healing services that involve Hindus. Of course, Hindu exorcists, particularly Dalit exorcists (*ojhe*), are the primary rivals of Catholic charismatic healers (see Schmalz 2002b). Jude most certainly did not realize, consciously at any rate, the extent to which his healing ministry had assumed a distinctively North Indian idiom. The repetition of Jesus' name, his references to divine heat, his use of water and other "unmarking" elements (see Marriot 1990), and his threatened or, at times, actual application of physical force to the possessed (Schmalz 2002a, 181) would all find parallels within what he would understand as the "surrounding" Hindu culture. But the play of charismatic healing is fundamentally about the improvisational power of a single, inspired "self." Indeed, one could say that the successful charismatic healer has gained so much power by playing within the rules that the rules themselves no longer apply.

## III. Play

Jude's encounter with Bhim was also as much about comedy as it was about healing. Huizinga (1950, 144–45), of course, mentions comedy as play in the sense of drama and competition, with specific reference to Attic culture. To be sure, Jude and Bhim's healing play had a number of dramatic elements. But from another perspective, the entirety of charismatic play appears as comedy in the sense of a sham. Not only did many Dalits find Jude's specific claims dubious, but many clergy did as well. The claims of being able to read minds and the strong sexual content of many of Jude's counseling sessions struck many priests in the diocese as being beyond the bounds of credulity and propriety. In Bhim's specific case, there were numerous elements that critics would have doubtless identified as emblematic of the farcical nature of much charismatic healing. Bhim, of course, was not "healed" in a conventional sense—he still experienced back pain, for example. With regard to Bhim's sperm count, it was unclear whether healing was necessary at all. In any case, the spectacle of Jude using the doctor's report as a surrogate or proxy for the supposedly afflicted organ would have seemed bizarre and ludicrous.

It was this understanding of charismatic healing as frivolous that formed the subtext when I was told of Jude's death. I wrote Jude regularly after I returned from India, but I never received a response. When I traveled back to India in December 2000 as part of a different project, I was eager to meet Jude again. While in a village in Bihar, I telephoned a Catholic priest to ask if he knew Jude's current whereabouts. Speaking to me in English, the priest told me matter of factly, "He is no more." The priest then reflected, "It's too bad, since he never really accomplished anything." In making this comment, the priest was not only referring to Jude's inability to find employment to support his family but also to Jude's healing ministry itself. For the priest, charismatic healing was indeed play, but only in the sense of nonproductive or useless activity.

One night during my research, I shared a room with Jude at a Catholic ashram as I had many times before. When Jude would retire for the night, he would often fall asleep while rhythmically saying the name of Jesus. That night, his repetition of the divine name seemed more earnest than usual. When I asked him about this, Jude spoke of a counseling session with a young boy earlier in the day. The boy had severely weakened legs and could walk only with difficulty. I remember watching Jude pray over the boy and then saying in Hindi, "It's OK now, you can run—run with me!" Jude jogged off through the ashram, with the smiling boy following, struggling to keep pace. When Jude mentioned the boy, I commented, "Oh, because his legs weren't healed, you're praying for them to be healed now, perhaps by taking his suffering upon yourself?" "Oh no," Jude said, "He was completely healed, completely." Jude did not explain further, nor did I press him about what, if anything, he was praying for as he went to sleep. But in some ways, Jude's allusion to the boy could be interpreted to challenge the priest and other critics who believe charismatic healing to be either a farce or a sham. Jude saw as well as I did that the boy still could not walk without pain, let alone run. Yet the boy was smiling and happy as he followed Jude throughout the ashram's compound. Perhaps for Jude, charismatic healing was a way of entering into levity, into hope beyond hope. From this perspective, to be healed is simply and earnestly to act as if one has been healed—in other words, "to play." To heal and be healed, then, is to be constantly playing and at play within and through the inevitability of human suffering and death. His fellow charismatics told me that as Jude lay on his deathbed, kidneys failing and his body wracked by fever, he continued to repeat the name of Jesus. Perhaps Jude was playing until the very end.

Huizinga would surely agree that Jude's deathbed refrain was a form of play, for the transition from life to death, or from affliction to healing, would represent precisely that kind of liminal state to which play or levity beckons. But such romanticism would not find much resonance in the writings of Georges Bataille, another scholar similarly fascinated by play. For Bataille (1997, 328), Christianity itself prevents any real understanding of play, or "the game," precisely because it speaks only of pain and death—although Bataille's own valorization of horror and ecstasy could be seen to praise Catholicism as much as it explicitly condemns it. In his writings on laughter, Bataille (59–63) calls our attention to how levity mocks and excludes that which is "other." With Jude we have found how the "play" of charismatic healing cloaks power and contest. As Bataille also observed, there is also "violence" to laughter, and to be sure there is a transgressive quality to Jude's account of his aggressive sessions of "charismatic counseling." From this perspective, levity assumes both freedom and power that make possible certain ways of acting that would otherwise be impossible. Of course, the desire for freedom and power is often born in the painful experience of seemingly unalterable limitation. To study ritual levity in religion is, then, perhaps to understand how the lightness of play is always connected to the heaviness of ordinary human life.

## Works Cited

Alland, Alexander. 1962. "Possession in a Negro Revivalist Church." *Journal for the Scientific Study of Religion* 1: 204–13.

Bataille, Georges. 1997. *The Bataille Reader*. Edited by Fred Botting and Scott Wilson. Oxford: Blackwell.

Boudewijnse, Barbara, Andre F. Droogers, and Frans Kamsteeg. 1998. *More Than Opium: An Anthropological Approach to Latin American and Caribbean Pentecostal Practice*. Lanham, MD: Scarecrow Press.

Brende, Joel O., and Donald B. Rinsley. 1979. "Borderline Disorders, Altered States of Consciousness, and Glossolalia." *Journal of the American Academy of Psychoanalysis* 7: 165–88.

Geertz, Clifford A. 1973. "Deep Play: Notes on a Javanese Cockfight." In *Interpretations of Cultures*, 412–54. New York: Basic Books.

Huizinga, Johan. 1950. *Homo Ludens: A Study of the Play-Element in Culture*. Boston, MA: Beacon Press.

Kris, Ernst. 1953. "Aesthetic Ambiguity." In *Psychoanalytic Explorations in Art*, 243–74. London: Allen and Uwin.

Lombard, Emile. 1907. "Essai d'une classification des phénomènes de glossolalia." *Archives de Psychologie* 7: 1–51.

Lombard, Emile. 1910. *De le glossalalie: Chez less premiers Chrétiens et des phénomènes similaires: Études d'exégè et de psychologies*. Lausanne: Briedel.

Malony, H. Newton, and A. Adams Lovekin. 1985. *Glossolalia: Behavioral Science Perspectives on Speaking in Tongues*. New York: Oxford University Press.

Marriot, McKim. 1990. "Constructing an Indian Ethnosociology." In *India through Hindu Categories*, ed. McKim Marriot, 1–39. New Delhi: Sage Publications.

May, L. Carlyle. 1967. "A Survey of Glossolalia and Related Phenomena in Non-Christian Religions." *American Anthropologist* 58: 75–96.

Pattison, E. Mansell. 1968. "Behavioral Science Research on the Nature of Glossolalia." *Journal of American Scientific Affiliation* 20: 73–86.

Schmalz, Mathew N. 2001. "American Catholic, Indian Catholics: Reflections on Religious Identity, Ethnography, and the History of Religions." *Method & Theory in the Study of Religion* 13: 91–97.

Schmalz, Mathew N. 2002a. "Charismatic Transgressions: The Life and Work of an Indian Catholic Healer." In *Popular Christianity in India: Riting between the Lines*, ed. Selva J. Raj and Corinne G. Dempsey, 163–87. Albany: State University of New York Press.

Schmalz, Mathew N. 2002b. "Dalit Christian Pentecostalism in a North Indian Village." *Dalit International Newsletter* 7 (October): 7–9.

Schmalz, Mathew N. Forthcoming. "Boundaries and Appropriations in North Indian Charismatic Catholicism." In *Engaging South Asian Religions: Boundaries, Appropriations, and Resistances*, ed. Mathew N. Schmalz and Peter Gottschalk. Albany: State University of New York Press.

Schmalz, Mathew N., and Peter Gottschalk. Forthcoming. "On Method and Narrative, or How a Textualist Gave Birth to Two Ethnographers." In *Notes from a Mandala: Essays in Honor of Wendy Doniger*, ed. Laurie Patton and David Haberman. Newark: University of Delaware Press.

Stirrat, Robert L. 1992. *Power and Religiosity in a Post-Colonial Setting*. Cambridge: Cambridge University Press.

# 12

# Response

Jonathan Z. Smith

There is nothing particularly surprising about a set of proposals linking ritual to play. What is novel, indeed, at first glance, startling, is this collection of chapters joined together by an exploration of the notion of "ritual levity."

Theories characterizing religion as play, either in origin or in form, are chiefly of the aesthetic sort that take play to be in opposition to seriousness, most particularly the seriousness attendant on the workaday, mundane world—that is, on the "profane." Within Western philosophical discourse, beginning with post-Kantian German Romanticism,[1] two elements stand out: first, that play is understood in relation to freedom; second, that this freedom is marked off from whatever names or characterizes the sphere of determinate existence. In some proposals, both being free and being marked off are associated with the sacred and, hence, with religion. In other iterations, a third element is added to establish the connection with (religious) ritual, namely, that play as free and marked off is also a punctual, temporary state. In reading classes, modern formulations of this view, in works such as those by Johan Huizinga (1939) or Roger Caillois (1950, 1967),[2] it becomes clear that, in fact, the model for ritual is not free play but rather the game, its rules and moves. It is in the game that one finds that paradoxical combination of arbitrary moves and determinate limits that give rise to strategies and ingenuities that are carefully reflected on and repeatedly rehearsed.[3] It is this series of elements that permits the comparison to ritual.[4]

If this line of reflection be continued, one might be led to a discussion of Claude Levi-Strauss's suggestive, brief reflections on, and distinctions between, games, ritual games, and rituals (1962, 44–47)[5] or to John MacAloon's careful differentiations between ritual, drama, festival, and spectacle (1984, 241–80), a set of categories not at all irrelevant to some of the chapters in this book. One might go farther and propose some wider lucid category, inclusive of subcategories ranging from jokes and riddles to reversals and rebellions.[6] However, this volume demands that attention be paid to its provocative juxtaposition of levity and ritual.

"Levity" is a light-word (leg^wh)—not in the sense of "illumination" but rather in the sense of "lightness," of "weightlessness" (Pokorny 1959, 660).[7] The antonym of "levity" is "gravity." As such, levity may take on aspects of freedom that have been associated with play, as the presence of the same light-root in words such as "alleviate," "elevate," "leaven," "levitate," and "relieve" suggests. Alternatively, "levity" takes on that experiential element designated in the vernacular expressions "getting" or "being high"—a semantic field that ranges from solemn liturgical formulae such as "exaltations" to that Durkheimian characteristic of ritual "effervescence" (1925, 295–314)[8]—the latter, a term that has been replaced and enlarged, in contemporary French discourse since the 1970s, by the more fluid and sexual "jouissance."[9]

Alas, we must also take note of the negative valence that invades the field of "levity" from the standpoint of the moral extension of its "air-head," a "light-weight"; or, to be "light-headed," "light-minded," or "flighty." It is this moral evaluation with respect to being light when one ought to be grave that makes for the apparent incongruity of associating levity with ritual as a focus for this volume.

In dictionaries of contemporary English usage, "levity" is described as that which is inappropriate, largely in terms of situation or of time. Levity is "unseasonable gaiety" (*Webster's New Dictionary of Synonyms*, 1968 edition). A paradigmatic case within a ritual occasion would be the not-uncommon occurrence of giggling at a funeral. The earliest citation in the *Oxford English Dictionary* for "levity" in this sense of the term is a 1546 reformist tract attacking Anglican clergy who refused to wear clerical garb. These individuals were "as though they were ledde with a certayne erreligious leuitie to overthrow and abolyshe all thynges vsed before in religion."[10] What is here stated with indignation is described positively in the chapters in this book: levity, at times serving as a point of "leverage," becoming an occasion for (apparent) critical reflexivity, a defamiliarizing moment, which, moreover, is not "unseasonable" but rather is often calendrical; which is not individual or spontaneous (as is the case with the funeral giggle) but, rather, is collective and can be counted upon as occurring beforehand—key elements in what makes rite correct.

There is no way in a brief chapter to reflect adequately the textual and ethnographic richness of the thick description that characterizes these chapters. Nor am I able to engage the several authors at the level of explicit or implied theory, except to applaud their consistent and appropriate impatience with Anglo-American and Soviet functionalist-homeostatic explanations for levity (or license) in ritual as providing a "safety value for passions the common people might otherwise direct to revolution" (Holquist 1984, xviii).[11] Rather, in the remainder of the space allotted to me, I propose to generate some groupings of the chapters that might encourage readers to construct conversations between the chapters. To this end, and in keeping with the lucid spirit of the volume, the chapters will be enumerated in a different order than they appear in this volume. This revised order is intended, as well, to illustrate the semantic field of the term *levity* as our authors have construed it.

At one end of this continuum, I would place Tracy Pintchman's description of sociable pleasure in interpersonal relations among a group of women ritual participants that temporarily brackets a variety of socio-religious cleavages (chapter 6). Pintchman's male assistant's dismissive comment, "just gossip," reminds one of Samuel Heilman's important ethnography, *Synagogue Life*, in which he develops a positive theory of gossip as the most adequate category for interpreting the interactions of religious life in a contemporary American Jewish *shul* (Heilman 1976). The role of informal communication and speech, often playful, within the context of ritual contributes as much to social cohesion, to the often temporary solidarity characteristic of rituals, as does the more often studied patterned, liturgical speech.[12] In Pintchman's example, the relevance is strengthened by the women's object of devotion, the mythic figure of Krishna at play with the gopi cowherdesses.

At the other end of the continuum, I would place Corinne Dempsey and Sudharshan Durayappah's description of self-conscious acts of trespass and reversal, at once both serious and playful in execution, which serve as cognitive tools by a ritual leader with the potentiality of permanently affecting the participants' understanding and progress in their religious tradition (chapter 5). Between these two poles, I would cluster the chapters as follows.

Close to Pintchman should be placed Jonathan Walters's comparisons between "Theist" and Buddhist Sinhalese ritual levity in a rural village (chapter 8). In choosing this topic and setting, Walters immediately makes impossible explaining the differences in terms of contrast between "folk" and "elite" or "canonical" traditions. I locate his ethnographic essay adjacent to Pintchman because of his first interpretative move with respect to ritual levity in the Theistic context, ritual as entertaining to the gods, although the analysis emphasizes not so much sociability as it does control, particularly in the case of "possessed people, that is the gods themselves," who act, in turn, in an entertaining, even if aggressive, manner. In the Buddhist context, on the other hand, levity is better understood as an internal condition, as "joy," as "merit is earned when the mind delights in ritual," and as that "mental happiness which their rebirth precursors experienced."

Next I would place Rachel McDermott's presentation of a Durga festival in Bengal (chapter 9). Here, too, elements of sociable pleasure recur, but now the levity is generated in some of the *pandal* displays by incongruous juxtaposition, all the more striking within an overall context of order and seriousness. In McDermott's analysis, it is "fluidity" in relation to the more "frozen" conceptions of divinity rather than in contrast to more "frozen" conceptions of social relations that is highlighted—although one may wonder whether this reflects more the difference between emic and etic perceptions. By the nature of the festival, McDermott introduces a key element in games and play somewhat muted in the other chapter: competition. (Note Pintchman's description of women bringing extra *puja* supplies, with no apparent potlatch-style contest as to who brought and gave more surplus.) Recall that a key paradigm for play in Huizinga was the contest, the *agon*, including even riddle contests in which death was the price of losing.

Multiple dimensions of contestation also figure in Mathew Schmalz's description of a North Indian Catholic charismatic healer in Varanasi (chapter 11): combat/contest between the healer and the "demoniac"; between castes and forms of Christianities; as well as between devotees (in the chapter, exemplified as that between "Jude" and the "young catechist"); as well as between healers.

In Selva Raj's treatment of the "men who cook," rather than levity reflecting implicit differences between the social relations of quotidian life and those during ritual (chapter 6) or the implied criticism of quotidian categories through ritual juxtaposition (chapter 9), Raj focuses on an explicit reversal of ordinary, socially defined gender roles—once a year: men [this one time] cook/women [this one time] do not (chapter 2). It is the paradox of such rituals that they, counterintuitively, affirm the social categories by the act of reversal. In Raj's example, cooking remains a gender-specific act. The ritual, by temporarily switching the gendered actors, makes this point all the more forcefully. That is, the structure not only survives the switch, but it is reinforced by it.[13]

The same issue of reversals returns in A. Whitney Sanford's presentation (chapter 3) of a local "unique to Baldeo" form of the widely distributed Holi festival in the Braj region. Here, the "license" characteristic of rituals in spring agricultural festivals[14] is tied to local forms and variations of a mythic complex centered on the return of Balarama and that deity's alteration of the Yamuna River's course. Rather than emphasize the worn, inadequate notion that ritual mirrors myth, Sanford emphasizes the work of this ritual play. While not innocent of the thesis that the ritual is linked to "the maintenance of social ties," Sanford usefully emphasizes the intellectual labor of the rituals. They provide an occasion at which "ties between social bonds and agriculture are worked out"; they "work out tensions . . . the flexibility and freedom to work out ambivalences." This language should give pause to the more utopian understanding of such carnivalesque occasions, as well as the sharp differentiation between official and folk rituals, between the "culture of the serious" and the "culture of laughter" that has preoccupied contemporary scholarship since Mikhail Bakhtin's 1930s dissertation, published in Russian as *Francois Rabelais and the Folk Culture of the Middle Ages and Renaissance* (1965), which was first translated into English in 1984 as *Rabelais and His World.* Nevertheless, the problem for ritual theory remains: the required anti-nomianism, the commandment, "Thou shalt commit thou shalt nots," in Saturnalianism, Mardi Gras, Holi, Carnival, and the like, appear to be destructuring reversals but remain a part of the structure rather than its critique.[15]

While different than Sanford's chapter, where a local understanding of a mythic scenario provides a key to the interpretation of a local version of Holi's lucid ritualized behaviors, William Harman's (chapter 7) and Liz Wilson's (chapter 4) contributions share an interest in the complex relationships between myth and ritual, an interest that is not foregrounded in the other chapters. Both share as well, at least at the interpretative level, an understanding of ritual as addressing, as solving problems.

Harman's chapter is analytically complex in several respects. There is the diachronic complication of two rival mythologies, Shiva and Vishnu, being brought into relation; and there are several frames of native interpretation (Shaivite, Vaishnavite, Muslim), each with its own "take" on the ritual, while having their own "take" on the others' "takes." If there is a solution to what Harman describes as the problem of the "integration of proximate disparate religious elements," then it is a short-term one; one of imagination and not of fact; one that works, in each case, only from the point of view of the relatively dominant group.

In contrast, in Liz Wilson's Newar example, the problem is solved through the ritual, and not only for the duration of the ritual. The problem is the status of widows. In this instance, the ritual appears to be self-consciously addressing the problem (the Parvati myth), as well as being equally self-conscious about the differences between the "mock" marriage rite, which unites the bride to her family, and the "actual" marriage rite, which separates the bride from her family. Part of the levity, in Wilson's analysis, arises from the play between this difference. I contrast this emic self-consciousness with, for example, Vincent Crapanzano's (1980) well-known revisionist account of Moroccan male circumcision, where the contrast between emic and etic understandings is highlighted. The ritual and native understanding states that the young boy has become an adult; the ethnographer observes the opposite effect—through the ritual, the boy has become infantilized.[16]

Amy Bard's chapter (10) sets a new direction within this volume: not levity in ritual but rather ritual as an object of levity; not so much collective, public acts of levity but rather individual, private, or domestic ones. What she treats are *parodia sacra*, and not the individual, spontaneous but, nevertheless, required *risus paschalis*, the Easter laughter within the church, by clergy and laity, in the context of a liturgical commemoration of death and resurrection, which, along with the earlier Mardi Gras, brackets the more austere and mournful rituals of Lent and Good Friday.[17] In Bard, the emphasis is often on laughing as a response to the discomfiture of distance, whether the practice involved is different than one is used to (the bride, though Shi'i, from a different locale) or reflects another point of view (Shi'i, Sunni). The result conforms to the lexical understanding of levity, discussed earlier, "unseasonable gaiety." Given its occurrence with the context of the Muharram, the levity is quite literally "giggling during a funeral," as discussed previously. The issue for Bard, I would suggest, is one of more precision in terminology. She rather consistently speaks of parody, without, for example, distinguishing between parody and related genres such as burlesque, ridicule, satire, and even irony.[18] Nevertheless, in contrast to a number of the other instances in this book, the levity she describes does not diffuse and defuse tensions but rather expresses and inscribes them.

Finally, Corinne Dempsey and Sudharshan Durayappah's chapter (5) presents a complex account of the self-conscious violation of rules and elements within ritual in a dominant school of esoteric tradition by an individual religious leader of a "marginal" Shri Vidya congregation within their diasporic temple. While there are clearly spontaneous actions and utterances, much appears to be part of a deliberate pedagogical strategy of intended transgressive actions and expressions. Taken as a whole, the ritual surprises, as described by Dempsey and Durayappah, appear to be a mode of spiritual disciplining not unlike the fabled Zen practice of a master slapping a disciple. In their example, gravity does not overcome levity. This success, one might suppose, is made possible in part because this particular temple, from an Other's dominant and traditional Shri Vidyan perspective, is itself in an inappropriate place where its rituals are being enacted by an inappropriate set of participants.

Two final observations. First, we have before us a volume on ritual levity, ritual play, which discusses its topic, although mentioning the term in passing, without once invoking the usual appeal to a cosmologized and an ontologized notion of *lila* (divine play) as an explanatory principle. I, for one, am grateful.

Second, I am by no means persuaded that, as yet, a single second order term or theory can encompass this range of rituals and ritual behaviors. This is indicated by the variety of disparate, largely undefined terms, employed for what the editors have here stipulated as "levity." An effort at compiling a by no means complete concordance of the chapter would note the presence of various terms, each one partially embedded in a set of heterogeneous theories: "play," "game," "joke," "pun," "parody," "mock," "reversal," and "rebellion," to name but a few. To have placed such issues on the agendum for ritual studies is one of the achievements of this book.

## Notes

1. For convenience, this understanding can be dated as beginning with Friedrich von Schiller's *Briefe uber die asthetische Erziehung des Menschen* (1794–95), found in the useful bilingual edition edited by E. M. Wilkinson and L. A. Willoughby (1983), a product of Schiller's third and most Kantian period. A valuable history of the conceptualization of play, by one in the service of a particular point of view, is provided by Spariosu (1989).

2. For English translation of Huizinga (1939), see Huizinga (1949). For English translation of Caillois (1950, 1967), see Caillois (1959, 1961).

3. Given its necessity, it is surprising that there are so few ethnographic studies of ritual rehearsals. Richard Schechner (1985) is the only figure I know to have theorized ritual rehearsal in relation to his notion of performance as "restored behavior." See especially pages 35–44. His profession as a theatre

director as well as a drama theorist clearly informs his understanding of rehearsal.

4. For surveys of games and play in relation to ritual, with excellent bibliographies, see MacAloon (1987) and Handelman (1987).

5. See also the less than satisfactory English translation, *The Savage Mind* (1967, 30–33).

6. The theoretical foundations for such an enterprise have been laid in Mary Douglas's (1968) seminal article, "The Social Control of Cognition: Some Factors in Joke Perception."

7. It would be difficult to improve on the stunning meditation, "Lightness," by Italo Calvino (1993 [1988]).

8. See also the English translation, *The Elementary Forms of Religious Life* (2001, 211–21). It is worth calling attention to Durkheim's own theory of play (1925, 542–48; 2001, 383–87).

9. The origin of the currency of the term in French discourse most likely results from its persistent use in Lacan (1999). See the partial English translation of some of the relevant passages in J. Mitchell and J. Rose (1985, 137–61). Roland Barthes's (1973, 82–84) contrast between "*plaisir du texte*" and "*texts de jouissance*" all but guaranteed its importance. Barthes references Lacan early in his discussion of *jouissance* (1973, 36); see also the English translation (Barthes 1975, 51–53, 21). The genealogy from Lacan is supported by Roudiez (1980) in his editor's "Introduction" to the English translation of J. Kristeva, *Desire in Language: A Semiotic Approach to Literature and Art.*

10. The OED cites the text as published in 1564. I cite an apparently later printing: (Anon.), (R. Jugge [publisher], n.p., n.d. [1566?]): sig. Aiij. Cf. *A briefe Examination for the Tyme, of a certaine Declaration lately put into print in the name and defence of certaine Ministers in London, refusing to weare the Apparrell prescribed by the Lawes and Orders of the Realme*, the summary in the form of an unpaginated table comparing the original *Declaration*, which I have been unable to locate, with the arguments in the *Examination* in (Anon.), *An Answere for the Tyme, to the Examination put in print, without the Authores name, pretending to mayntayne the Apparrell prescribed against the Declaration of the Mynisters of London* (n.p., 1566).

11. Holquist here refers to the 1935 statements by Anatoly Lunacharsky, then the Soviet Commissar of Enlightenment. Bakhtin, throughout his work, consistently challenges this interpretation. Among British functionalists, this position is best articulated in Max Gluckman's 1952 Frazer Lecture, "Rituals of Rebellion in South and South-west Africa," reprinted in Gluckman (1963b: 110–36). Gluckman's chief examples are the reversal in the Swazi Ncwala as described by Kuper (1980) *An African Aristocracy*, especially pp. 197–225. See now the important reexamination of this royal ritual by Lincoln (1989, 54–74). Given the theme of this present volume on ritual levity, note should be taken of Gluckman's popular 1955 BBC broadcast talk, "The License in Ritual," in Gluckman (1963a).

12. On gossip's role in social cohesion, see especially D. Jones, "Gossip: Notes on Women's Oral Culture" (1981, 193–98). John Beard Haviland, best

known for his important ethnographic monograph, *Gossip, Reputation and Knowledge in Zinacantan* (1977), has presented a fascinating account of native transcribers editing tape recordings of oral gossip sessions so as to lessen their informal character (Haviland 1996, 45–78).

13. On the power of mixing structural or classificatory categories to reinforce those very same categories, see the important meditation on the significance of hybrid masks in initiation rituals in Turner (1967, 104–108). Turner here draws on William James's "law of dissociation" (see further, J. Z. Smith 2004, 162–72 and notes 14 and 15).

With less explicit theoretical discussion, see also the observation embedded in the important intracultural comparative essay by Roberto Da Matta (1977), "Constraint and License: A Preliminary Study of Two Brazilian National Rituals," comparing Brazilian Independence Day with the Brazilian Carnival. While Da Matta begins by contrasting the two festivals as "symmetrical but inverted rituals," with Independence Day as a "sacred, formal rite which celebrates structure, in opposition to Carnival, which is a profane, informal rite creating communitas" (250–51, emphases omitted), he concludes with the observation that Carnival "is an event of communitas which at the same time—given the conditions of Brazilian social organization and its division into classes—serves to maintain the hierarchy and position of those classes. In short, the communitas of Carnival is a function of the rigid social condition held in everyday life by those groups involved. It is the universality and homogeneity of everyday life" (251). I see nothing in this interpretation that cannot be generalized to other comparable data.

14. For an elderly comparative survey of lucid elements in spring festivals, see the chapter "The Magical Significance of Games in Primitive Agriculture" in Frazer 1912a; also see Frazer 1912b, 1: 92–112.For a useful general survey of the Indic rituals, see Bose (1953, 73–102).

15. The most suggestive structural proposal on the topic of license, reversals, and masquerades at seasonal festivals is the extraordinarily brief theoretical essay by Leach (1961 [1966]).

16. Crapanzano's article is also conveniently reprinted in Ronald Grimes (1995); see also, Crapanzano (1985, 47–52).

17. See the brief discussion in Bakhtin (1984, 78–79). Bakhtin refers (79, n. 25) to J. P. Schmidt's *De risu paschalis*, which I have not seen. In addition to this Catholic practice, compare the British lucid Hock-day or Hoketyde, part of a complex of English jocular practices associated with Easter Monday and Tuesday in Brand (1854, 99–105), s.v. Hoke Day; Walsh (1907, 368–72), s.v. Easter Monday and Tuesday, 533–34, s.v. Hock or Hoke Day. Because of their close calendrical proximity, All Fools' Day, April Fools' Day, or the Feast of Fools seem a displacement of these paschal rites and practices.

18. On the genre question, see, among others, the important survey by Hutcheon (2000). Note as well the careful distinctions as to parodic types in the 1929 essay by Bakhtin, "Discourse Typology in Prose" (Bakhtin 1971 [2002], 176–96, esp. pp. 178–80, 192), and in his later work of the 1940s, "From the

Prehistory of Novelistic Discourse," published posthumously in Russian and translated into English (Bakhtin 1981, 41–83, esp. pp. 51–82).

## Works Cited

Anonymous. 1566. *An Answere for the Tyme, to the Examination put in print, without the Authores name, pretending to mayntayne the Apparrell prescribed against the Declaration of the Mynisters of London*. n.p.

Bakhtin, M. 1971 [2002]. "Discourse Typology in Prose." In *Readings in Russian Poetics: Formalist and Structuralist Views*, ed. Ladislav Matajka and Krystyna Pomorska, 176–96. Normal, IL: Dalkey Archive Press.

Bakhtin, M. 1981. *The Dialogic Imagination*. Edited by Michael Holquist, translated by Caryl Emerson and Michael Holquist. Austin: University of Texas Press, Slavic series no. 1.

Bakhtin, M. 1984. *Rabelais and His World*. Translated by Helene Iswolski. Bloomington: Indiana University Press.

Barthes, Roland. 1973. *Le Plaisir du texte*. Paris: Éditions du Seuil.

Barthes, Roland. 1975. *The Pleasure of the Text*. Translated by Richard Miller. New York: Hill and Wang.

Bose, Nirmal Kumar. 1953. *Cultural Anthropology and Other Essays*. Calcutta: Indian Associated Publishing Company.

Brand, John. 1854. *Observations on Popular Antiquities*. Revised by Sir Henry Ellis. London: Henry G. Bohn.

Caillois, Roger. 1950. *L'Homme et le sacre*. Paris: Gullimard.

Caillois, Roger. 1959. *Man and the Sacred*. Translated by Meyer Barash. Glencoe, IL: Free Press.

Caillois, Roger. 1961. *Man, Play and Games*. 2nd ed. New York: Free Press.

Caillois, Roger. 1967. *Les Jeux et les Hommes:Le Masque et le Vertige*. 3rd ed. Paris: Gullimard.

Calvino, Italo. 1993 [1988]. "Lightness." In *Six Memos for the Next Millennium: The Charles Eliot Norton Lectures 1985–86*, ed. Italo Calvino, 3–29. New York: Vintage Press.

Crapanzano, Vincent. 1980. "Rite of Return: Circumcision in Morocco." *The Psychoanalytic Study of Society* 9: 15–36.

Crapanzano, Vincent. 1985. *Tuhami: Portrait of a Moroccan*. Chicago, IL: University of Chicago Press.

Da Matta, Roberto. 1977. "Constraint and License: A Preliminary Study of Two Brazilian National Rituals." In *Secular Ritual*, ed. Sally Falk Moore and Barbara Meyerhoff, 244–64. Amsterdam: Van Gorcum.

Douglas, Mary. 1968. "The Social Control of Cognition: Some Factors in Joke Perception." *Man: The Journal of the Royal Anthropological Institute* 3: 361–76.

Durkheim, Emile. 1925. *Les Formes Elementaires de la vie Religieuse: Le Systeme Totemique en Australie*. 2d ed. Paris: Librairie Felix Alcan.

Durkheim, Emile. 2001. *The Elementary Forms of Religious Life*. Edited by Mark Cladis, translated by Carol Cosman. New York: Oxford University Press.

Frazer, James George. 1912a. *The Golden Bough*. 3rd ed. London: Publisher unknown.

Frazer, James George. 1912b. *Spirits of the Corn and of the Wild*. Publisher unknown.

Gluckman, Max. 1963a [1956]. *Custom and Conflict in Africa*. New York: Basil Blackwell.

Gluckman, Max. 1963b. *Order and Rebellion in Tribal Africa: Collected Essays with an Autobiographical Introduction*. Glencoe, IL: London, Cohen & West.

Grimes, Ronald L. 1995. *Readings in Ritual Studies*. Upper Saddle River, NJ: Prentice Hall.

Handelman, David. 1987. "Play." In *Encyclopedia of Religion* 11, ed. Mircea Eliade, 363–65. New York: Macmillan.

Haviland, John Beard. 1977. *Gossip, Reputation and Knowledge in Zinacantan*. Chicago, IL: University of Chicago Press.

Haviland, John Beard. 1996. "Text from Talk in Tzotzil." In *Natural Histories of Discourse*, ed. Michael Silverstein and Greg Urban, 45–78. Chicago, IL: University of Chicago Press.

Heilman, Samuel. 1976. *Synagogue Life: A Study in Symbolic Interaction*. Chicago, IL: University of Chicago Press.

Holquist, M. 1984. "Prologue." In *Rabelais and His World*, ed. Mikhail Bakhtin, xviii, trans. Helene Iswolsky. Bloomington: Indiana University Press.

Huizinga, Johan. 1939. *Homo Ludens: Versuch einer Bestimmung des Spielelements der Kultur*. Amsterdam: Pantheon academische verlagsanstalt.

Huizinga, Johan. 1949. *Homo Ludens: A Study of the Play-Element in Culture*. London: Routledge and K. Paul.

Hutcheon, Linda. 2000. *A Theory of Parody: The Teachings of Twentieth Century Art Forms*. Champaigne-Urbana: University of Illinois Press.

Jones, D. 1981. "Gossip: Notes on Women's Oral Culture." In *The Voices and Words of Women and Men*, ed. Cheris Kramarae, 193–98. Oxford: Pergamon Press.

Jugge, R. [publisher], n.p., n.d. [1566?]): sig. Aiij. Cf. *A Briefe Examination for the Tyme, of a certaine Declaration lately put into print in the name and defence of certaine Ministers in London, refusing to weare the Apparrell prescribed by the Lawes and Orders of the Realme.*

Kuper, Hilda. 1980. *An African Aristocracy: Rank among the Swazi*. Oxford: Holmes and Meier.

Lacan, J. 1999. *Encore: Le Seminaire livre XX, 1972–73*. Paris: Seuil.

Leach, Edmund. 1961 [1966]. *Rethinking Anthropology*. London School of Economics Monographs on Social Anthropology. London: Berg.

Levi-Strauss,Claude. 1962. *La Pensee sauvage*. Paris: Librairie Plon.

Levi-Strauss, Claude. 1967. *The Savage Mind*. Chicago, IL: University of Chicago Press.

Lincoln, Bruce. 1989. *Discourse and the Construction of Society: Comparative Studies in Myth, Ritual and Classification*. New York: Oxford University Press.

MacAloon, John J. 1984. "Olympic Games and the Theory of Spectacle in Modern Societies." In *Rite, Drama, Festival, Spectacle: Rehearsals Toward a Theory of Culture Performance*, ed. John J. MacAloon, 241–80. Philadelphia, PA: Institute for the Study of Human Issues.

MacAloon, John J. 1987. "Games." In *Encyclopedia of Religion* 5, ed. Mircea Eliade, 744–48. New York: Macmillan.

Mitchell, Juliet, and Jacqueline Rose, eds. 1985. *Feminine Sexuality: Jacques Lacan and the ecole freudienne*. New York and London: W. W. Norton and Company.

Pokorny, Julius. 1959. *Indogermanisches etymologisches Worterbuch*. Bern: Francke Verlag.

Roudiez, Leon. 1980. "Introduction." In *Desire in Language: A Semiotic Approach to Literature and Art*, by Julia Kristeva, ed. Leon Roudiez and Alice Jardine, 1–22, trans. Thomas Gora. New York: Columbia University Press.

Schechner, Richard. 1985. *Between Theatre and Anthropology*. Philadelphia: University of Pennsylvania Press.

Schmidt, J. P. 1847. *De risu paschalis*. Rostock, Germany: Publisher unknown.

Smith, J. Z. 2004. *Relating Religion: Essays in the Sturdy of Religion*. Chicago, IL: University of Chicago Press.

Spariosu, Mihai. 1989. *Dionysus Reborn: Play and the Aesthetic Dimension in Modern Philosophical and Scientific Discourse*. Ithaca, NY: Cornell University Press.

Turner, Victor. 1967. *The Forest of Symbols: Aspects of Ndembu Ritual*. Ithaca, NY: Cornell University Press.

von Schiller, Friederich. 1983. *On the Aesthetic Education of Man in a Series of Letters*. Edited by E. M. Wilkinson and L. A. Willoughby. New York: Oxford University Press.

Walsh, W. S. 1907. *Curiosities of Popular Customs and of Rites, Ceremonies, Observances, and Miscellaneous Antiquities*. Philadelphia, PA: J. B. Lippincott.

# About the Contributors

**Amy C. Bard** teaches at Wellesley College and Harvard University. She has published articles on Urdu poetry, Shi'i Islam in South Asia, and women's poetic performance. Much of her research explores how gender, regional identity, and sectarian tensions mediate poetic production, appreciation, and meaning in contemporary South Asia. Her writings also engage the anthropology of emotion/affect.

**Corinne Dempsey** is associate professor of religious studies at the University of Wisconsin, Stevens Point. Her publications include *Kerala Christian Sainthood: Collisions of Culture and Worldview in South India* (Oxford University Press, 2001) and *The Goddess Lives in Upstate New York: Breaking Convention and Making Home at a North American Hindu Temple* (Oxford University Press, 2006). She has coedited two other volumes with Selva Raj: *Popular Christianity in India: Riting between the Lines* (State University of New York Press, 2002) and *Miracle as Modern Conundrum in South Asian Traditions* (State University of New York Press, 2009).

**Sudharshan Durayappah** is an adjunct instructor at the University of Toronto and graduate student at York University in Toronto. His areas of interest include ritual studies, diaspora studies, and religion and art.

**William P. Harman** is professor of religion at the University of Tennessee, Chattanooga. He teaches comparative religion with specific training in Tamil Hinduism. His publications include a monograph, *The Sacred Marriage of a Hindu Goddess* (Indiana University Press, 1989), and a volume coedited with Selva Raj, *Dealing with Deities: Religious Vows in South Asian Religions* (State University of New York Press, 2006), as well as numerous articles focusing on the study of religion.

**Rachel Fell McDermott** is associate professor of Asian and Middle Eastern Cultures at Barnard College. She is the author of *Mother of My Heart, Daughter of My Dreams: Kali and Uma in the Devotional Poetry of Bengal* (Oxford University Press, 2001) and *Singing to the Goddess: Poems to Kali and Uma from Bengal* (Oxford University Press, 2001), as well as several articles and two edited volumes.

**Tracy Pintchman** is professor and director of Asian studies at Loyola University, Chicago. Her research focuses on goddesses and women in Hinduism. Her publications include *The Rise of the Goddess in the Hindu Tradition* (State University of New York Press, 1994), *Seeking Mahadevi: Constructing Identities of the Hindu Great Goddess* (State University of New York Press, 2001), and several articles. Her recent book, *Guests at God's Wedding: Celebrating Kartik among the Women of Benares* (State University of New York Press, 2005), is an in-depth treatment of women's Kartik puja traditions.

**Selva J. Raj**, who received his PhD in history of religions from the University of Chicago, was chair and Stanley S. Kresge Professor of Religious Studies at Albion College. He published many articles on Hindu-Catholic ritual exchange in India and edited three volumes with Corinne Dempsey: *Popular Christianity in India: Riting between the Lines* (State University of New York Press, 2002) and *Miracle as Modern Conundrum in South Asian Traditions* (State University of New York Press, 2009). He also edited, with William Harman, *Dealing with Deities: The Ritual Vow in South Asia* (State University of New York Press, 2006) and, with Knut Jacobson, *South Asian Christian Diaspora: Invisible Diaspora in Europe and North America* (Ashgate Press, 2008).

**A. Whitney Sanford** is assistant professor of religion at the University of Florida. Her first book, *Singing Krishna: Sound Becomes Sight in Paramanand's Poetry* (State University of New York Press, 2008), explores the role of devotional poetry in ritual practice. Her manuscript, *Transforming Agriculture: Hindu Narrative and Ecological Imagination*, explores how Hindu agricultural narratives provide the foundation to expand the ecological imagination and rethink agricultural practice. Her new project, "Gandhi's Environmental Legacy: Food Sovereignty and Social Movements," investigates Gandhi's influence on sustainability and food and water sovereignty movements.

**Mathew N. Schmalz** received his PhD in history of religions from the University of Chicago. He is presently an Edward Bennett Williams

Fellow and an associate professor of religious studies at the College of the Holy Cross, where he also serves as director of Asian studies. He has published over fifteen articles, among which two discuss the charismatic healer "Jude."

**Jonathan Z. Smith** is Robert O. Anderson Distinguished Service Professor of the Humanities at the University of Chicago. A Fellow of the American Academy of Arts and Sciences, he served as the general editor of the *Harper Collins Dictionary of Religion* (HarperOne, 1995) and has most recently published *Relating Religion: Essays in the Study of Religion* (University of Chicago Press, 2004).

**Jonathan Walters** is professor of Religion and Asian Studies and chair of the Division of Humanities and Arts at Whitman College. He is the author of *Querying the Medieval: Texts and the History of Practices in South Asia* (Oxford University Press, 2000), *Finding Buddhists in Global History* (American Historical Association, 1998), and *Buried Treasure in Sri Lankan History* (Social Scientists' Association Occasional Papers Series, 1998), coeditor of *Constituting Communities: Theravada Buddhism and the Religious Cultures of South and Southeast Asia* (State University of New York Press, 2003), and has written numerous articles on Sri Lankan Buddhism.

**Liz Wilson** is professor and chair of the Department of Comparative Religion at Miami University. She is the author of *Charming Cadavers: Horrific Figurations of the Feminine in Indian Buddhist Hagiographic Literature* (University of Chicago Press, 1996) and editor of *The Living and the Dead: Social Dimensions of Death in South Asian Religions* (State University of New York Press, 2003).

# Index